American
Political
Prisoners

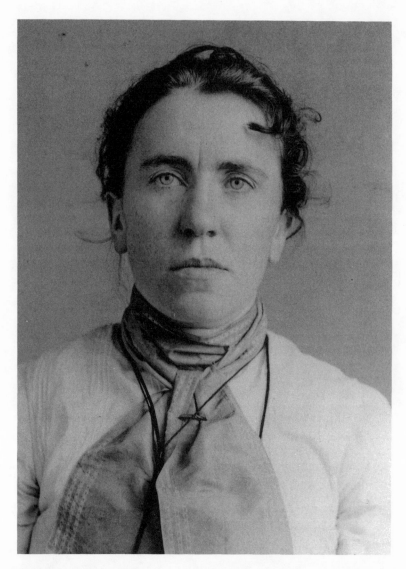

Emma Goldman, anarchist and free speech advocate, served two years in Missouri State Penitentiary for conspiracy to obstruct the draft. Photo taken by the Chicago Police Department in 1901. Courtesy of the author.

AMERICAN POLITICAL PRISONERS

Prosecutions under the Espionage and Sedition Acts

Stephen M. Kohn

Foreword by Howard Zinn

PRAEGER

Westport, Connecticut
London

Library of Congress Cataloging-in-Publication Data

Kohn, Stephen M. (Stephen Martin)
  American political prisoners : prosecutions under the espionage
and sedition acts / Stephen M. Kohn; foreword by Howard Zinn.
    p. cm.
  Includes bibliographical references and index.
  ISBN 0–275–94415–8 (alk. paper)
  1. Political prisoners—United States—History. 2. World War,
1914–1918—Conscientious objectors—United States. 3. World War,
1914–1918—Protest movements—United States. I. Title.
HV9466.K64 1994
365'.45'0973—dc20   93–37883

British Library Cataloguing in Publication Data is available.

Library of Congress Catalog Card Number: 93–37883
ISBN: 0–275–94415–8

First published in 1994

Praeger Publishers, 88 Post Road West, Westport, CT 06881
An imprint of Greenwood Publishing Group, Inc.

Printed in the United States of America

The paper used in this book complies with the
Permanent Paper Standard issued by the National
Information Standards Organization (Z39.48–1984).

10 9 8 7 6 5 4 3 2 1

This book is dedicated to my loving wife,
Leslie M. Rose

Contents

Foreword

In the pages that follow, the reader will be confronted with enormous crimes against the constitutional principle of free speech in a country that prides itself on its freedom and declares itself a model for democracy all over the world. The result of those crimes, for thousands of Americans, was persecution, imprisonment, sometimes torture and death. For many more, the result was to create an atmosphere of fear, the fear of expressing one's honest opinions, the kind of fear we usually attribute to totalitarian states.

In this case, however, the crimes against free speech and against human beings were committed by the U.S. government and various state governments during the first World War. They were crimes made legal by acts of Congress, by Presidential affirmation, and by Supreme Court decision—a troubling commentary on the much-praised "separation of powers," which is presumably a hallmark of our presumably democratic government.

What Stephen Kohn has done is to document what happened, with the kind of specific detail—names, places, punishments, the feelings of prisoners, the rationales of wardens and politicians—that brings history alive in the most immediate way, that goes behind statistics to individual human beings. He has been able to do this by an extraordinary feat of research, extracting from a reluctant government the records that are published for the first time in this book.

It is important to know exactly what motivated these thousands of vocal dissenters and their hundreds of thousands of sympathizers (half a million Americans were subscribing to the anti-war Socialist newspaper *Appeal to Reason*). They were protesting against the horrors of a war that had been going on in Europe since August 1914, in which young men on both sides were being sent to their deaths in huge numbers for reasons which, after the war, no one could rationally explain. I will take the liberty of quoting from my book *A People's History of the United States*, where I discuss the first World War:

For three years the battle lines remained virtually stationary in France. Each side would push forward, then back, then forward again, for a few yards, a few miles, while the corpses piled up. In 1916 the Germans tried to break through at Verdun; the British and French counterattacked along the Seine, moved forward a few miles, and lost 600,000 men. One day, the 9th Battalion of the King's Own York-shire Light Infantry launched at attack with eight hundred men. Twenty-four hours later, there were eighty-four left.

Not long after the slaughter at Verdun, a U.S. Senator, James Wads-worth of New York, proposed compulsory military training for all males. "We must let our young men know," he said, "that they owe some re-sponsibility to this country."

I suggested, in *People's History*, what that "responsibility" meant:

Ten million were to die on the battlefield; 20 million were to die of hunger and disease related to the war. And no one since that day has been able to show that the war brought any gain for humanity that be worth one human life. The rhetoric of the socialists, that it was an "imperialist war," now seems moderate and hardly arguable. The advanced capitalist countries of Europe were fighting over bound-aries, colonies, spheres of influence; they were competing for Alsace-Lorraine, the Balkans, Africa, the Middle East.

But what was the United States' interest in the war? It is not easy to unravel, from the knot of factors, a single clear thread. That the war was totally irrational from the standpoint of ordinary Americans does not mean that it was, therefore, totally rational from the standpoint of the nation's ruling class.

One strand of explanation, however, seems to be what the historian Richard Hofstadter (*The American Political Tradition*) saw as "economic necessities." When the war began in Europe American business was de-pressed, and there was much unemployment. (As the banker J. P. Morgan testified later: "the heavy industries were working far below capacity and bank clearings were off." But by 1915 war orders were coming from Eng-land and the economy was being given a boost. By April 1917 more than $2 billion worth of goods had been sold to the Allies. Hofstadter con-cluded: "America became bound up with the Allies in a fateful union of war and prosperity."

President Woodrow Wilson, campaigning in 1912, had said: "Our do-mestic markets no longer suffice; we need foreign markets." The war in Europe made England a market for American goods and profitable loans. The banking house of J. P. Morgan acted as agent for the Allies, and loaned them money in great amounts, thus tying the American economy closer and closer to a British victory over the Germans.

There is another strand in that admittedly tangled knot of explanation. The start of the war in Europe coincided with a growing fear by the American government of growing radicalism inside the country. Class warfare was not just a threat, it was an actuality in the violent clashes between working people and corporations that had grown in intensity through the second half of the nineteenth century and reached a crescendo in the years just before the war.

In 1905, two hundred socialists, anarchists and radical trade unionists met in Chicago, with Socialist leader Eugene Debs and legendary labor organizer Mother Mary Jones sitting on the platform, to form the Industrial Workers of the World. The mood was set by Big Bill Haywood, leader of the Western Federation of Miners, who picked up a piece of board, used it as a gavel to open the convention, and said: "Fellow workers. . . . This is the Continental Congress of the working-class. . . . The aims and objects of this organization shall be to put the working-class in possession of the economic power, the means of life, in control of the machinery of production and distribution, without regard to the capitalist masters."

The I.W.W. (the "Wobblies" as they came to be known) did not just organize workers. They threatened the system. In 1909, in McKees Rocks, Pennsylvania, they led a strike of six thousand workers against an affiliate of U.S. Steel, and defied the state troopers who were called out to break the strike. They promised to take a trooper's life for every worker killed (in one gun battle four strikers and three troopers were killed) and managed to keep picketing the factories until the strike was won. In 1912, they led a tempestuous strike of textile workers in Lawrence, Massachusetts, and the workers, holding out against the immense power and wealth of the mill owners, finally won their demands.

The I.W.W. had goals beyond strikes. It said: "Strikes are mere incidents in the class war . . . to prepare the masses for the final 'catastrophe,' the general strike which will complete the expropriation of the employers." Is it any wonder that, as the U.S. government contemplated entering the war in 1917, it saw an opportunity to destroy the I.W.W., using wartime patriotism as its weapon?

In 1914, southern Colorado erupted in a huge walkout of workers from the coal mines owned by the Rockefeller family. John Reed, the radical journalist who visited the scene, wrote an article about the strike, entitled, "Class War in Colorado." It was one of the most violent and dramatic labor struggles in American history, culminating in a military assault on men, women, and children living in a strikers' tent colony (the "Ludlow Massacre"), and then a violent rampage of miners through the mine districts in their fury against the burning of women and children at Ludlow.

The Socialist Party was seen by the government as a major threat. It reached its height of influence in the nation in the years before the war. At one time it had 100,000 members, and had elected over a thousand Socialists to office in 340 municipalities around the country. There were Socialists in Congress, and Socialist literature reached perhaps a million people.

When Woodrow Wilson, who had run for President in 1916 on a peace platform, decided after his election to ask Congress for a declaration of war, he understood that he would have to mobilize an unenthusiastic citizenry for war. Despite his call to arms "to make the world safe for democracy," Americans did not rush to enlist. A million men were needed, but in the first six weeks after the declaration of war only 73,000 men volunteered. Men would have to be drafted, and so Congress voted overwhelmingly for conscription.

A combination of persuasion and coercion was necessary to get the country behind the war. A Committee on Public Information was established to persuade Americans the war was worth fighting. The Committee sponsored 75,000 speakers, who gave 750,000 four-minute speeches in five thousand cities and towns.

It was clear that there was resistance to going to war. In the summer of 1917, Socialist anti-war meetings in Minnesota drew tens of thousands of farmers. In the municipal elections of 1917, many Socialists were elected to office on anti-war platforms. Ten socialists were elected to the New York State legislature.

This was the situation in June of 1917, when Congress passed the Espionage Act to enable prosecution of anyone speaking against the war. The fact that people continued to speak against the war, risking imprisonment, is a testament, not just to the work of the Socialist Party, of pacifists and radicals, but to a fundamental fact about the American people—their reluctance to kill and be killed in wars overseas. It has always taken a combination of enticements, propaganda, and compulsion to get participation in wars of dubious moral standing.

Stephen Kohn's meticulous research gives us glimpses into the courageous resistance of thousands of Americans. That courage should be inspirational to a new generation which may face similar moral choices.

I first knew Steve Kohn when I was a faculty member and he was a student at Boston University. Not an ordinary student, he was a founder and editor of an intrepid campus newspaper called the *Exposure*. It dared to challenge and continually *expose* the authoritarian administration of John Silber with a series of bold, ingenious investigations. As a result, newspaper censorship was introduced, the *Exposure*'s funds were cut off, but it persisted. Eventually, it went to court with the aid of the Civil Liberties Union and won a settlement.

Steve went on to law school, and I was not surprised when, after graduation, he became a successful counsel for "whistleblowers"—people who challenged their own employers whom they found guilty of unethical practices. With this book he is, in a sense, blowing a whistle on a very large wrong, on behalf of a more democratic America.

Howard Zinn

Acknowledgments

Since I began work on this project in 1980, many individuals and organizations have provided invaluable assistance and encouragement. These include Michael D. Kohn, Estelle S. Kohn, Corinne M. Kohn, Margareta Margiotta, Nataleigh Rose Kohn, Emily Light Rose, David K. Colapinto, Samuel G. Rose, William Worthy, Howard Zinn, Mari J. Buhle, Harold Dressler, Tia Broadway, Barbara Wien, Ann Kiefer, Linda M. Nunes-Schrag, Elizabeth Nobbe, the National Endowment for the Humanities Youth Grants Program (which provided an initial grant), Northeastern University School of Law, Antioch School of Law, the National Whistle-blower Center, Glen Marcus, Mark Toney, Sam Daoud, Penny Sippel, Dan Eades, Michael Clagett, Ana Maria Ramos, Michael Rose, Jim Pfeiffer, and Michael Meltsner.

American
Political
Prisoners

Introduction

Certain chapters in U.S. history are deliberately ignored. What they tell us about our conduct toward one another and about our political and social development does not square with the conventional account of our democratic processes. Yet, like personal traumas that haunt us when we try to avoid them, the social and political traumas of these unspoken experiences continue to linger and haunt our society.

One such ignored chapter of our history concerns the U.S. government's destruction of the lives of thousands of American dissidents, anti-war activists, Socialists, trade union leaders and pacifists who were arrested under federal laws during World War I. Those idealists were systematically arrested and in some cases died at the government's instigation and with its legal sanction. As a result, a developing human rights movement was uprooted and disposed of in an unmarked grave.

I was first drawn to the study of World War I because of the era's social and political ferment, especially its flourishing dissident movement whose supporters were prosecuted and imprisoned by the U.S. government for opposing or resisting the draft. Political scientists still debate the influence of the pre-1917 dissident movement in the United States and the extent to which it wrought changes in our social and political institutions. What is certain is that at the time of the United States' entry into World War I, there was an expanding anti-war movement that brought together a diverse group of political activists.

The powers of government swiftly combined to destroy this movement through a Congress that passed anti-sedition laws, through a "liberal" Democratic president who signed them into law and then vigorously enforced these laws and through a Supreme Court that unfailingly upheld the constitutionality of these laws when they were challenged. Whether this dissident movement would have survived and expanded but for the repression will never be known. But what cannot be denied is the legal terror visited upon all of its adherents—from the leaders to the rank and file.

American Political Prisoners provides a missing chapter on the repression that occurred from 1917 to 1932. The core of the book is based on formerly inaccessible files belonging to the Federal Bureau of Prisons, the Federal Bureau of Investigation (FBI) and other divisions of the Department of Justice. Some of these files were made available to me in response to my Freedom of Information Act requests after I successfully sued the FBI.

American Political Prisoners consists of three parts. The first chronicles the history and application of the laws used to imprison anyone solely on the basis of religious or political belief. These laws, many of which remain on today's statute books, represent an overt and serious threat to freedom of thought and expression. The fact that they were systematically used in the past and their constitutionality was upheld by the Supreme Court of the United States speaks to the ominous potential for their misuse in the future.

The second part of the book offers a glimpse into the prison life of the political prisoners. It is based on the actual words of the prisoners, their families, prison guards, prison doctors and the warden of Leavenworth Penitentiary, culled from prison records. In it, I hope to present the reader with a dramatic re-creation of the actual experience of the political prisoners. Chapters 4 to 7, 9 and 10 are based on materials heretofore unavailable to historical researchers or the public.

In the federal system, prison records are routinely destroyed every twenty-five years. Thus, when I began my research, the custodian of documents at the Federal Bureau of Prisons informed me that all the records had been destroyed in the 1950s as part of standard prison procedure. But through perseverance and luck, many of the old, rotted and forgotten records from Leavenworth and Atlanta Penitentiaries were located and released, one by one, and to my amazement were released uncensored.

The boxes of prison files held standard prison information—work orders, slips regarding dates of release and entry, medical records, and so on. From these records, the experiences of many of the prisoners surfaced. The documents included confiscated prison letters, medical reports on inmates who died from abuse, background memoranda on why prisoners were arrested, Department of Justice memoranda on the legal cases and disciplinary records from the many prisoners placed in "the hole," the epithet prisoners gave to solitary confinement. It almost goes without saying that none of these documents was intended for publication, and, in fact, many were confiscated by prison authorities to prevent them from being read even by the inmates themselves or by their families.

The third part of the book documents the hundreds of union leaders, anti-war activists, Socialists and other dissidents rounded up and arrested under the sedition laws. The lengths of the entries are uneven, determined as they are by the availability of information. Nevertheless, I have tried to provide particulars on who was arrested, where they came from, what they believed, how long they were imprisoned and how they were treated in prison.

Although tens of thousands of activists were arrested from 1917 to 1932, I have accounted only for political prisoners who were convicted under the federal or state espionage and sedition acts and who actually served a year or more in prison. The number of political dissidents who served less than a year in prison, yet were arrested, indicted, fined or deported, is simply too great to document in this book. Additionally, thousands of conscientious objectors were arrested under the Selective Service Act. Other than conscientious objectors who died in prison, these cases will be presented in a forthcoming book.

Part I

Background to the Sedition Laws and Their Use During the World War I Era

Chapter 1

The Espionage and Sedition Acts of 1917 and 1918: Then and Now

The advent of World War I led to the creation of the first federal police system designed to monitor, infiltrate and destroy groups of dissenters in the United States. As the U.S. Senate Select Committee to Study Governmental Operations with Respect to Intelligence Activities would conclude in its 1976 report documenting the abuses of this police system, "The first substantial domestic intelligence programs of the federal government were established during World War I."[1]

World War I gave birth to the network of laws and institutions that provided precedent during the 1950s for the anti-communist witch hunts led by Senator Joseph R. McCarthy and that were used during the 1960s and 1970s to discredit and "neutralize" grass-roots movements for peace, civil rights, women's rights and other activities protected by the First Amendment.[2] The network of repressive laws and institutions created during World War I still exists and has been strengthened over time.[3]

The World War I period also gave birth to a series of laws and judicial interpretations of the First Amendment to the U.S. Constitution that legalized the investigation and imprisonment of thousands of Americans because they held unpopular beliefs or political affiliations. This legalization of political repression provided the ideological and legal underpinnings not only of the Red Scare, but also of all future governmental intrusions into the political and religious dissent activities of millions of Americans.[4]

CONGRESSIONAL PASSAGE OF
REPRESSIVE LEGISLATION

At the time the United States entered World War I, there was a very large American peace movement. Congress, aware of this movement, passed two laws intended to suppress "disloyal" or anti-war activity.

On June 15, 1917, Congress passed the now infamous Espionage Act.[5] This law, which had nothing whatever to do with espionage, made it a felony to make "false statements" or statements that might cause "insubordination" or "disloyalty" in the armed services or statements that could "obstruct" enlistment into the armed services.[6] A "conspiracy" to cause such "disloyalty," "insubordination" or "obstruction" was likewise criminalized.[7] Anyone found guilty under the law was subject to heavy fines and imprisonment of up to twenty years.

The congressional supporters of this law specifically pointed to the anti-war resolution passed by the Socialist Party in a special St. Louis convention and to the radical labor union activities of the Industrial Workers of the World (IWW) as justification for passing the Espionage Act.[8] For example, Congressman Albert R. Johnson from the state of Washington complained of the pre-war labor-organizing activities of the IWW within the lumber industry. On the floor of Congress he noted that "all of the lumber manufacturers" had sent him telegrams requesting federal action against the IWW. Johnson spoke in support of the bill as a means of eradicating the "nonloyal agitators" and "outlaw leaders" of the IWW.[9]

In the Senate Lee S. Overman of North Carolina warned that the Espionage Act was needed to prevent "papers" from being "circulated all through the South urging Negroes to rise up against white people."[10]

A minority of congressmen and senators unsuccessfully opposed passage of the Espionage Act. Senator William E. Borah of Idaho warned:

I am afraid of the . . . unconstitutional, un-American, unwise, and unnecessary scheme. It is fundamentally and essentially wrong, and being wrong in principle, no one can foresee all the evils to flow from it.[11]

Congressman William J. Cary of Wisconsin opposed the law as a "menace to every vital principle of liberty" and "contrary to every precedent and tradition of our past history." Congressman Cary condemned the "denaturing" of "representative democracy" and the fettering of the "spirit of American liberty."[12]

The elected Socialist Party congressman from New York, Meyer London, bemoaned the passage of the law: "There is nothing more oppressive in the world than a democracy gone mad."[13]

On May 16, 1918, Congress amended the Espionage Act, broadening its prohibitions. The May 16 amendment made it a felony, punishable by twenty years in prison, when the United States is at war, [to] wilfully utter, print, write or publish any disloyal, profane, scurrilous, or abusive language about the form of government of the United States, or the Constitution of the United States, or the military or naval forces of the United States, or the flag of the United States, or the uniform of the army or navy of the United States, or any language intended to bring the form of government of the United States, or the Constitution of the United States, or the military or the naval forces of the United States, or the flag of the United States, or the uniform of the army or navy of the United States into contempt, scorn, contumely or disrepute.[14]

The congressional debate over the May 16 amendment left no doubt as to Congress' intent. Senator Kenneth McKellar of Tennessee put it simply: "If we cannot reason with men to be loyal it is high time we forced them to be loyal."[15] Congressman William Green of Iowa "heartily" commended the bill: "For the extermination of these pernicious vermin [i.e., members of the IWW] no measures can be too severe."[16] Congressman W. B. Walton of New Mexico condemned "pacifist demonstrations" and declared that the twenty-year sentence contained in the bill was "too mild": "Twenty years! Twenty years in the penitentiary for men who ought to be shot within twenty-four hours after their crime is discovered."[17]

The law was intended not only to prohibit speech, but also to eliminate thoughts and ideas deemed disloyal. As Congressman Percy Quin of Mississippi stated on the floor of Congress: "I want to curb these fellows who are disloyal in their hearts."[18]

FEDERAL PROSECUTION OF THE DISSIDENTS

Even before the implementation of the Espionage Act, federal prosecutors indicted outspoken anti-war activists under a general criminal conspiracy law. On May 18, 1917, Congress passed the Selective Service Act, the first compulsory military draft law since the controversial Civil War conscription laws.[19]

Unlike the Selective Service Acts of 1940 and 1948 (the latter of which remains in effect today), the 1917 draft law did not explicitly criminalize opposition to the draft. Instead, federal prosecutors utilized a general conspiracy law that made it a felony, subject to two years in prison, to "conspire" to violate any federal law. Consequently, federal prosecutors used this conspiracy law to indict anti-war activists for speeches made after the passage of the draft law on April 28, 1917, but before the passage of the far more restrictive Espionage Act in June 1917.

Among the first persons convicted under the conspiracy statute were the outspoken anarchist leaders Emma Goldman and Alexander Berkman. The indictments on June 15, 1917, came in response to their public speeches and magazine articles against the war and charged them under the Selective Service Act with "conspiracy to induce persons not to register."[20]

The prosecution never accused either Goldman or Berkman of actually advising any draft-age person against registering for the draft. It was sufficient to accuse them of publicly expressing their strong views against conscription, war and militarism to warrant conviction under the general conspiracy statute.[21]

Additionally, the conspiracy statute did not require the government to prove that anybody actually failed to register for the draft as a result of listening to the public speeches of Goldman and Berkman. The alleged "conspiracy" to urge persons not to register—accomplished solely through public speeches and articles—was sufficient to justify a conspiracy conviction.[22] The government was under no obligation to introduce any evidence that anyone was influenced by Goldman's and Berkman's speeches or that they in fact actually counselled any individual to violate any law. The U.S. Supreme Court unanimously upheld the use of the general conspiracy statute to convict anti-war leaders.[23]

After passage of the Espionage Act, the government used the broad language and strict sentencing provisions of that law to indict thousands of dissidents. The U.S. Department of Justice used the Espionage Act to prosecute unmercifully anyone who held anti-war sentiments or who advocated radical social change. The primary institutional victims of the law were the American Socialist Party, then headed by Eugene Victor Debs, and the Industrial Workers of the World, then headed by William D. Haywood. The Department of Justice prosecuted thousands of individuals, ranging from national figures (including a congressman) to ordinary men and women whose sole crime was to criticize the war to a neighbor or a friend.

Like the earlier prosecutions under the Selective Service Act, almost all Espionage Act indictments were based on a "conspiracy" to violate the law. Conspiracies under the Espionage Act carried a twenty-year sentence, but significantly reduced the burden of proof for local U.S. attorneys seeking convictions. In fact, the Department of Justice privately commented on "how little evidence" was needed "to connect most" of the persons convicted under the Espionage Act "with any direct and substantial violation of that act."[24]

Generally the federal courts followed the Justice Department's lead in upholding prosecutions under the Espionage Act. For example, a federal district court in Syracuse, New York, declined to dismiss the prosecution of André Boutin. Boutin had circulated a pamphlet entitled "Pure Common Sense," which, according to the federal court, stated:

We need preparedness, not to kill one another, but to live peacefully, happily, and equally. . . .

[W]e should treat each other like brother and sister, whether we are born on this side or the other side of the iron post.... We should all respect and help one another. War is pure ignorance.[25]

The federal court judge who heard the case concluded that the pamphlet "tend[ed] to suppress patriotic feelings" and thus could cause a "refusal to duty." The judge considered the pamphlet "pernicious" and wrote that it could "destroy military ardor and inclination to cheerfully perform military duty."[26]

Individuals were prosecuted for publishing newspapers critical of the war,[27] showing a movie critical of Great Britain's actions during the American Revolution (*The Spirit of '76*),[28] sending telegrams critical of the treatment of persons imprisoned under the Espionage Act,[29] circulating the American Socialist Party's "anti-war proclamation"[30] and using a "loud voice" to state that the draft law was unconstitutional.[31]

Although the vast majority of federal courts uncritically prosecuted cases under the Espionage Act, some district judges refused to allow the sedition cases to go to trial.[32] For example, in *Wolf v. United States*, a U.S. court of appeals overturned the conviction of John H. Wolf, who had received a five-year sentence, in part for calling World War I "unjust."[33] The court recognized that "when patriotic sentiment is high," it may be "particularly difficult to secure a fair trial" in sedition act cases: "Patriotism must not become, even innocently, a cloak for injustice."[34]

One federal district court in Butte, Montana, severely criticized the "governmental despotism" involved in the anti-sedition prosecutions. Judge George M. Bourquin boldly stated that the "so-called 'Reds' " who were persecuted during the World War I period were "less a danger to America" than those who used legally questionable tactics to persecute them. According to Judge Bourquin, the "spirit" of "intolerance" was the "most alarming manifestation" in the United States:

Far worse than the immediate wrongs to individuals that they do, they undermine the morale of the people, excite the latter's fears, distrust of our institutions, doubts of the sufficiency of law and authority; they incline the people toward arbitrary power, which for protection cowards too often seek, and knaves too readily grant, and subject to which the people cease to be courageous and free, and become timid and enslaved.... Doubtless some of those, of some variety of prestige, who horrify the thoughtful lovers of America by their loose suggestion and advocacy of stone walls, shootings at sunrise, and other lynch law, are animated by sincere, but mistaken, concern for national welfare; but equally doubtless many of them are incited by unholy desire for personal advantage—money profit, popular approval, or political preferment. They are breeders of suspicion, fear, anger, revenge, riot, crime, class hatred, "Reds," despotism, threatening, if aught can, civil anarchy and revolution, and they and the government by hysteria that they stimulate are more to be feared than all the miserable, baited, bedeviled "Reds" that are their ostensible occasion and whose sins they exaggerate.[35]

Initially, the Supreme Court of the United States unanimously upheld the Espionage Act convictions. In March 1919, the Supreme Court upheld the convictions of Charles T. Schenck, the general secretary of the Socialist Party; Elizabeth Baer, an Executive Board member of the Socialist Party; Jacob Frohwerk, a Missouri newspaper publisher; and Eugene V. Debs, the Socialist Party's presidential candidate and the leader of the famous Pullman strike.[36] The rulings on this trilogy of cases—*Schenck v. United States, Frohwerk v. United States,* and *Debs v. United States*—became the collective standard courts applied in deciding sedition cases.

Justice Oliver Wendell Holmes, who wrote all three decisions, rejected the defendants' First Amendment argument on the grounds that if Congress has the "right to prevent" a certain evil, then Congress could legislate against speech that "create[d] a clear and present danger" that they would "bring about" the Socialist/pacifist "evil."[37]

Ironically, within a matter of months Justice Holmes found himself in the minority on the Court. In his dissenting opinion in *Abrams v. United States* (a case concerning the conviction of five "anarchists" who distributed two leaflets critical of the U.S. government), Justice Holmes, with Justice Louis D. Brandeis' support, argued that the "clear and present danger" standard should be narrowly applied.[38] The Supreme Court, however, upheld the convictions, citing Justice Holmes' own standard.

The next year, 1920, a divided Supreme Court again upheld the constitutionality of an Espionage Act conviction. In that case, *Pierce v. United States,* the defendants were convicted of circulating the anti-war leaflet entitled "The Price We Pay."[39] The pamphlet, written by an Episcopal clergyman, was a "highly colored" "protest" against the "further prosecution of the war by the United States."[40] The defendant, Clinton H. Pierce, and four other members of the Socialist Party were charged with and convicted of "distributing the pamphlets" "throughout the city of Albany," New York.[41]

Ironically, in an earlier case (1917), a federal district court in Maryland threw out an indictment against two individuals charged with circulating the very same pamphlet.[42] In that case, *United States v. Baker,* the court pointed out that prosecuting individuals for distributing the pamphlet would be "going very far indeed."[43] The court explained its reasons for refusing to allow the case to go to trial:

You may have your own opinions about that circular. I have very strong individual opinions about it, and as to the wisdom and fairness of what is said there; but so far as I can see it is a circular principally intended to induce people to subscribe to a Socialist newspaper and to get recruits for the Socialist party. I do not think that we ought to attempt to prosecute people for that kind of thing. It may be very unwise in its effect, and it may have been unpatriotic at that particular time and place; but it would be going very far indeed, further, I think than any law that I know of would justify, to hold that there has been made out any case here, even tending to show that there was an attempt to persuade men not to obey the law. There is a very lurid description of the horrors of war in that circular—some of it well written; some of it not so well written. But, after all, there is no difference of opinion that war is a terrible catastrophe, and involves many terrible things.[44]

The defendants in *Pierce* had put off distributing the pamphlet *until* they were informed of the Maryland court's decision. Unfortunately for Pierce and his codefendants the federal district court in Albany did not agree with the Maryland district court's decision, and the convictions were upheld under the Espionage Act.

The *Pierce* convictions were also upheld by the Supreme Court of the United States. Once again, Justices Holmes and Brandeis dissented when the majority of the Supreme Court held that a jury may "fairly" infer that, based upon the content of the pamphlet and the circumstances surrounding its distribution, the content of the material could have a "tendency" to cause "individual disloyalty" or "refusal of duty." In a strongly worded dissent, Justice Brandeis, noting that the pamphlet had not been distributed to men of the military, called attention to the "total lack of evidence" that any of the defendants intended to cause any form of "refusal of duty," "disloyalty" or "insubordination." Justice Brandeis stated:

The fundamental right of free men to strive for better conditions through new legislation and new institutions will not be preserved, if efforts to secure it by argument to fellow citizens may be construed as criminal incitement to disobey the existing law—merely because the argument presented seems to those exercising judicial power to be unfair in its portrayal of existing evils, mistaken in its assumptions, unsound in reasoning or intemperate in language. No objections more serious than these can, in my opinion, reasonably be made to the arguments presented in "The Price We Pay."[45]

The Supreme Court has never formally overturned its rulings in *Schenck*, *Debs*, *Frohwerk*, *Abrams* and *Pierce*. Since then, however, the Court has critically reviewed the convictions obtained during that period. In his concurring opinion in *Dennis v. United States*, Justice Robert H. Jackson noted that the World War I convictions under the *Schenck* "clear and present danger" test were "loosely construed" and used to "punish socialism, pacifism and left-wing ideologies." Justice Jackson noted that the "charges often" rested on "far fetched inferences which, if true, would establish only technical or trivial violations."[46] In his concurring opinion in *Brandenburg v. Ohio*, Justice William O. Douglas acknowledged the abusive potential inherent in the "clear and present danger" standard.[47]

The dissents in *Abrams*, *Schaefer* and *Pierce* show how easily "clear and present danger" is manipulated to crush what Brandeis called "the fundamental rights of free men to strive for better conditions through new legislation and new institutions" by argument and discourse, even in time of war.

In all, approximately two thousand cases were filed under the Espionage and Sedition Acts. The victims of the law ranged from pacifists, to anarchists, to religious zealots, to Socialists and trade union leaders. In addition to the prosecution of various individuals, the law was used to systematically destroy the large Socialist Party then existing in the United States and the IWW.

The government succeeded in using the law to ban both organizations' distribution of literature through the mails, to raid their national offices and to indict or convict almost all their leaders. In less than a decade the federal government had succeeded in using these laws to destroy popular dissident organizations and imprison their leaders throughout the United States.[48]

THE MASS IWW TRIALS

Most of the Espionage Act cases involved the trial of an individual or a small group of individuals for speaking or writing against the war. But in the case of the IWW, the government targeted an entire labor organization, rounding up its national and local leaders and holding them for mass trials in the cities of Chicago, Illinois; Wichita, Kansas; Sacramento, California; and Omaha, Nebraska. Summaries of these proceedings are presented below. For facts about the convicted IWW members, see Chapter 12.

The Indictment and Trial in Chicago

On September 5, 1917, the federal campaign to close down the IWW began with the arrest of the IWW's national and regional leaders, its major newspaper editors and its Executive Board members. In this first indictment, the Department of Justice named 166 alleged union leaders.

As would be true in all the other federal cases against the IWW, the indictments (and sustained convictions) were based on the union's "public distribution" of statements and speeches against war in general or against the United States' participation in World War I specifically. The major conspiracy indictments were based exclusively on speech-related crimes. In relevant part, the federal indictment against the union leaders stated:

By means of personal solicitation, of public speeches, of articles printed in certain newspapers [here twelve newspapers are named, of which eight are foreign language editions], circulating throughout the United States, and of the public distribution of certain pamphlets entitled, "War and the Workers," "Patriotism and the Workers" and "Preamble and Constitution of the Industrial Workers of the World," the same being solicitations, speeches, articles and pamphlets persistently urging insubordination, disloyalty and refusal of duty in said military and naval forces and failure and refusal on the part of available persons to enlist therein.[49]

Of those indicted, eighty-seven were confined for over a year in the Cook County Jail while awaiting trial, and bail was arranged for twenty-six members. Of the remaining fifty-three indicted IWW members (often referred to as Wobblies), four received a severance of their cases and eventually had their cases dismissed, one was found dead at the time of the indictment and the remaining defendants were never apprehended.[50]

The Chicago trial lasted from March 23 until August 30, 1918. The only evidence submitted against the IWW members consisted of newspaper articles, letters and organizational literature—most of which were printed *before* the United States entered into World War I. According to an American Civil Liberties Union (ACLU) study of the trial:

No member of the IWW was convicted in any court of any crime involving the organization in violence. . . . No connection whatever was found between German agents or German money and the IWW . . . most of the charges of obstruction against the IWW during this war were part of an organized campaign by war-profiteers and employing interests to use the war to crush this labor organization.[51]

Despite the lack of evidence against them, the IWW leaders were found guilty and sentenced severely—fifteen were sentenced to twenty years, thirty-seven to ten years, thirty-four to five years and eighteen to two years. Total fines were over $2.5 million. The convictions under the Espionage Act were upheld by a federal appeals court.[52]

While the IWW leaders languished in jail, the weaknesses of the government's case were publicly exposed. For example, Alexander Sidney Lanier, a former major in the Bureau of Military Intelligence, reviewed the entire 40,000-page court record of the Chicago trial and concluded the following in testimony before the U.S. House Judiciary Committee:

It is my opinion that none of these men were properly convicted, because I think that the indictments were vitally defective. I do not think that if I had been on the jury, I would have convicted a single one of them, because there was no evidence . . . that those men were guilty of the conspiracy with which they were charged.[53]

Even more revealing as to the weakness of the government's case was a confidential Department of Justice memorandum of December 10, 1920, prepared for attorney general, which admitted that the cases against the

IWW defendants were completely lacking in evidence. In one case, the DOJ admitted that the trial was a "farce."[54]

The Trial in Wichita

In late November and early December 1917, approximately fifty IWW leaders as well as activists from the Oil Workers and Agricultural Workers Industrial Unions were arrested in Kansas and Oklahoma.

They were held in three county jails in Kansas for two years until they were tried under the Espionage Act for urging people to violate the Selective Service Act and causing "insubordination in the military" by "public speaking" and by publishing "articles printed in certain newspapers." The charges were almost identical to those of the Chicago indictment.

The Kansas county jails—Shawnee, Sedgwick and Wyandotte—were reported to be among the vilest penal institutions in the country. Winthrop D. Lane, a reporter for *Survey* magazine, was commissioned by *Survey* and the National Civil Liberties Union (the forerunner of the ACLU) to investigate these jails. Lane found that of the twenty-eight IWW members confined in Kansas county jails, one died, four contracted tuberculosis and two were transferred to insane asylums. Lane described the jails as overcrowded, rat-infested and "disease breeding" and reported that the prisoners were kept idle and sometimes spent fifty consecutive days in solitary confinement. Lane wrote that the Sedgwick County Jail was the worst he had ever seen:

The Sedgwick County jail is the worst place for incarcerating human beings that I have ever been in. . . . It is filthy with the accumulated filth of decades. . . . The toilets throughout are covered with dirt. Many of them are encrusted with excreta and a few actually stink. The men declare that they do not dare to sit down on them, because of the vermin.

The age of the jail has produced crevices and openings in the brick walls through which rain and, in winter, melting snow pour in. . . . Rats issue through these holes and through the crevices in the steel flooring. At evening, when the prisoners have quieted down, these rats come forth in great numbers. It is not uncommon for a prisoner to be awakened by a rat running over his bed or even across his face.[55]

On December 1, 1919, the defendants were tried. Twenty-five were found guilty on four counts—all relating to their opposing World War I—and were transferred to the federal prison in Leavenworth. Nineteen of these inmates were freed in May 1921 after the federal circuit court of appeals overturned their conviction on the first count of the indictment—the only part of the indictment for which they were serving time. The remaining six Wichita defendants were slowly released through pardons or through the expiration of their sentences in 1922 and 1923.

The Sacramento Trial and the "Silence Defense"

Between September 1917 and June 1918, fifty-three IWW leaders and activists, all active members on the West Coast, were arrested. Among those incarcerated was the secretary of the committee set up to defend those indicted; the secretaries of the Stockton, Los Angeles, Oakland and Sacramento IWW locals; and officials of the Construction Workers, the Agricultural Workers and the Marine Transport Workers Industrial Unions. Like the IWW unionists in Chicago and Wichita, they were charged with conspiracy to obstruct the war effort and the military draft.

The allegations against the IWW members indicted in Sacramento were more frenzied than those in other cities where arrests of IWW members took place. These included accusations that the IWW was responsible for an alleged assassination attempt against California's Governor-Elect William D. Stephens, based in part on the arrest of two members, employed as miners, who were carrying dynamite (a routinely and legitimately used material in mining). The *Sacramento Bee* called for shooting the IWW prisoners, "the sooner the better!"[56] No evidence linking the IWW to the alleged assassination attempt was ever produced, however. In fact, according to Melvyn Dubofsky's classic study of the IWW, the so-called assassination plot was fictional; "federal officials learned that the entire assassination affair had been arranged by a corrupt San Francisco district attorney."[57]

While the defendants awaited trial in jail, their defense efforts were undermined by federal agents. The first of the federal attempts to sabotage the defense consisted of a series of raids on the defense office: seven raids in six months.[58] Next, a union supporter was arrested when she entered the county jail with bail money for two of the IWW defendants. Federal agents struck again after defense secretary Fred Esmond wired the U.S. attorney general to protest the inhumane treatment of the unionists in prison. Esmond was arrested and held in jail for eight months incommunicado, and his telegram was introduced as evidence against him at the Sacramento sedition trial, where he was convicted along with the other defendants.

Five Sacramento defendants died in jail while awaiting trial. An account of the prison conditions, which some of the defendants endured for a year, went as follows:

These men were thrown into a city jail cell, 21 × 21 feet. All of them could not lie down at once. It was winter. One cotton blanket was given each. Their food was about two ounces of mush in the morning, less than two ounces of bread, and at night three fetid little smelts and less than two ounces of potatoes, with "coffee" twice a day. In the fold they shivered. Day by day they starved. By relays they slept at night; the bedlam of a city drunk tank soothed slumbers wooed in frost and starvation.[59]

The IWW defendants went to trial on December 7, 1918, in the federal court in Sacramento. Forty-three of the forty-six defendants who were actually brought to trial conducted a "silent defense." They refused counsel and refused to speak throughout the trial; they conducted no cross-examination and called no witnesses. They felt a fair trial was impossible and refused to participate in a "kangaroo court." At the end of the trial the defendants' elected spokesman, Mortimer Downing, explained why this silent defense was used:

We decided upon the silent defense because we despair of justice for the working man being achieved through the courts. . . . We are tried in a prejudiced community. Some of our men have been held incommunicado. They have been prevented by United States agents from mailing courteous appeals to the court. Some of them have been confined, untried, for a year. These conditions are intolerable, and this "silence strike" is to preserve the self-respect of ourselves as members of organized labor.[60]

All the defendants were found guilty. The three Wobblies who conducted a defense received lenient jail sentences. Of those who participated in the silent defense, twenty received ten-year terms, and the remainder were sentenced to three to five years in prison. After sentencing, the "silent" defendants were transferred to Leavenworth Penitentiary.

The Omaha Roundup

On November 13, 1917, sixty-four IWW members arrived in Omaha, Nebraska, for a special convention of the Agricultural Workers Industrial Union. Upon their arrival in Omaha they were summarily arrested, although there was no evidence of their having committed any crime. They waited in jail for eight months before their case was even sent before a grand jury for indictment, and they remained in jail for an additional ten months while awaiting trial. In April 1919, prior to taking the case to trial, the government dismissed all charges. No evidence was ever collected to incriminate—even under anti-war legislation—the activities of these union men.

RELEASE OF THE ESPIONAGE ACT PRISONERS

At the end of World War I, the federal government gradually began to release these prisoners. Many were released at the expiration of their sentences. Others were pardoned on the condition that they would be deported from the United States or would agree to resign from membership in various radical organizations and become "law-abiding citizens."

Many prisoners adamantly refused to compromise their beliefs.[61] Among them were fifty-two members of the IWW who on August 22, 1922, issued a statement about their refusal to even apply for individual pardons or clemency:

We know that we are now in prison solely for exercising the constitutional right of free speech at a time when discretion might have been the better part of altruism. If it is a crime to exercise the right for which our fathers laid down their lives, then we have no apology to offer. Free speech has always been the one thing we have prized above all others. In this regard we are unchanged. And we cannot bring ourselves to make application for clemency because we wish to avoid being forced into an action that would make hypocrites of us all.

Liberty is sweet to any man in prison, but not sweet enough to us to be purchased at the price of principle. We feel we owe it to the loyal men and women outside of these walls who still believe in freedom of speech, assemblage and the press, to remain steadfast and uphold these ideals even at the cost of continued incarceration. We cannot do otherwise than refuse to recant. We must continue to refuse to beg for a pardon which in common justice ought to have been accorded to us long ago.

In the face of such an alternative, we have decided to stand by our principles, no matter the cost. . . . [IWW] members have always stood firm whenever the right of free speech was threatened. We are standing firm now. . . . But in matters of principle, conscience and civil rights, we believe men can serve best by unfaltering devotion to the ideas they are committed to uphold. . . . We serve notice upon the men who directed our inquisition that medieval methods of seeking to change the convictions of human minds by force have failed. If it is their intention to keep us in prison until we admit we are wrong about those things, they might as well throw away the keys at once. They will never need them.[62]

By December 1923, the U.S. government concluded that the purposes behind the original arrest and persecution of persons under the Espionage and Sedition Acts had been achieved. In a confidential memorandum to the attorney general, the U.S. pardon attorney declared victory in the government's war against the radicals and anti-war activists. "It is exceedingly fortunate that the government has . . . kept a sufficient number of them in prison to set an example of firmness that will go down in history as a warning to those who in the future might be inclined to harbinger and harass the government."[63]

The pardon attorney praised the imprisonment of these dissidents, while conceding that in most cases related to the remaining prisoners "it [would] be difficult" to "find justification in the evidence" to support the original charges filed against them.[64] For reasons unrelated to individual justice or the merits of the prisoners' claims, the pardon attorney recommended that all the remaining prisoners held under the Espionage and Sedition Acts be granted an "unconditional" commutation of their sentences and that they be immediately released from prison:

Further imprisonment would not add appreciably to [the government's interests] but would be a constant source of contention and dissatisfaction and also of misunderstanding among many of our really good citizens and furnish material for those who openly or covertly are seeking to break down and overturn our present form of government.[65]

Soon after this recommendation was issued by the Justice Department, unconditional commutations of sentences were issued to all remaining political prisoners. In June 1924, Nicholas S. Zogg, an anarchist, was the last inmate held under the Espionage and Sedition Acts to be released from a federal prison.

STATE PROSECUTION OF DISSIDENTS

A majority of states and territories passed anti-sedition legislation similar to that of the federal government. For example, in 1917, Alaska made it a crime to make "utterances or publications tending to excite discontent, trouble, ill feelings, or hostility against the United States" (see Alaska statutes, chap. 50). Twenty-nine other states followed Alaska's example and passed anti-sedition laws, commonly referred to as anti-anarchy or criminal syndicalism laws.[66] Many states also passed laws prohibiting the display of a red flag. Between 1917 and 1920, the following states and territories passed repressive legislation: Alaska, Arizona, California, Connecticut, Delaware, Hawaii, Idaho, Illinois, Indiana, Iowa, Kansas, Louisiana, Michigan, Minnesota, Montana, Nebraska, Nevada, New Jersey, New Mexico, New York, Oklahoma, Oregon, Pennsylvania, South Dakota, Utah, Vermont, Washington, West Virginia, Wisconsin and Wyoming.[67]

Due to the local nature of prosecutions under criminal syndicalism and state sedition acts, the actual scope of prosecutions under these laws is impossible to determine. According to Eldridge F. Dowell's 1939 study on state criminal syndicalism legislation, California, Washington State and Idaho prosecuted the greatest number of individuals under these laws.[68] Between 1917 and 1933, the number of imprisonments was highest in California (135),[69] followed by Washington State (52).[70] Scores of other states, including Nevada, Pennsylvania, Oregon, New York and Michigan, incarcerated persons under these laws.

Unlike the federal anti-sedition laws, the state anti-anarchy or criminal syndicalism laws were not limited in their application to periods of declared war. The state sedition laws were also applicable during peacetime, and a majority of prosecutions under the state laws occurred after World War I had ended. Most of those convicted were members of the IWW and the early Communist Party.[71]

Federal and state courts uniformly upheld the constitutionality of these laws.[72] In 1927, the U.S. Supreme Court, in *Whitney v. California*, broadly interpreted the rights of states to criminalize the utterance of certain ideas, even if those utterances created no "clear and present danger" to national security. The Court ruled that it was no longer even "open to question" that a person could be prosecuted merely for "utterances inimical" to "organized government."[73]

THE PRESENT STATUS OF SEDITION LEGISLATION

In 1919, the year after the end of World War I, U.S. Attorney General A. Mitchell Palmer requested that Congress follow the lead of numerous states and pass legislation applicable in peacetime that would make "sedition and seditious utterances and publications a crime."[74] On that occasion Congress declined to follow this recommendation. By 1924, the new attorney general, Harlan Fiske Stone, acknowledged in a letter that many of the actions by the Department of Justice against dissidents had been "brutal and tyrannical in the extreme" and warned that when government becomes involved in the "opinions of individuals," its "police system" becomes "dangerous to the proper administration of justice and human liberty."[75]

Attorney General Stone's words were not long heeded. In 1940, Congress passed a peacetime federal anti-sedition law, modeled after the state of New York's anti-anarchy law and commonly known as the Smith Act. In the 1940s and 1950s, many Socialists and Communists were imprisoned under its provisions.[76] For example, between 1940 and 1956 over 185 leaders of the Socialist Workers Party (SWP) and Communist Party (CP) were indicted under the Smith Act. Among those imprisoned were James P. Cannon, the National Secretary of the SWP; Felix Morrow the editor of the *Militant* newspaper; the leadership of Local 544 of the Teamsters Union (one of the largest and most progressive locals of that union); the General Secretary and entire national leadership of the CP; Benjamin Davis, a former elected New York City Council member; and Elizabeth Gurly Flynn, a former leader of the IWW union and a founding member of the ACLU.[77] Federal courts initially gave the Smith Act an even broader interpretation than had been given the Espionage Act.[78]

In the late 1950s and 1960s, the Supreme Court gradually narrowed the applicability of peacetime sedition laws[79] and even reversed the *Whitney v.*

California decision.[80] Significantly, the Supreme Court did not overturn the *Schenck* and *Abrams* decisions and did not address the open issues related to wartime sedition laws.

The Espionage Act, the Smith Act and most state criminal syndicalism laws are still in effect. Given the past history of these laws and the Supreme Court's failure to unequivocally declare such laws unconstitutional on their face, the future abusive application of sedition legislation is a realistic possibility. Worse, since 1917, the investigatory powers and prosecutorial authority of federal and state police agencies have massively increased. The ability of the government to punish political dissidents is far greater today than it was in 1917.[81] For example, during the 1950s, 1960s and early 1970s, the FBI, CIA and other police agencies utilized their vast investigatory and prosecutorial powers to "neutralize," "discredit" and undermine the major civil rights organizations and leaders (including Dr. Martin Luther King), women's rights organizations, peace groups and the so-called "New Left." By 1973 the FBI alone, using paid informants, wiretaps, illegal break-ins, secretly installed microphones and the indiscriminate opening of political subjects' mail, had created political intelligence files on over 500,000 American citizens. The U.S. Senate Select Committee to Study Government Operations concluded that many of the actions of the Federal police agencies "adopted tactics unworthy of a democracy," and "reminiscent" of those of "totalitarian regimes."[82] Perhaps most significantly, the Committee found that the "Constitutional system of checks and balances" did "not adequately" work.[83]

The legal history of political imprisonment demonstrates that, in time of crisis, all three branches of the U.S. Government have aggressively used repressive legislation to silence dissent.

NOTES

1. Senate Select Committee to Study Governmental Operations with Respect to Intelligence Activities, *Book II, Intelligence Activities and the Rights of Americans,* 94th Cong., 2d sess., 1976, S. Rept. No. 755, 23.

2. Ibid.

3. See, e.g., Amnesty International, *Proposal for a Commission of Inquiry into the Effect of Domestic Intelligence Activities on Criminal Trials in the United States of America* (Nottingham, England: Russell Press Ltd., 1981); Robert J. Goldstein, *Political Repression in Modern America: 1870 to the Present* (New York: Schenkman Publishing Co., 1978); Lennox S. Hinds, *Illusions of Justice: Human Rights Violations in the United States* (Iowa City: School of Social Work, University of Iowa, 1978).

4. See, e.g., *Brandenburg v. Ohio,* 395 U.S. 444, 450–457 (1969) (Douglas, J., concurring).

5. 40 Stat. 217 (1917).

6. Ibid., 219, Sec. 3.

7. Ibid., Sec. 4.

8. See, e.g., Remarks of Senator Paul O. Hustings, May 11, 1917, *Cong. Rec.*, 55:2087.

9. Remarks of Congressman Johnson, May 3, 1917, *Cong. Rec.*, 55:1758.

10. Remarks of Congressman Overman, May 10, 1917, *Cong. Rec.*, 55:2062.

11. Remarks of Senator Borah, May 11, 1917, *Cong. Rec.*, 55:2120.

12. Remarks of Congressman Cary, May 4, 1917, *Cong. Rec.*, 55:152–155.

13. Remarks of Congressman London, May 3, 1917, *Cong. Rec.*, 55:1779.

14. 40 Stat. 553 (1918).

15. Remarks of Senator McKellar, April 6, 1918, *Cong. Rec.*, 56:4718.

16. Remarks of Congressman Green, May 7, 1918, *Cong. Rec.*, 56:6181.

17. Remarks of Congressman Walton, May 7, 1918, *Cong. Rec.*, 56:355.

18. Remarks of Congressman Quin, May 7, 1918, *Cong. Rec.*, 56:6185.

19. 40 Stat. 76 (1917).

20. Harry Weinberger, "The Case of *U.S. v. Emma Goldman and Alexander Berkman*," undated, from Atlanta Penitentiary file on Alexander Berkman.

21. Ibid.

22. See *Goldman v. United States*, 245 U.S. 474 (1918).

23. Ibid., 40 Stat. 217 (1917).

24. U.S. Department of Justice, memorandum from U.S. Pardon Attorney to U.S. Attorney General, December 6, 1923, 6, National Archives.

25. Quoted in *United States v. Boutin*, 251 F. 313, 315 (N.D.N.Y. 1918).

26. *Boutin*, 251 F. at 315.

27. *Stilson v. United States*, 250 U.S. 583 (1919).

28. *Goldstein v. United States*, 258 F. 908, 909 (9th Cir. 1919).

29. *Anderson v. United States*, 269 F. 65, 70–71 (9th Cir. 1920).

30. *Debs v. United States*, 249 U.S. 211 (1919); *Schenck v. United States*, 249 U.S. 47 (1919).

31. *Anderson v. United States*, 264 F. 75, 78 (8th Cir. 1920).

32. See, e.g., *Von Bank v. United States*, 253 F. 641 (8th Cir. 1918); *Dickson v. United States*, 278 F. 728 (8th Cir. 1921); *United States v. Mayer*, 252 F. 868 (W.D. Ky. 1918).

33. *Wolf v. United States*, 259 F. 388, 391 (8th Cir. 1919).

34. *Wolf*, 259 F. at 394.

35. *Ex Parte Jackson*, 263 F. 110, 113–114 (D. Mont. 1920).

36. *Schenck*, 249 U.S. 47; *Frohwerk v. United States*, 249 U.S. 204 (1919); *Debs*, 249 U.S. 211.

37. *Schenck*, 249 U.S. at 52.

38. *Abrams v. United States*, 250 U.S. 616, 624–631 (1919) (Holmes, J., dissenting).

39. *Pierce v. United States*, 252 U.S. 239 (1920).

40. *Pierce*, 252 U.S. at 245.

41. *Pierce*, 252 U.S. at 240–242.

42. See *United States v. Baker*, 247 F. 124 (D. Md. 1917).

43. *Baker*, 247 F. at 125.

44. *Baker*, 247 F. at 125.

45. *Pierce*, 252 U.S. at 273 (Brandeis, J., dissenting). In *Schaefer v. United States*, 251 U.S. 466 (1920), Justices Holmes and Brandeis (along with Justice Clark) also dissented in the conviction of these defendants under the Espionage Act.

46. *Dennis v. United States*, 341 U.S. 494, 567–568 (1951) (Jackson, J., concurring).

47. *Brandenburg v. Ohio*, 395 U.S. 444, 452 (1969) (citations omitted).

48. Goldstein, *Political Repression in Modern America*, 103–136; Daniel Bell, *Marxian Socialism in the United States* (Princeton, N.J.: Princeton University Press, 1967), 102–106; Howard Zinn, *A People's History of the United States* (New York: Harper and Row, 1980), 355–367; Melvyn Dubofsky, *We Shall Be All: A History of the IWW* (New York: Quadrangle, 1969), 398–444.

49. American Civil Liberties Union [hereafter ACLU], "The Truth About the IWW Prisoners" [Pamphlet] (New York: ACLU, 1922), 42.

50. Ibid., 16.

51. Ibid., 8.

52. *Haywood v. United States*, 268 F. 795 (1920).

53. ACLU, "The Truth," 29. Also see "Letter to President Wilson," *New Republic*, April 16, 1919.

54. U.S. Department of Justice, memorandum to U.S. Attorney General, December 10, 1923, National Archives; also see Senate Select Committee, *Book II, Intelligence Activities*, 23–24.

55. Winthrop D. Lane, "Uncle Sam: Jailer," *Survey*, September 1919, p. 800.

56. Quoted in ACLU, "The Truth," 25.

57. Dubofsky, *We Shall Be All*, 439.

58. Ibid., 18.

59. Industrial Workers of the World [hereafter IWW], "The Silent Defense" [Pamphlet] (Chicago: IWW, undated), 5.

60. Quoted in ibid., 18.

61. H. F. Kane, "Why Eleven Members of the IWW Imprisoned at Leavenworth Refused Conditional Pardon" [Pamphlet] (New York: "Printed free of charge by a friend," 1923).

62. IWW General Defense Committee, "An Open Letter to President Harding" [Pamphlet] (Chicago: IWW, 1922).

63. U.S. Department of Justice, Memorandum from U.S. Pardon Attorney to U.S. Attorney General, December 6, 1923, National Archives.

64. Ibid., 2.

65. Ibid., 1.

66. Remarks of Congressman Kelly, February 6, 1920, *Cong. Rec.*, 59:2577–2578. By 1956, the number of states and territories with sedition laws had increased to forty-four; *Pennsylvania v. Nelson*, 350 U.S. 497, 514 n.4 (1956) (Reed, J., dissenting).

67. Remarks of Congressman Kelly, February 6, 1920, *Cong. Rec.*, 59:2577–2578.

68. Eldridge F. Dowell, *A History of Criminal Syndicalism Legislation in the U.S.* (Baltimore: Johns Hopkins University Press, 1939).

69. Ibid., 122 n.46.

70. Ibid., 131 n.102.

71. See, e.g., *Gitlow v. New York*, 268 U.S. 652 (1925); *Whitney v. California*, 274 U.S. 357 (1927).

72. See, e.g., Dowell, *History of Criminal Syndicalism*.

73. *Whitney*, 274 U.S. at 371.

74. U.S. Attorney General A. Mitchell Palmer to Congress re Activities of the Department of Justice, November 17, 1919, 66th Cong., Sess., 19, S. Doc. 153, 4.

75. Senate Select Committee, *Book II, Intelligence Activities*, 23.

76. 42 U.S.C. §2385.

77. James T. Farrell, "Our Fight to Free the 18" (New York: Social Workers Party, 1944): Simon W. Gerson, Record of Smith Act Cases (New York: Joint Self-Defense Committee, 1956).

78. *Dennis v. United States*, 341 U.S. 494 (1951) (upholding prosecution of Communist Party leaders); *Dunne v. United States*, 138 F. 137 (8th Cir. 1943) (upholding convictions of Socialist Workers Party leaders).

79. See, e.g., *Noto v. United States*, 367 U.S. 290 (1961); *Scales v. United States*, 367 U.S. 203 (1961); *Yates v. United States*, 354 U.S. 298 (1957); *Pennsylvania v. Nelson*, 350 U.S. 497 (1956).

80. *Brandenburg v. Ohio*, 395 U.S. 444 (1969).

81. See, e.g., Senate Select Committee, *Book II, Intelligence Activities*.

82. Ibid., 3.

83. Ibid., 6.

Chapter 2

The Selective Service Act

The largest number of political cases arising during World War I concerned prosecutions under the Selective Service Act, or military draft law. In the first year of the war alone there were over eight thousand indictments under the Selective Service Act.[1] Many of those arrested were members of the Socialist Party, pacifist religions or the IWW.

Thousands of conscientious objectors protested the war by refusing to register for the draft.[2] The maximum sentence for failing to register was twelve months in jail. Additionally, the U.S. military court-martialed a large number of conscientious objectors for their anti-war activities or for their religious objection to military service.[3]

Unlike draft laws in previous times of war, the Selective Service Act of World War I placed thousands of conscientious objectors under military authority before they obtained a religious exemption to military service. While the failure to register for the draft was considered a civil offense under the Selective Service Act and subjected the nonregistrant to relatively mild penalties in federal court, a conscientious objector who registered as such immediately fell under military authority and became subject to military justice.

Consequently, many World War I conscientious objectors were first inducted into the army and then court-martialed for offenses such as "refusal to obey orders," "desertion" and "disloyal statements." Military courts ignored most of the basic legal protocol designed to guarantee civilians fair trials. There were no juries, many objectors had no attorneys or counsel and the judges often were military officers. After a year of adjudicating objectors without a uniform mechanism for doing so, the War Department set up a board of inquiry to judge individual cases of war objection and determine whether these men were legally eligible for noncombat service.[4]

In total, over 450 objectors were found guilty at court-martial hearings. In most of these cases the Department of War recognized the genuineness of the objectors' anti-war principles and would offer them alternative service within the military. Most of these objectors refused noncombat service and were subsequently convicted. According to the Department of the Army's *Statement Concerning the Treatment of Conscientious Objectors in the Army*, the original sentences given to conscientious objectors were extreme: 17 sentenced to death, 142 sentenced to life in prison, 73 sentenced to twenty years, and so on.[5] All had their sentences commuted after the war ended.

The arrested objectors were initially housed in military stockades at numerous military camps, including Custer, Devens, Funston, Upton and Meade. From these camps they were transferred to two major military prisons, Alcatraz Island, in San Francisco Bay, and Fort Leavenworth, Kansas. After the strikes at Fort Leavenworth in 1919, the remaining objectors were transferred either to Fort Douglas, Utah, or to Alcatraz.

Treatment of the imprisoned objectors was barbaric. At least seventeen objectors died in jail; others were driven insane. Norman Thomas—in his study of World War I conscientious objectors, *Is Conscience a Crime?*— stated that the War Department admitted to confining conscientious objectors

in unsanitary guardhouses—sometimes in unheated cells during the winter months, without blankets; and long hours of standing at attention, in bitter cold or in blinding heat. Men were forcibly clad in uniform, beaten, pricked or stabbed with bayonets, jerked about with ropes round their necks, threatened with summary execution, tortured by various forms of the "water cure." In at least two cases men were immersed in the filth of latrines, one of them head downward.[6]

Solitary confinement consisted of two consecutive weeks on a bread-and-water diet, in completely darkened cells, while chained or handcuffed to the cell walls for nine hours a day.

World War I objectors were subjected to a brutish prison environment mainly because they directly resisted war and military authority. Many objectors refused to cooperate in any capacity with the military system. Not only did they refuse to fight, but also they refused to salute officers, wear proper uniforms or work on noncombat projects. Although the resistance of the objectors did not stop or hinder the U.S. war effort, the military feared the potential threat these objectors posed to the "effective conduct of the war."

In an extremely revealing letter, Major General Leonard Wood, the commanding officer at Camp Funston, Kansas, justified the abusive treatment that objectors experienced at Funston. This treatment included starvation-level diets, beatings and water torture (keeping prisoners in cold showers until they were on the verge of collapse). According to Wood, objectors who refused alternative service and urged others to stop cooperating with the military were sowing "dissension in our military establishment and opposing an effective conduct of the war." Continuing his attack on the objectors, Wood wrote:

They are, as shown in their words and acts, avowed enemies of the government and are opposing the government in the efforts which it is making to crush autocracy. Not only are they refusing to play the part of loyal citizens, but they are also, by work and example, spreading discontent among other men. Their conduct is reprehensible in the highest degree, and if men of this character, in fact, enemies of the government, are not dealt with vigorously, their evil influence will be far reaching. Fortunately for the nation and for our institutions, men of this type . . . are rare. If this were not the case our government would soon cease to exist.[7]

Those who violated the law, but did not publicly oppose the war or resist military authority, suffered little. For example, the War Department estimated that 171,000 people silently evaded the draft. Few evaders were ever arrested or prosecuted. Also, 3,500 conscientious objectors accepted alternative service with the military, and most were treated civilly. The court-martials and mistreatment were primarily reserved for the type of objector who challenged the military—the "absolutists" and the political resisters.

Most of the objectors sentenced between 1917 and 1918 received very long sentences. Almost all the sentences were commuted by the army, however, and the last conscientious objector held in a military prison was released from Alcatraz Island on December 6, 1920.

Except for the conscientious objectors who died while in military prisons or camps, the biographical histories of these persons will be discussed in a forthcoming book.

NOTES

1. Remarks of Congressman John E. Raker, July 13, 1918, *Cong. Rec.*, 56:528.

2. Arrests for draft law violations numbered in the thousands. The experiences of the more than five hundred conscientious objectors who served long-term sentences will be treated in a forthcoming book documenting imprisoned conscientious objectors during World Wars I and II and the Korean and Vietnam Wars.

3. See Stephen M. Kohn, *Jailed for Peace* (Westport, Conn.: Greenwood Press, 1986).

4. Norman Thomas, *Is Conscience a Crime?* (New York: Vanguard, 1927), 73–104.

5. Secretary of War, *Statement Concerning the Treatment of Conscientious Objectors in the Army* (Washington, D.C.: Government Printing Office, 1919).

6. Thomas, *Is Conscience A Crime?* 144.

7. Quoted in *New York Call,* January 11, 1919.

Part II

Inside Golgotha: The Prison
Experience of the World War I
Sedition Act Inmates

Chapter 3

The Convictions

The grounds for opposing the war of those tried and convicted under the sedition laws were as diverse as the creeds they espoused. Some cited religious faith; others named socialist, anarchist and humanitarian principles. Many were skeptical of electoral politics. Each trial had its own drama in which the powers of government directly confronted the rights of the individual. Some defendants represented themselves; others hired expert lawyers. A small minority refused to present any case whatsoever, believing that they could not obtain justice through the courts.

In one of the first sedition cases, Alexander Berkman and Emma Goldman were charged with conspiring to violate the Selective Service Act (i.e., the wartime draft law) and were tried jointly before a federal court in New York City. Both defendants represented themselves before a jury of twelve men. Below are excerpts from the closing argument Alexander Berkman delivered to the jury in July 1917.

Alexander Berkman's Remarks to Jury

The charge against us [i.e., Berkman and Goldman] as you know from the indictment is that we conspired to advise and to urge men of conscriptable age not to register. . . . The question now is, Did the prosecution prove the alleged conspiracy? Did the prosecution prove that we urged people not to register? Did it prove any overt acts in furtherance of that alleged conspiracy? Did it even attempt to prove or to demonstrate that we are guilty as charged? Oh no.

. . . I personally do not believe in this war. I do not believe in any war of that character. I believe the war is merely for the purpose of furthering capitalistic interests. I believe the people have

Alexander Berkman leaving the federal court house after his indictment on June 20, 1917 for anti-war activities. Courtesy of the Library of Congress.

nothing to gain from this war, neither the people of Europe nor
the people of America. I believe in universal peace. But I am not
a pacifist. I am a fighter and all my life I have been fighting for
liberty. . . . [T]oday . . . barbarism persists and one nation fights another nation with bloodshed, with force, with dynamite, with infer-
nal machines, with all the greatest inventions of the human mind,
inventions intended for the benefit of mankind, not for his destruction. But the time will come when the nations . . . will develop their
constructive tendencies, will realize that men in Russia or in Germany or in France or America have the same aim to live, to support
themselves, to enjoy life and liberty and sunshine, that all humanity
is kin. . . . [T]he . . . nations of Europe and America and of all other
countries will realize that . . . it was better to co-operate, to work together, to help together with mutual effort for a common good,
rather   than   to   murder   and   slaughter   each   other.
. . . We are . . . internationalists and I am sure that some day the
nations will become international in the sense that they will do away
with all hatred, with all strife, with all this ugliness, with all this murder, and slaughter, and with all this violence. And you accuse us of
violence, us who stand for the principle of universal peace?
Ridiculous!

I am proud to stand here as a believer in the highest ideal that
the human mind ever conceived, the very highest ideal, the ideal of
sunshine for everyone, the ideal of the rights of the child, the right
of the child who today works in the factories and the mills and is
exploited day after day; the right of the woman, equal rights of the
woman in every way; the right of the man not alone to an empty
political liberty, but the right of the man to the resources of life, the
right of the working class to be able to produce for the general
benefit, not for the profit of this or that monopolist, the right of
humanity to enjoy the wealth of the world. . . .
. . . The No Conscription Manifesto [the leaflet circulated by
Goldman and Berkman, which the government used to indict them]
. . . was sent out in 50,000 copies all over the country. . . . And what
does this No Conscription Manifesto say in essence? "Liberty of
conscience is the most fundamental of all human rights, the pivot
of all progress. No man may be deprived of it without losing every
vestige of freedom of thought and action. In these days when every
principle and conception of democracy and of liberty is being cast
overboard under the pretext of democratizing Germany it behooves
every liberty loving man and woman to insist on his or her rights of
individual choice in the ordering of his [or her] life and actions."
And here is again a passage that gives the very gist of the matter in

one sentence: "The No Conscription League is to be the voice of protest against the coercion of conscientious objectors to participate in the war. . . . The whole no conscription movement in this country and all through the country was and is for the purpose of giving voices of protest, expressing the opinions of the conscientious objectors who did not want to participate in the war, their reasons for objecting to the war; people who are opposed to bearing arms for reasons of conscience. That was the purpose of the no conscription movement.

. . . [W]e believe that free speech is the very foundation of any liberty in this country or any other country; and I believe that the moment we begin to limit free speech, the moment you begin to persecute those who believe in the use of free speech, that moment you are committing the worst crime against liberty, the worst crime against true democracy, the worst crime against the traditions in which you believe, the worst crime against the best interests of this country, the best interests of this people, because the abolition of free speech is a bad thing, gentlemen. Free speech is a sacred thing. . . . And you, gentlemen of the jury, are intelligent enough to know that this country was originally founded upon the liberty of conscience, upon free speech, upon the free expression and discussion of opinion. We may be wrong. Maybe anarchism is all wrong. Maybe all our ideas are wrong. But I claim even the right of being wrong. I may express any opinion. If I am wrong I am willing to discuss with you, willing to discuss with anyone on the platform. . . . I believe free discussion and free speech should not be limited under any consideration. It is a dangerous thing to do. It is the murder of liberty.

Suppose we are wrong. Suppose our ideas are wrong. Is that any reason why we are guilty of conspiracy on this charge? Is that the reason to say that we conspired or told people not to register? Why, gentlemen of the jury, many of the idealists of the past, were told they were wrong—maybe they were wrong. But consider, maybe they were not; and what then?

. . . I . . . explained to you . . . that I am opposed to war, to capitalist war, that I believe in universal peace and [the] constructive tendencies of man, I believe that through education, through organization, through enlightenment we will bring people to the point where it will not be necessary to have war, where all the destructive tendencies will be abolished, where even crime will be abolished, where misery and desperation and poverty, the sources of crime, will be abolished. I believe that in my heart as I believe anything. Maybe I shall not see it in my own lifetime. But that makes no difference.

I believe these things are absolutely true. It has been shown to you that I believe them and it has also been shown by ourselves that we do not believe in war, we do not believe in conscription. I consider conscription the deathblow to American liberty or to any other kind of liberty. . . .

. . . I am willing to suffer for my ideas in prison if necessary. Life is dear, but not so dear that I should be at liberty without self-respect. I would rather be in prison with my ideals, with my convictions, true to myself than be outside with my soul damned in my own estimation. So I am not pleading to save ourselves from prison. . . . The question here is, have we got free speech and liberty of expression in this country, or not? That is the real question at issue, over and above this indictment, over and above all these things that have been quoted by the District Attorney. And it is up to you as representatives just now of the American people, it is up to you as the jury in this case to tell the world by your verdict whether you believe that free speech is necessary, whether you believe that free speech is a good thing.[1]

Berkman (along with codefendant Goldman) was found guilty of conspiring to interfere with the draft and was sentenced to two years in Atlanta Penitentiary. In Atlanta he was "placed in solitary confinement" for calling the warden a "hypocrite." The warden ordered Berkman disciplined for "carrying on revolutionary propaganda among the inmates" and placed him in "isolation" from the general prison population because he was a "menace to the Institution."[2]

After completing his sentence, Berkman, along with Goldman, was deported to Russia. In Russia, they actively advocated the civil liberties of political dissidents in that country and were forced to flee from the Communist authorities in 1921.

NOTES

1. Closing Statement of Alexander Berkman, July 1917, Paul Munter Shorthand Reporter, Tamiment Collection, New York University.
2. A. Berkman prison record from Atlanta Penitentiary #7422.

Chapter 4

Prison Discipline

Commencing in November 1917, prisoners convicted under the Sedition Act began to enter Leavenworth, Atlanta and other federal penitentiaries. Regardless of their background, education or age or the paucity of evidence presented against most of these prisoners, they were assigned a number and work duties (usually rock breaking) and were required to comply with prison discipline. The Sedition Act prisoners would receive hundreds upon hundreds of official reprimands for disobeying various rules; a sampling of these is presented below, drawn from the records of Leavenworth Penitentiary in the year 1919. These disciplinary reports are representative of the treatment all federal political prisoners faced during their incarceration.

Disciplinary Action Against No. 13133 (J. A. MacDonald), January 24, 1919

Became sarcastic and ridiculed the laws and system of Government of the United States. Isolation on restricted diet and removed as a school teacher.

Disciplinary Action Against No. 13162 (Morris Levine), January 29, 1919

Refusing to work. Refused to go out with #3 gang, giving two reasons: 1st that he thought that one of his fellow IWW's had been placed in isolation unjustly, and secondly that he would not work under Certain Gun Guards. Reprimanded and placed in Isolation on restricted diet and thirty (30) days good time taken.

Disciplinary Action Against No. 13162 (Morris Levine), February 15, 1919

Disobedience of orders. Coming on sick call this morning for treatment and positively refusing to take same. Reprimanded and placed on restricted diet.

Disciplinary Action Against No. 13126 (Ben Fletcher), February 15, 1919

Hammering on plate with fork so it rang all over the mess hall. Reprimanded and placed in isolation on restricted diet.

Disciplinary Action Against No. 13577 (John Potthast), March 31, 1919

The above prisoner left his plate full of meat and bread at dinner time today. Reprimanded and two weeks yard and amusement privileges taken.

Disciplinary Action Against No. 13592 (Otto Elsner), April 11, 1919

The waiters in the mess hall have orders to put one spoonful of eggs on each plate. The above cursed him for not putting more on his plate this a.m. Reprimanded and placed in isolation on restricted diet.

Disciplinary Action Against No. 13147 (John Walsh), April 14, 1919

A serious disturbance occurred in the mess hall. After careful investigation I am convinced it was prearranged by a number of prisoners the majority of whom were I.W.W.'s. The disturbance consisted of yelling and breaking cups and plates and the yelling continued after they got in the cell house. Isolation restricted diet, reduced to 3rd grade indefinitely. After being released from restricted diet this prisoner will be segregated indefinitely as a dangerous and irresponsible character.

Disciplinary Action Against No. 13582 (Caesar Tabib), May 3, 1919

Refusing to work. I asked the above prisoner to help unload cement. He complained of lung trouble and refused to work. He will be placed in a cell on full rations and hand cuffed to the grated door during working hours until further notice.

Disciplinary Action Against No. 13103 (Richard Brazier), May 16, 1919

This man was talking and laughing in the dining room at breakfast this date. Reprimanded and two weeks yard and amusement privileges taken.

Disciplinary Action Against No. 13565 (Pete De Bernardi), June 25, 1919

Refusing to break their rock smaller and laughed at the guard when ordered to do so on this date, breaking them to suit himself. Reprimanded and placed on restricted diet. (Already in segregation).

Disciplinary Action Against No. 13568 (Frank Elliott), June 26, 1919

The above prisoner is useless for anything in the shape of work. He can only boast of one good quality and that is his ability for talking. Reprimanded and reduced to third grade.

Disciplinary Action Against No. 13568 (Frank Elliott), July 12, 1919

The above prisoner is absolutely useless and has no earthly intentions of working and I consider it wise to have him segregated from the gang. Reprimanded and placed in isolation on restricted diet.

Disciplinary Action Against No. 13162 (Morris Levine), August 2, 1919

This man was laying in bed at the time the count was going on. I have told him to get up. Reprimanded.

Disciplinary Action Against No. 13591 (Joseph Carroll), August 21, 1919

Did strut himself out aisle and turn up his trouser bottom. Reprimanded.

Disciplinary Action Against No. 13568 (Frank Elliott), August 21, 1919

This man rolled a cigarette in the dining room and did not try to hide it but let everyone see that he was making a cigarette. Reprimanded.

Disciplinary Action Against No. 13570 (John Grave), September 15, 1919

Indolence. The above prisoner failed to break his share of rock on this forenoon, when I spoke to him with reference to the matters, he replied; "I have broken all the rocks I intend to break." Reprimanded and placed in isolation on restricted diet.

Disciplinary Action Against No. 13103 (Richard Brazier), September 17, 1919

Not getting up at the bugle call. I found this man in bed 5 minutes after the last bugle call. Reprimanded.

Disciplinary Action Against No. 13572 (Henry Hammer), September 18, 1919

Inclined to be playful during working hours. The above prisoner started to throw rock at a lamp post on this afternoon. I reprimanded him for so doing and as a result he was inclined to be insolent. He is one of those men who would like to turn this institution into a Sporting Club. Reprimanded and reduced to second grade.

Disciplinary Action Against No. 13565 (Pete De Bernardi), October 17, 1919

The above prisoner called me a dirty stinker and also made an attempt to hit me with his clenched fist. Note: This prisoner is confined in a segregated cell and has been very insolent complaining of his food. At various times and has provoked the guard almost beyond endurance, on this occasion he was very insolent, kept calling for an unusual amount of food and kept complaining about it, until the guard opened the door to investigate. At this time the prisoner seems to have assumed a threatening attitude and the guard struck him with his stick. Action: Reprimanded, removed to another cell and placed on restricted diet.

Disciplinary Action Against No. 13591 (Joseph Carroll), October 23, 1919

Indolence. The above prisoner scarcely broke a half barrow of rock on this afternoon, likes to exercise and roam about and do things to suit himself. Reprimanded and placed in isolation on restricted diet.

Disciplinary Action Against No. 13111 (Manuel Rey), October 25, 1919

The above prisoner read considerably on the forenoon. He is one of the men who takes literature out and distributes it among the other prisoners. Reprimanded and reduced to Second Grade.

Disciplinary Action Against No. 13582 (Caesar Tabib), October 25, 1919

Refusing to break their rock smaller and laughed at the guard when ordered to do so on this date, breaking them to suit himself. Reprimanded and placed on restricted diet. (Already in segregation.)

Disciplinary Action Against No. 13162 (Morris Levine), October 28, 1919

Willful waste of food. The above prisoner just ate the outer edges off 4 pieces of bread at supper today and at noon day meal he had bread crumbled up on the floor under where he was sitting. Reprimanded and reduced to Second Grade.

Disciplinary Action Against No. 13175 (James Phillips), November 1, 1919

The above prisoner left the gang on this forenoon without permission evidently he went to the toilet but he failed to notify us. Reprimanded and reduced to second grade.

Disciplinary Action Against No. 13568 (Frank Elliott), November 25, 1919

Indolence, defiance and loafing. This prisoner has visited the entire day and done hardly nothing. He has kept the rest of the men around him from working, and seems to defy us and absolutely does not make any pretense to do his work. Reprimanded and placed in isolation on restricted diet, and handcuffed to grated cell door during working hours.

Disciplinary Action Against No. 13575 (Phil McLaughlin), December 31, 1919

This prisoner did willfully and maliciously turn his back upon his work and stare at us in a very defiant manner. Reprimanded and placed in isolation on restricted diet.

Chapter 5

A Transfer to St. Elizabeth's Hospital for the Insane

Between October 6, 1918, and December 19, 1918, Mrs. Edward Johnson corresponded with the warden of Leavenworth Penitentiary concerning her husband. Edward Johnson, a farmer from Barronet, Wisconsin, had been sentenced to the federal penitentiary at Leavenworth for a year and a day for "obstructing military service." Besides his wife he left behind seven young children. In a letter to the warden, the federal judge who had heard Johnson's case, the Honorable Evan A. Evans, wrote that Johnson had been "teaching and preaching that it is unlawful to kill, even in war." The judge acknowledged that Johnson had a "very enviable reputation" in his community before he "became obsessed" with religion. Judge Evans recommended parole for Johnson if he would "get over" his "religious notions." Johnson was not listed as a member of any political organization. The following written exchange took place between Mrs. Johnson and the warden.[1]

Mrs. Edward Johnson to William Morgan, Warden, U.S. Penitentiary, Leavenworth, October 6, 1918

Dear Warden: Would like to know how my husband is and if there is not some way to get him home. He has been sick so much. And to be away from his little ones at home he worry about us. I have 7 little children to take care and the oldest is 10 years, and the baby 2½ months. I am not able to go out and work. So I have nothing but what little is given to me. So some time it looks bad. Can my husband come home. There is plenty of work for him as a carpenter. Please let me know what I can do at once please. Mrs. E. Johnson

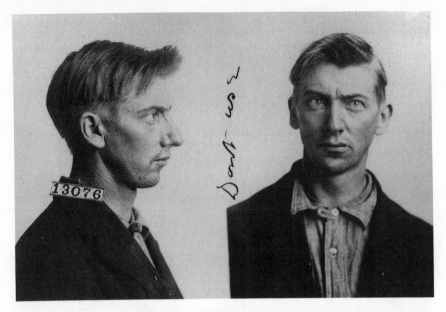

Leavenworth prison photo of Edward Johnson, a religious opponent of war, who had been arrested for "teaching and preaching that it is unlawful to kill." Johnson broke down in prison and was transferred to St. Elizabeth's Hospital for the Insane. Department of Justice photo.

Warden to Mrs. Johnson, October 11, 1918

Dear Madam: There has been some question raised as to the soundness of mind of your husband. It will be of material assistance to us if you can give any information as to previous physical or mental condition of the young man prior to his coming here.

You certainly have my heartfelt sympathy and with it the assurance that everything consistent with prison rules will be done to promote the health of your husband. Respectfully, Warden

Mrs. Johnson to Warden, October 16, 1918

Dear Warden: My husband has been troubled with cataracts and stomach ulcers since we were married. But my husband got bad last spring. They arrested him on the 14th of May and took him away from his work. They put him in jail for 90 days and gave him bread and water for ten days. He was not allowed to talk to anyone or write. On the second day of bread and water they told him his wife was sick. This was not so, but it worried him and he could not find out.

This was the first time I learned there was anything wrong with his mind. It all comes from worry. He always takes everything to heart. Some can take it light, but he never done that. Please let me know how he is. Mrs. Edward Johnson

Warden to Mrs. Johnson, October 19, 1918

Dear Madam: In reply to your letter of the 16th, your husband appears to be very despondent due to a belief that his friends have forgotten him. In order to ease his condition the physician has kept him in the hospital where the noise and bustle of the regular routine would not reach him. This is, no doubt, the cause of his neglect to answer your letter. Respectfully, Warden

Mrs. Johnson to Warden, December 15, 1918

Dear Warden: Would like to ask a question concerning my husband. Has he gotten my letter or not? Does he seem to remember anything about home? I heard some one saying that he didn't seem to know if he had a wife and children or not. Wish he would come a little closer to home so I could go and see him as we love our dear husband and father. [Leavenworth is over 300 miles from the Johnson home in Barronet, Wisconsin.] Mrs. Edward Johnson

Warden to Mrs. Johnson, December 19, 1918

Dear Madam: In response to your communication of the 15th, it is quite probable that your husband will be transferred to St. Elizabeth's Hospital in Washington, D.C.

I am informed by the Prison Physician that he often speaks of you and his children but on account of his mental condition probably, he seems to have no inclination to write. Very truly yours, Warden

Medical Certificate, St. Elizabeth's Government Hospital for the Insane, January 18, 1918

Name: Edward Johnson
Age: 36
Religion: Christian
Date of Transfer to Hospital for Insane: January 18, 1918
History of Insanity: No record
Previous peculiarities of patient: no record
Evidence of abnormal sexual habits: no record
History of previous attacks: no record

Present symptoms: Suicidal, dementia praecox, paranoid, emotional, depressed, cries frequently, apprehensive and suspicious, delusions of persecution
Probable causes of present attack: unknown

Johnson's files were unobtainable from St. Elizabeth's Hospital, and it is unknown whether he and his family were ever reunited.

NOTE

1. The material in this chapter was obtained from the Leavenworth Penitentiary file of Edward Johnson. The letters were edited by the author.

Chapter 6

A Death

On March 23, 1918, the forty-four-year-old Mexican writer and editor Ricardo Flores Magón was arrested and charged with conspiracy to obstruct military service. The sole basis of his conviction was a radical anti-war editorial he wrote in his Los Angeles–based newspaper, *Regeneración*. Magón, a disciple of Tolstoy, had participated for years in Mexican revolutionary activities and opposition to the Díaz regime. He entered Leavenworth Penitentiary on November 3, 1919, to begin a twenty-one-year sentence. He would never leave the penitentiary.[1]

Ricardo Flores Magón to Friends[2]

Dear Friends: The Government machine will never pay heed to my sufferings. Humane interests have nothing to do with Government officials. They are part of a huge machine which has no heart, nor nerves, nor conscience.

That I am going blind? The machine will say with a shrug of its shoulders, "So much the worse for him." That I shall die here? "Well," the machine will say, "there will be room enough in the prison graveyard to accommodate a corpse."

Had I a friend with political influence, I could be set free even if I had stepped upon one or all of the Ten Commandments. But I have none, and for expediency's sake I must rot and die, pent up like a wild beast in an Iron cage, far away from the Innocent creatures I love.

My crime is one of those which have no atonement. Murder? No; it was not murder; human life is cheap to the machine's eyes, and

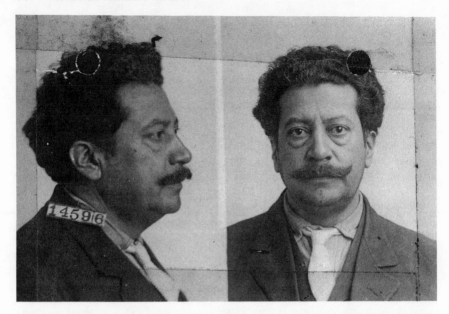

Leavenworth prison photo of Ricardo Flores Magón, a Mexican disciple of Tolstoy arrested in Los Angeles for publishing an anti-war article. Magón was denied medical attention in Leavenworth and died in prison on November 21, 1922. Department of Justice photo.

thus a murderer gets easily released, or if he has killed by the wholesale he will never dwell in an Iron cage but will be laden with honorific crosses and medals instead.

Swindle? No; if this were the case I would have been appointed President of one big corporation or other.

I am a dreamer. This is my crime. Yet my dream of the beautiful and my cherished visions of a humanity living in peace and love and freedom, dreams and visions which the machine abhors, shall not die. It's with one, for so long as there should be upon this earth an aching heart or an eye full of tears, my dreams and my visions shall live.

Warden W. I. Biddle to Attorney General H. M. Daugherty, June 9, 1922[3]

Dear Sir: Enclosed please find copy of telegrams relative to having an outside physician make a physical examination of Ricardo Flores Magón.

Magón is a well-educated, cunning Mexican who has made false statements relative to his physical condition.

I finally concluded not to allow an outside physician to make this examination.

Magón to Attorney Harry Weinberger[4]

There are pus cells present in my sputum. I am afflicted with a dangerous disease of my respiratory organs. The tissues of these organs are rotting and disintegrating. I request a physical examination from an outside physician.

Prison Physician's Report, March 20, 1922[5]

I have the honor to state that the records of this office and complete physical examination show that the man is in good health; he is standing confinement well, there is nothing critical or dangerous in his condition, and there is no probability of deleterious effect resulting from confinement during the remainder of his term.

Magón to Weinberger[6]

I have exophthalinia [bulging of the eyes, caused by a deficiency of the endocrine system or by a tumor] which is not reported. Exophthalinia is a severe sickness of the eyes.

Prison Physician's Report, April 8, 1922[7]

Today's physical examination verifies our previous reports that there is no evidence whatsoever of failing health.

Magón to Weinberger[8]

From time to time and for several days blood is present in the sputum, especially in winter the pains in the regions of my heart is always present and so is the one in my kidneys. Nothing is said in the report as to how irregular my bowels move. They move every four, five or six days which means that I am suffering from something of a very grave character. The slight cough is so intense and continuous as to keep me awake nights.

Prison Physician's Report, August 30, 1922[9]

Magón has no trouble in getting around without glasses. His general health is very good. He is in no way failing physically and is standing confinement well.

Magón to Weinberger[10]

In my medical report there is no indication of diabetes. Could diabetes disappear in a diet mostly composed of starches and syrups? The prison physician at McNeil Island Penitentiary diagnosed diabetes and the doctor at the service of the United States District Court diagnosed the same when requested to do so by Federal Judge Oscar Trippett to have me examined while awaiting trial in Los Angeles County Jail.

Report of Doctor J. H. Langworthy, M.D., October 16, 1922[11]

Prisoner Ricardo Flores Magón is standing his confinement well. His general physical condition is good. The only serious defect I find in him physically is partial cataract in each eye which is unusual in a man of his age. This is progressing very slowly and there is apparently no danger of his becoming blind in the near future, though ulteriorly this will probably take place.

Magón to Friend[12]

I have no more paper to continue writing on my dear friend but I think that you and all honest people that reason is against the absurd statement that my health is good. I am sick and very sick.

Letter from W. I. Biddle, Warden to Attorney General Daugherty[13]

Dear Attorney General Daugherty: It is with regret that I inform you of the death of Ricardo Flores Magón, Register No. 14,596 of this institution, which occurred this morning. Enclosed please find a letter from Dr. A. F. Yohe, prison physician, relative to the death of Magón. Respectfully, Warden

Prison Physician's Report, November 21, 1922[14]

In compliance with your request for report of circumstances in the death of Ricardo Flores Magón, Register 14596, advise that the night attendant at the hospital was called by guard Lewis in Cell House "B" about 4:15 o'clock this morning. The attendant went over promptly and found Magón suffering with distress and pain about the heart, he examined him and returned to the hospital for medicine. While the attendant was returning to the hospital the guard called again and stated that Magón was dead.

You will, no doubt, recall that Magón had been recently examined by both the doctors Langworthy and myself and in those examinations we were unable to find any evidence of disease of heart. Prompt service was always rendered Magón and he was not neglected in any way.

Ricardo Flores Magón's body was shipped to Mexico where over a quarter of a million people attended his funeral.

NOTES

1. The material in this chapter was obtained from the Leavenworth Penitentiary file of Ricardo Flores Magón and from "Why Mexican Red Was Kept to Die in Prison a Mystery," *New York World*, November 21, 1922.

2. Excerpted from undated letter by Ricardo Magón, quoted in "Why Mexican Red Was Kept to Die in Prison a Mystery," *New York World*, November 21, 1922 (no by-line).

3. W. I. Biddle to H. M. Daugherty, June 9, 1922.

4. Magón to Harry Weinberger, November 5, 1922.

5. A. F. Yohe to W. I. Biddle, March 20, 1922.

6. Magón to Harry Weinberger, November 5, 1922.

7. Stewart McKeen Acting Physician to W. I. Biddle, April 8, 1922.

8. Magón to Harry Weinberger, November 5, 1922.

9. A. F. Yohe to W. I. Biddle, August 30, 1922.

10. Magón to Harry Weinberger, November 5, 1922.

11. Report of Dr. J. H. Langworthy, October 16, 1922.

12. Magón to Harry Weinberger, November 5, 1922.

13. W. I. Biddle to Attorney General H. M. Daugherty, November 21, 1922.

14. A. F. Yohe to W. I. Biddle, November 21, 1922.

Chapter 7

The Most Indolent Man
at Leavenworth

Caesar Tabib, a member of the IWW, was arrested under the Espionage Act in August 1918 and sentenced to ten years in prison at the mass trial of IWW members in Sacramento, California. At the age of twenty-four he entered Leavenworth Penitentiary on January 25, 1919. The following reports on his confinement were recorded by his guards, the prison warden, the prison physician and an outside doctor retained to examine Tabib.[1]

Report of Prison Guard O. Driscoll, April 25, 1919

[Caesar Tabib] is the most indolent man in this Institution. He tries his utmost to keep willing workers from doing their share. Reprimanded, reduced to third grade.

Report of Prison Physician Dr. A. F. Yohe, May 2, 1919

Complete physical examination of Tabib, No. 13582, shows the man has no disease of the lungs or heart to bear out his claims of bad lungs and shortness of breath. It is my opinion that he is able to perform any ordinary manual labor to which he is assigned.

Report of Prison Guard O. Driscoll, May 3, 1919

Refusing to work. I asked the above prisoner to help unload cement. He complained of lung trouble and refused work. He will be placed in a cell on full rations and hand cuffed to the grated door during working hours until further notice.

Prison Record Notation, June 8, 1919

Admitted to hospital.

Prison Record Notation, June 9, 1919

Returned to isolation.

Report of Prison Guard Robertson, June 25, 1919

Refusing to break rock smaller and laughed at the guard when ordered to do so on this date, breaking them to suit himself. Reprimanded and placed on restricted diet. Already in segregation.

Report of Prison Guard Robertson, August 14, 1919

Refused to work. Reprimanded and placed on restricted diet. Already in segregation.

Notation to Prison Record, February 5, 1920

Admitted to hospital. Tubercle test—positive. Transferred to TB Annex.

Dr. A. F. Yohe to Warden A. V. Anderson, June 10, 1920

Dear Warden: In response to your request for report as to the physical condition of Caesar Tabib, #13582, I will state that is affected with mild chronic pulmonary tuberculosis. His general physical condition is fully as good as when he entered this Institution. There is nothing specially critical in his condition and he is standing confinement quite well.

Report of Deputy Warden L. J. Fleicher, June 13, 1920

Abusing writing privilege. Using obscene language in his correspondence with woman. Writing privileges suspended.

Report of Prison Guard Lucas, October 3, 1921

Habitual agitator and trouble maker. This prisoner claimed that he did not have good eggs. Also that his plate was dirty. This man is continuously trying to stir up trouble and discontent among the patients and helping the Annex.

Report of Deputy Warden F. G. Zerbst, November 4, 1921

Abusing writing privilege. This prisoner wrote a letter to a lady friend in which he referred to General Pershing as "notorious murderer." Reprimanded and reduced to third grade.

Dr. Yohe to Warden W. I. Biddle, March 1, 1922

Dear Warden Biddle: It is my opinion that Tabib, #13582, has a mild type of chronic pulmonary tuberculosis. Confinement in this institution has not been injurious and the outcome, while problematic, is not altogether unfavorable. Respectfully, Dr. A. F. Yohe, Physician

Dr. Yohe to Warden Biddle, October 28, 1922

Warden Biddle: In response to your request for report to remark, as to the physical condition of Caesar Tabib, #13582, I have the honor to state that I have again carefully examined this man and find no extension of diseased lung. He has stood this summer very well with the exception of a mild attack of malaria. Judging from the way he has stood confinement up to this time I do not believe that any special deleterious effect will result from its continuance.

Warden Biddle to Superintendent of Prisons Heber H. Votaw (Washington, D.C.), November 17, 1922

Your letter of November 13, 1922 has been received.

Dr. A. F. Yohe, prison physician, says there is nothing new to add to the physical condition report on prisoner Tabib. He is receiving the best of care possible in the prison hospital annex. It might be added that Tabib has been a trouble maker for the annex attendants.

Dr. Yohe has been prison physician here for eighteen years, he has given satisfactory service in looking after the health of the inmates and never shows any prejudice or preference in his treatment of prisoners. It can be stated that about the only prisoners making complaints about Dr. Yohe are the IWW's, who are backed up by outside IWW's and Socialist agitators.

In regard to the alleged bad treatment of Tabib in May, 1919, will state that this took place under the former warden of the penitentiary, but I am convinced that, forming my judgment from the record sheet, it was necessary to handle him in a firm manner to maintain discipline here. At that time many IWW prisoners were refusing to work, trying to get up prison strikes, riots in the dining room and make all trouble possible.

We have had to keep a very careful watch on the letters of the IWW prisoners, as some of them made attempts to send out false statements about government officials.

Dr. Yohe to Warden Biddle, January 20, 1923

Dear Warden: In response to your request for report and remarks as to the physical condition of Caesar Tabib, #13582, he still carries afternoon rise in temperature, considerable soreness in chest, slightly reduced in flesh and is inclined to be somewhat neurotic. If the confinement is long continued, this man will finally break down under the strain. Respectfully, A. F. Yohe, Physician.

Letter from Allen L. Porter, M.D., to Dr. Yohe, January 26, 1923

My Dear Doctor: Enclosed please find report on Tabib. Hoping this meets with your approval and that I said nothing that would involve you or the institution. Fraternally yours, Allen L. Porter, M.D.

Report on Medical Consultation by Dr. Porter on Tabib's Condition for U.S. Prison at Leavenworth, January 26, 1923

Complying with your request on January 23rd, I examined Caesar Tabib in the U.S. Prison at Leavenworth, Kansas. Patient was located in the Tubercular Ward. DIAGNOSIS: Pulmonary tuberculosis. PROGNOSIS: Unfavorable. This patient has an active form of tuberculosis and it is a mere guess as to how long he will live. It will be of material advantage to him to be moved to a different climate and there is no doubt his life would be prolonged if such could be accomplished.

Tabib was kept in prison until December 23, 1923, when he was released along with the last remaining IWW defendants held under the Espionage Act.

NOTE

1. The material in this chapter was obtained from the Leavenworth Penitentiary file of Caesar Tabib #13582.

Chapter 8

Military Justice

In December 1917, Philip Grosser, a twenty-seven-year-old conscientious objector, was arrested in Boston, Massachusetts, for failing to report for military duty. Under existing regulations, although a conscientious objector, Grosser was forcibly inducted into the armed services and required to adhere to all military rules, such as wearing a military uniform, standing in formation and standing at attention in the presence of military officers. He was court-martialed and sentenced to thirty years of hard labor on August 25, 1918, for "refusal to obey a lawful command" and "attempting to create mutiny" in the army by "writing letters" in support of conscientious objectors. From his various military prisons, Grosser was able to smuggle out letters that chronicled his treatment.[1]

Report from the *Boston Advertiser*, August 31, 1917

Philip B. Grosser of the West End, for whom Federal authorities have had a warrant out for a week charging him with refusing to submit himself for the physical examination for the National Army, surrendered himself at the Marshal's office yesterday afternoon and was placed under arrest by Deputy Marshal Scully. . . .

Grosser told the Commissioner that he had refused to appear for examination because he is an internationalist and a non-militarist. He declared that he was willing to stand any punishment the law might impose on him. . . .

Grosser's arrest followed the receipt of a letter by Chairman Burroughs of Division 5 exemption board in which Grosser declared that he was determined not to obey any military orders and would not submit to a physical examination for military purposes.[2]

Letter from Philip Grosser to His Brother David,
February 24, 1918

Dear Brother: . . . February 10th I was searched, all personal letters, newspapers, clippings were confiscated. I was arrested and imprisoned by orders of the NO. Eastern Department. I am not allowed to communicate with the outside world. My palace is a cell 7 × 6. Reading, writing and smoking are not allowed. No chance for exercise . . . [My prison friends] may write about dogs, cats, the weather, etc. In fact this is my only recreation; to read and reread the letters I receive. No politics or philosophy or free speech stunts. You know it is quite tiresome to have too much leisure. Do not worry, I am resigned to my faith. I refuse to do any kind of work and do not participate in their military ritual. Soldiers with loaded rifles carry me out to retreat once in a while. But when they dump me on the floor, I lay there until the ceremony is over and then I go back to my cell. I laugh at their implements. I know that my will power is stronger than the bayonet and that my ideas will not be shot out of my head by bullets. Do not wait for my letter. Write and tell everybody to write . . . Phil

Grosser to His Brother David, February 28, 1918

Dear Brother: I received your registered letter. Since Sunday Feb. 10, I am imprisoned. They torture me. I am not allowed to write to anybody. My mail is given to me. I think some provocateur posing as a C.O. who came to the camp Friday the 8th framed something on me. Not allowed to leave my cell for a minute even for exercise. No reading writing or smoking. Do not mention in your letters to me that you received a letter.

Instances of brutality. On my refusal to perform a military trick, soldiers with loaded rifles and bayonets came to my cell, kicked me and dragged me out to the guard room, dumped me on the floor. I picked myself up and sat on a cot until their ceremony was over. Provost Cop. Beerchfield wanted to play the hose on me for refusing to work under military authorities. . . .

You ask what I do all the day? Old Ben Johnson of Dictionary fame used to complain, "How the days pass away and nothing done." I cannot get rid of the days. "Every day is like a year. A year whose days are long." Phil

Grosser to His Brother David, March 6, 1918

What happened? Feb. 10 (Sunday 3 P.M.) I was taken to Headquarters by Lt. Barker. He called the Adjutant. Two sentries (soldiers) were also present. They made me undress and searched me. . . .

Brutalities which can be proven. Lt. Barker an officer of the day in prison ordered me to work. "As a C.O.," I replied, "I refuse to work under military control." He ordered two soldiers to load their rifles and get their bayonets ready for action. Armed to their teeth they came to my cell. The door was opened. Barker asked the soldiers whether they have power enough to work me. They replied "yes." I had my arms folded and said that no power in this world can make me work against my will. Barker said "we have the authority and power to make you obey orders. I will not employ that power now." He locked the cell and dismissed the soldiers.

Sergeant Kelly ordered me out to stand reveille. I said that as a non-militarist I can not participate in any of the military rituals. A corporal and three soldiers with loaded rifles came to my cell, grabbed me by the neck, kicked me and carried me out to the guard room. They dumped me on the floor. I picked myself up, sat on a cot until the ceremony was over. Then went back to my cage.

Today they let me out for exercise for about fifteen minutes. I was also allowed to go for my meals.

I am well. Write write   P. B. Grosser

Grosser to His Brother David, March 7, 1918

David: Do everything possible right away. They are trying to pull over something in the dark. I ask the officers several times to let me write and they say "we have no authority. It is up to the commanding officer." I promised not to tell anything about the treatment I receive, just to notify that I am still alive. But they refuse. It seems as if they are afraid of the light. They can, however, do almost anything and make a good report. Next time you see Major Baker you might tell him that you heard rumors that I am tortured. Do not mention that I sneak out a letter once in a while. Do something before it is too late. Write. Make others write. Any nonsense will be good.

Grosser to His Brother David, March 26, 1918

David: The policy of the authorities now seems to be to starve me into submission. . . .

Of course you know what happened Monday March 11th. The hemp man's band was put around my neck and I was made to swing. The only bad thing about it, is that they did not let me hang a few minutes longer and be through with it all. I was beaten black and blue, kicked and jumped upon.

How . . . about Dr. Keppel's promise, that the case will be taken up without delay? I made it clear to the authorities that I am perfectly willing to serve a prison sentence after I am tried and convicted. Nay I am even ready to suffer the supreme penalty with a smile on my face. But damn it if they will make me observe military rules by force. The authorities, however, have not preferred any specific charges against me and keep up their inquisition in the name of Democracy.

Philip Grosser would spend three years in various military prisons, including Forts Jay and Leavenworth. In June 1919, he was transferred to Alcatraz Island, where he was held in solitary confinement—"the hole"—and placed in a segregation unit for "degenerates." As additional punishment for failing to comply with military orders Grosser was placed in a twenty-three-inch by twelve-inch iron "coffin cage." Over the protest of the Alcatraz military authorities, Grosser was released on December 2, 1920, along with all remaining conscientious objectors confined in military prisons.[3]

NOTES

1. The material in this chapter was obtained from 4:2292–2299, ACLU Archives (Seeley G. Mudd Manuscript Library, Princeton University; published with permission of Princeton University Libraries); *Boston Advertiser*, August 31, 1917; and Philip Grosser, "Uncle Sam's Devil's Island" [Pamphlet] (Boston: published by friends, 1933).

2. *Boston Advertiser*, August 31, 1917.

3. Grosser, "Uncle Sam's Devil's Island."

Chapter 9

Isolation

Roy P. Connor was twenty-seven years old when he entered the federal penitentiary at Leavenworth on January 25, 1919. He had left his home in Kennesaw, Georgia, in 1912, and had lost touch with his family; until joining the IWW Agricultural Workers Industrial Union in 1916, he had wandered across the United States. After joining the union, he became an organizer and delegate. Connor was arrested in a roundup of numerous IWW activists in California. He was convicted in 1918 at the Sacramento trial for "conspiracy" and other violations of the Espionage Act and was sentenced to ten years' imprisonment. He would spend over four years in isolation and segregation. In 1922, he began the first of several hunger strikes to protest his treatment. The letters in this chapter were written in 1922 and 1923.[1]

Letter from Roy P. Connor to Warden W. I. Biddle[2]

Dear Warden Biddle: Realizing from past experience the utter uselessness of appealing to you for anything, life, instead of a being a pleasure, has become one hellish nightmare. I have gone on what is known in everyday parlance as a "hunger strike." I will not eat until I am permitted to have the medical treatment I am in need of. You told me three months ago when I could hardly walk that I was in good health and nothing was wrong with me. That may have been your true opinion, but I doubt it like hell. A person with any intelligence, who has never even been inside a medical institution can tell by looking at me or listening to me cough that I have the T.B.

I am not so foolish as to think that I will gain anything by writing you this. It will only amuse you and give you an opportunity to take further revenge, but I do not care. You have forced me to pass the stage of caring a damn whether I live or not. You have carried your persecution to the extremes.

You have shown prejudice against me in more ways than one. You refused me medical treatment when I was damn sick. You refused to permit my application for clemency to go out for eleven days. You then suspended my mailing privileges indefinitely, which means permanent. The excuse you gave was phony. The real reason you did that was because you did not want me to communicate with people who are in a position to aid me in obtaining freedom.

This letter is only the expression of my true feelings, but if you feel insulted, you can chain me by the neck, eyes, ears for the rest of my natural life. It won't displease me in the least. I am either going to be permitted medical treatment or be made into a corpse. I don't give a damn which.

The pangs of hunger last but to the grave. In Disgust I am Roy P. Connor, Convict 13564, Isolation No. 2

Memorandum from Prison Physician Dr. A. F. Yohe to Warden Biddle[3]

Warden: In compliance with your request for information concerning the mental and physical condition of Roy Connor, register number 13564, permit me to advise that on December 31st, 1919, Connor was placed in permanent segregation for violation of prison rules, where he remained until April 22nd, 1922, when he was admitted to the Hospital as a result of a twelve day hunger strike.

Connor has shown evidence of being somewhat neurotic, and at such times mildly hysterical accompanied by insomnia, though he usually recovers in a few days, after taking food and rest. These attacks are evidently due to passing periods of mental depression caused from worry and do not amount to a true psychosis. Respectfully, Doctor Yohe

Connor to Dr. Yohe[4]

Doctor Yohe: Have just listened to the pitiful sobs of a Mexican prisoner who was beaten and choked by a convict nurse. This same prisoner was choked last night almost to death. Men are choked up here so often that the most heartrending cries attract but little attention. You brag about running the hospital in a humane manner so I am protesting to you against having to listen to such brutality.

Why not show a little of your humane feelings and kill a few of us in a humane manner.

It is true that others have not complained—who would they complain to? I fear that this will receive no more consideration than it would if I were to drop it down the sewer—still—duty calls. Roy P. Connor

P.S. The Poor Mexican is still sobbing.

Notation for Deputy Warden from Prison Guard H. Anderson[5]

Dear Sir: #13564 [Connor] started in after ten to yell out of his window, swear and cursing everybody. He was placed in straightjacket to keep him away from the window, but did not stop his tirade. H. Anderson, Captain Night Watch

Connor to Warden Biddle[6]

I don't blame you for not wanting decent citizens to know that a human being had been confined 3 years in isolation for refusing to break rock, but I do condemn and curse you as one of the biggest liars in the universe for saying "That I am on a hunger strike until I either get a pardon or croak." You know damn well that I wrote you two different times demanding to be given *medical treatment*. I even sent one of the letters to you via the Chaplain. You also know that I have not started on a hunger strike since coming back from the hospital October the 4th.

I have been trying to eat the damn diseased filth you sent us for past two weeks, but have not succeeded very well, as my stomach is not equal to the task.

If you have gall enough to look a man square in the face I would like to interview you and request that if an interview is granted please try to keep from making a damn ass out of yourself.

Yes you can call my hunger strikes jokes, moving picture shows, or anything else you like, but when I go on one I will either go to the hospital or to hell. Roy P. Connor 13564

Dr. Yohe to Warden Biddle[7]

In compliance with your request for report regarding Roy P. Connor, Register 13564, who is now on an alleged hunger strike, I beg to advise that Connor states he has eaten nothing for ten days and his reason for such is: "He just doesn't care to eat, feels better without food. . . . "

He is somewhat thin in flesh and slightly anaemic; there is nothing whatsoever critical or alarming in his condition, and there is no particular evidence of deleterious effect due to his abstinence from food, if it is a fact he has eaten nothing. Respectfully, Physician

Letter (Smuggled Out of Prison by Unknown Source)[8] from Connor to Senator Henry Cabot Lodge:

Dear Senator Lodge: Am writing you this letter in behalf of the score of human beings confined in what is known to prison officials as Permanent Isolation; but the prison inmates know as "The Slaughterhouse." This place of punishment is ruled by two "Negro Rioters" who were sentenced to life imprisonment for the wanton and indiscriminate murder of men, women and children in Houston, Tex.

Nothing these sluggers enjoy more than staining the walls and floor with the blood of men. Many have been beaten into insensibility only a few days before I came to the hospital. Willie Williams No. 13205 military prisoner, who weighs less than 115 pounds was attacked by both rioters, without warning. Brutally clubbed, kicked, stomped and beaten senseless. His cries and pleas for mercy was the most pitiful thing that I have ever heard it would have touched the heart of a savage; but not the two sluggers, they continued to rain blows upon him, after he had become unconscious, one of the prisoners begged the guard who stood silently by "to interfere" and for so doing he was also beaten. The crime for which Williams was beaten consisted of nothing more than complaining to the "Deputy" because the negroes would not give him salt, pepper and vinegar to go with his meals.

The sluggers were not even reprimanded. One of them after turning the hallway into a "pool of blood" put his cap on the side of his head and swaggered down the aisle grinning at us men locked in our cells, which are "chambers of horror."

I have been confined in the slaughter house for THREE YEARS for an offense generally punishable by FIVE DAYS in the hole, i.e. refusing to work in rock-gang.

Some of us have been there so long and witnessed so much brutality that we don't give a damn whether we are murdered or not.

I was warned and threatened a couple of days before coming over there but I promised the men in the "slaughterhouse" to do what I could so I am appealing to you to investigate the above statements and DEMAND that WE who are confined there permanently be treated like HUMAN BEINGS instead of like beasts. Respectfully, Roy P. Connor, No. 13564

Warden Biddle to Heber H. Votaw, Superintendent of Prisons, Department of Justice[9]

Your letter asking for a report on the cases and physical condition of Roy P. Connor, Register 13,564, was received today.

Connor's record sheet shows that he was reported frequently for violating prison rules, refusing to work, making trouble whenever possible. On December 31, 1919 he was ordered placed in permanent segregation by Former Warden A. V. Anderson, and he has been held there since. Under the rules governing this institution when a prisoner is placed in permanent segregation with the approval of the Attorney General, he is held there until the Attorney General orders his release.

Connor is probably the vilest prisoner confined in this penitentiary, and is looked on as a degenerate.

The "hunger strikes" on the part of Connor are intended for use as propaganda by IWW agitators on the outside. If Connor can win out by these methods it will mean that others confined in segregation for the safety of the institution, and the IWW prisoners generally, will resort to the same tactics and we will have a serious time in maintaining discipline here. Respectfully, Warden

Connor to Warden Biddle[10]

Skunk Warden: You are an insult to the human race. I wrote you when I was in the hospital and asked for my mailing privileges back. I also asked to be released out into the yard. I agreed to do a little work and obey rules. I now withdraw my request to go out and work. A dirty degenerate who will take a man's writing privileges for writing the truth about such a damn hypocrite and thief like you and then go and publish in paper like you did about me. You syphilitic bastard I wouldn't work for a lying prostitute like you. You scurvy specimen of degeneration. I don't care if I stay up here the rest of my life you damn platting inhuman barbarian. You are lower than any syphilitic whore who was ever born. You are a disgrace to the word human. You damn misfit. You thief.

I am on a hunger strike you god damn fruit merchant and I am demanding to be given medical treatment. You half breed cross between a skunk and a coyote. You lying diseased piece of filthy scum. You damn lover of stool pigeons and degenerates. You god damn unsophisticated, unprincipled narrow minded cock sucker.

You dirty bastard. You lying belly robbing thief. I want to interview you so I can tell you to your face just how low you are and if you got gall enough to look a man square in the face call me down to see you. The atmosphere in your presence will be obnoxious to me or any other decent person. You cowardly cur but I would stomach you long enough to tell you what every prisoner except degenerates and stool pigeons think of you as a lying degenerate prostitute.

With contempt for all fakers, degenerates, stool pigeons and diseased offspring, Roy P. Connor 13564, Isolation No. 2

Memorandum from Prison Guard Dempsey to Deputy Warden[11]

Sir: Roy Connor began his cursing at 10:30 P.M. and after I tried to quiet him without any success I and Queen and Leon Totten 17857 put him in straight jacket. He then made so much noise that I called Capt. Anderson and he came to the hospital and I wanted him to give me permission to gag Connors but he said he would not like to give permission, so I left him still hollering and in straight jacket with Guard Garret at 11:45 P.M. Respectfully, Guard Dempsey

NOTES

1. The material in this chapter was obtained from the Leavenworth Penitentiary file of Roy P. Connor #13564.
2. Connor to W. I. Biddle, July 6, 1922.
3. A. F. Yohe to W. I. Biddle, May 18, 1923.
4. Connor to Yohe, November 13, 1923.
5. Anderson to Deputy Warden, October 15, 1923.
6. Connor to Biddle, October 18, 1922.
7. Physician to Biddle, July 18, 1922.
8. Connor to Henry Cabot Lodge, December 22, 1922.
9. Biddle to Heber Votaw, November 9, 1922.
10. Connor to Biddle, October 21, 1922.
11. Memorandum from Guard Dempsey to Deputy Warden, October 15, 1923.

Chapter 10

Relief from the Psychopathic Ward

In June 1923, Roy P. Connor was confined in the prison psychopathic ward. While there, his parents first learned of his arrest and imprisonment.[1]

Mrs. P. L. Connor to Warden W. I. Biddle, June 23, 1923

Dear Warden: I have a son, Roy P. Connor, who left home in 1912 and I have not been able to locate him since. I have a letter from a parole board official who advises me that he is confined in Leavenworth prison. I write you to please give me what information you can on this man. My son is about 30 years old. Yours, Mrs. P. L. Connor

Warden Biddle to Mrs. Connor, June 25, 1923

Dear Mrs. P. L. Connor: In reply to your letter, please be advised that we have a man in this institution by the name of Roy P. Connor, alias Roy P. Conner. Respectfully, Warden

Connor to His Mother, July 2, 1923

Darling Mother: For twelve long years I have mourned you as dead. Would not believe that letter I have just received was from you if I did not recognize the hand-writing. I was in Winnipeg, Canada when I received a letter from a friend in Savannah with clipping enclosed out of the Atlanta Journal saying you were dying and wanted to see me. The letter had been forwarded from the States and the clipping was three weeks old; I figured that you had died and that I was morally guilty of murder. I quit working for the C.P.R. in the middle of the afternoon and for the next two years I was a drunken wreck just drifting from one state into another, not knowing where I was going and caring less, without either hope or ambition, nothing to look forward. I knew that I could never look any of the rest of the family in the face again, so I remained mute, though I longed to hear from them; the thoughts of what a return letter would bring robbed me of the courage to write and wait a reply.

As to my case I am enclosing a clipping which speaks for itself and I will write Dad as soon as I finish this and give him the particulars of my case in its entirety.

Now dear mother don't worry a bit about me; this place is not as bad as you might imagine.

As you can tell by this letter that I am not insane although I am confined in the psychopathic ward and have been for the past two months for mental observation.

Would like to hug and kiss you once more, but don't you make a visit to this place.

With love and best wishes, Roy P. Connor, Box 7 Leavenworth

Connor to His Father, July 2, 1923

Dear Dad: I gave up all hopes of ever hearing from or seeing any of my loved ones more than ten years ago, and though I wandered over the universe, I do not think that I committed any wrong, except the failure to write home.

When I first came here I had not recovered from the effects of Flu and Pneumonia, coughing almost continually, and felt very bitter over the injustice of my conviction. I had not the faintest glimmer of hope; thought I had T.B., and did not see any chance of ever getting out and having no wish to die a martyr . . . I think I was insane, but have pulled myself together since hearing from home, and, in future, I shall obey all prison rules. If I had not received letters from home I would have been a raving maniac in three months longer, but as it is I am seldom restless now as I know I have something to live for and to look forward to. I am anxious to make a sincere effort to be a worthy citizen.

I will give you my case in its entirety, and will be frank: I joined the I.W.W. in June or July, 1916 . . . in Nebr. In Jan. 1917, I went from Seattle to Portland and into Cal. When war was declared there was about forty of us working at Exeter, Cal. We all registered for the draft and claimed exemption on the grounds of being conscientious objectors. In July 1917 I became an organizer for the I.W.W. Everything was done in the open. The hall in Fresno was open for anyone who wished to come in, sit down and rest or read. In fact, it was more like a library than anything else.

We were indicted Oct. 4th and remained in jail until May 1918 when 12 of us were released on $1,000.00 bond each.

The trial started in Dec. We refused to accept counsel (43 of us) or say anything in our own behalf. The first two weeks of trial consisted of reading articles from I.W.W. publications.

Two constables identified me as being one of the pickets picketing a strike in Exeter. Their testimony was true. We won half of our demands and went back to work. With love and best wishes, your son, Roy P. Connor, Leavenworth, Kansas

Connor to His Brother, July 4, 1923

Dear Brother: Thanks for your letter of the 29th. It showed the true spirit of a loving brother. I neither feel guilty or ashamed of my imprisonment and was it not for the name of the family I would not care a damn who knew it. We were arrested indiscriminately. The indictment was a blanket one; anyone carrying an I.W.W. card with his name on it could be arrested; we were convicted of violating the espionage act but prosecuted for our activities in the industrial field; two men whose names were not even mentioned except to show their membership cards got ten years; the trial was a farce, a human tragedy. The indictment had been changed so many times that we refused to even read the new ones which included four counts and sometimes covering fifty pages and then again it would be 75 pages. Prior to trial most of the fellows had been in jail more than a year, 20 of us were down sick with the flu or pneumonia, 5 had died so when [our counsel] suggested that [our] case be postponed to give them time to prepare a defense we immediately fired them and decided that on account of the war hysteria and the lies of the newspapers, it would be useless to make a defense in an atmosphere of bias and prejudice. The case came up in Dec., we told them we were ready; we plead not guilty and remained silent during the four weeks of trial, ten or twelve who were sick slept during most of the proceedings. Senator Pepper of Pa. has just completed reviewing the records of our trial. He was requested to do this by President Harding and his report to the press was to the effect "that we should not have been convicted."

Though I am no longer a member of the I.W.W. I consider the members the finest men I have ever known. Honest, don't drink, clean morally and possess the highest ideals and intellectually superior to the average university professor. They are the super men of the labor movement. I refused to accept my freedom at their expense before the trial and I would do the same today.

Don't pay any attention to me being in psychopathic ward; it is only for short time. It is the very best place in Institution.

Hoping you are in good health and enjoying life, I am your loving bro, Roy Connor, Box 7, Leavenworth, Kans.

Warden to Pardon Attorney James A. Finch, November 5, 1923

This will acknowledge your letter of November 3, 1923 in which you state that the Governor of Georgia, and others are interesting themselves in behalf of Roy P. Connor.

In reply will state that Connor's actions of late have been very bad, and his vicious tendencies are coming out now as strong as they did during his first couple years confinement in the penitentiary.

When prison officials come near Connor he curses and calls them vile names. He has a low, vile mind and uses foul language that is a disgrace even to a penitentiary.

The letters from Connor's parents are filled with statements about their activities among Georgia politicians in getting recommendations to have him pardoned, and they have a tendency to arouse all the bad there is in him.

You asked for my views regarding Connor being law-abiding if released, and I will say that I do not believe he will work or try to become a useful citizen. All of the inmates know of Connor's bad behavior which resulted in former officials placing him in segregation, of his pretended hunger strikes and of the way he has been carrying on of late, and, in my judgment, if he is released on pardon it will have a very bad effect on the discipline of the prison. Very respectfully, Warden

Connor to His Father, November 20, 1923

Dear Papa: It is true that I have been in prison too long. Am extremely nervous at times and my mental faculties are subnormal but when I get outside for a couple of weeks I will be O.K. again. I have no fear of what the future holds.

There is no use to worry about me getting hurt or anything like that here. I am getting so I can sleep pretty well and I do not go out in the yard or anywhere else where there is any chance of trouble. Hoping to see all soon. With love and best wishes. Your son, Roy P. Connor

Over the objection of Warden Biddle, Roy P. Connor was released on December 24, 1923.

NOTE

1. The material in this chapter was obtained from the Leavenworth Penitentiary file of Roy P. Connor, #13564.

Chapter 11

Release

As the United States entered the 1920s, the ranks of federal political prisoners started to thin. Many of those convicted under the various antisedition laws completed their sentences. Others were released from prison upon the condition that they be deported from the United States or cease and desist from all dissident political activities. As for the long-term Sedition Act prisoners (i.e., those sentenced to between ten and twenty years who refused to agree to the various conditions offered by the Department of Justice), their sentences were gradually commuted by the president.

The Justice Department carefully weighed the merits of each commutation of sentence, an example of which is a December 23, 1921, memorandum written to President Warren G. Harding by U.S. Attorney General H. M. Daugherty, recommending the commutation of Eugene V. Debs' ten-year sentence.[1] President Harding agreed with this recommendation and commuted Debs' sentence on December 25, 1921.

Memorandum to President Warren G. Harding from Attorney General H. M. Daugherty, December 23, 1921

To the President:

Eugene V. Debs, hereinafter called the defendant, was convicted in the United States District Court for the Northern District of Ohio, at Cleveland, of violating Section 3, Title I, of the Espionage Act of June 15, 1917, as amended by the Act of May 16, 1918, and was sentenced September 14, 1918, to imprisonment for ten years in the State Penitentiary at Moundsville, West Virginia. The case was appealed to the Supreme Court, which affirmed the judgment of the

Socialist Party leader Eugene V. Debs as he stepped from Atlanta Penitentiary on Christmas day, pardoned by President Harding after serving two years of his ten-year sentence. Courtesy of the Library of Congress.

District Court March 10, 1919, and Debs began to serve his sentence April 12, 1919, in the penitentiary at Moundsville. Later he was transferred to the United States Penitentiary at Atlanta, Georgia, where he is now confined. He will be eligible for parole August 11, 1922. His term, with the allowances for good conduct, will expire December 28, 1925. . . .

Debs himself, so far as I know, has not applied for executive clemency and therefore no action would be taken in his case were it not for the enormous mass of communications received in his behalf by people who clearly regard Debs as a martyr to the cause of freedom of speech.

The basis of the indictment against Debs was a speech delivered by him before the State Convention of the Socialist Party of Ohio, at Canton on June 16, 1918. In his utterances Debs was most guarded, clearly attempting to keep within the law in order to avoid prosecution, but by subtle argument, innuendo, ridicule, and by commendation of unlawful acts in others, to prepare the minds of his hearers for similar disloyal and unlawful actions on their part. . . .

Debs' own speech clearly established the foregoing statement. Observe what he says: "There are certain limitations placed on right of free speech," and he must be extremely careful as to *what* he says. . . .

Having prepared the minds of his audience for the real and more important meaning and significance of his words, he says that he has just returned from yonder (the workhouse) "where three of our most loyal comrades are paying the penalty for their devotion to the cause of the working class."

What was the offense for which these persons were undergoing sentence? They were convicted of aiding and abetting, counselling and inducing another to refuse to register for military service in violation of the Draft Act, and they had been making speeches against the war and the draft. Continuing, in sarcasm, Debs said:

> They have come to realize, as many of us have, that it is extremely dangerous to exercise the constitutional right of free speech in a country fighting to make democracy free for the world.

thus leaving the impression that the constitutional guaranty of freedom of speech gave these men the right, in violation of law, to induce a man not to register for military service. Closing his eulogy on these "three loyal comrades," he said:

> I am proud of them. They are there for us; and we are here for them. Their lips, though temporarily mute, are more eloquent than ever before; and their voices, though silent, are heard around the world.

In the same manner he eulogized Kate Richards O'Hare as a woman of unimpeachable loyalty to the socialist movement and declared that—

> The United States, under the rule of the plutocrats, is the only country that would send a woman to the penitentiary for exercising the constitutional right of free speech. If this be treason, let them make the most of it.

Kate Richards O'Hare was convicted for wilfully obstructing the enlistment service of the United States.

It seems clear, therefore, from the foregoing, that Debs, by his speech, was actually and consciously attempting to influence and persuade his hearers to refuse to obey the laws of this country and thereby obstruct and hamper it in the prosecution of the war. In fact, he expressly so stated in his address to the jury. He said, "I have been accused of obstructing the war. I admit it". . . .

Debs, at the trial, admitted all the facts in the case and at the conclusion admitted that he had had a fair trial. He still admits his trial to have been fair. His defense was one of justification. He asserted that all he had said was true, but contended that the Espionage Act, on which he was indicted and tried, was unconstitutional, being in conflict with the first amendment of the Constitution which guarantees freedom of speech. This contention, however, was rejected by the Supreme Court, which has held that the Act is constitutional and that Debs' utterances constituted a violation of the Act. . . .

The fact that the crime is termed by the offenders and those who sympathize with them, a "political offense" does not alter the situation. Such offenses are crimes of far greater menace to society and to the Government at large than ordinary crimes, for they go to the life and strength of the nation.

. . . In the Debs case and other similar cases, a reasonable punishment is necessary as an example to others, and when that is accomplished, there is no justification for further imprisonment.

There is, however, in this particular case of Debs, a danger not often encountered and that is that his prolonged confinement will have an injurious effect on a large number of people who will undoubtedly regard his imprisonment unjustifiable. . . .

Debs is now about sixty-six years of age. He appears to be physically strong but as a matter of fact is not, and he is not a normal man mentally on this particular subject, his obsession clearly preventing him from acquiescing in the final decision of the Courts respecting the limitations of freedom of speech as guaranteed by the Constitution. He is a man of much personal charm and impressive personality. In the work he has undertaken, these qualities make him a very dangerous man, calculated to mislead the unthinking and afford an excuse for those with criminal intent. So far as he thinks correctly he may be conscientious, but he does not think correctly and apparently cannot do so on the questions involved in this case, and it must not be overlooked that under our form of Government his theories, which are in conflict with the highest constituted authority, are wrong and treasonable.

Aside from the offense of which Debs was convicted, his private life, so I am informed, has been irreproachable. His wife is quite as old as he is and she is failing in health.

In punishing those who have committed crimes, it is or should be the policy of those executing the law to consider how much or what percentage of the defendant's life period will be taken by the sentence. I feel that considering Debs' age in connection with all other matters set forth and discussed herein, the percentage of his life appropriated to this sentence is excessive.

A great lesson has been taught, not only to this country, but to the world and future generations, by the decision in this case. The decision was by a unanimous court and is sound. Too much credit cannot be given to the Judiciary and those connected with the Department of Justice, in seeing to it that justice was administered and that the law was interpreted aright, as it was essential it should be interpreted, for the protection and preservation of this nation in its extremity, when assailed by foes within as well as by foes without.

Victory has come, not only to the armies in the field but to the powers and instrumentalities within our nation which were essential to the protection and the safe-guarding of our own form of Government. Debs has been imprisoned over two years and eight months, the law in question has been vindicated and a lesson taught which will never be eradicated from the pages of history. . . .

Under these circumstances I am of the opinion that the time has come when it is not only proper but expedient that some action be taken in the Debs' case and his sentence materially reduced. . . .

As stated, Debs has now been imprisoned over two years and eight months. In my opinion, the ends of justice would be served and it would be a gracious act of mercy to release him in the near future. . . .

NOTE

1. U.S. Department of Justice, Attorney General H. M. Daugherty to President Warren G. Harding, "In the Matter of the Application for Pardon in Behalf of Eugene V. Debs," Department of Justice Memorandum No. 35–386–3336, December 23, 1921, Yale University Library.

The Socialist Party office in Boston after a raid by the U.S. Department of Justice. Courtesy of the National Archives.

Unidentified protesters being arrested at a "Woman's March" against World War I in New York City. Courtesy of the National Archives.

Anti-war activist Louis Kramer after his arrest for conspiracy to obstruct the draft. He served two years in Atlanta Penitentiary. Courtesy of the National Archives.

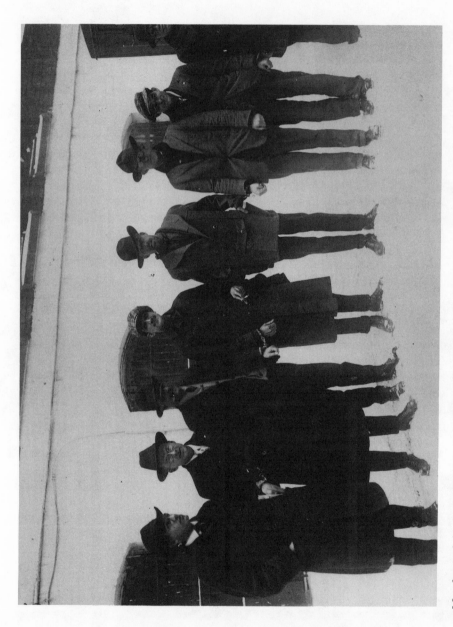

Members of the Industrial Workers of the World being detained in a county jail in New York. Courtesy of the National Archives.

IS THIS TO BE THE STORY OF
FREE SPEECH IN AMERICA?

Free Political
Prisoners by
Christmas ❦

What Can I Do to Help
in This Campaign?

Amnesty campaign brochure published by the General Defense
Committee. Courtesy of the author.

A prison cell in Sing Sing Penitentiary, where members of the early Communist Party were imprisoned under the New York Criminal Anarchy law. Courtesy of the Library of Congress.

William D. Haywood, General Secretary of the Industrial Workers of the World union. Photo taken upon his admission into Leavenworth Penitentiary in 1918. Department of Justice photo.

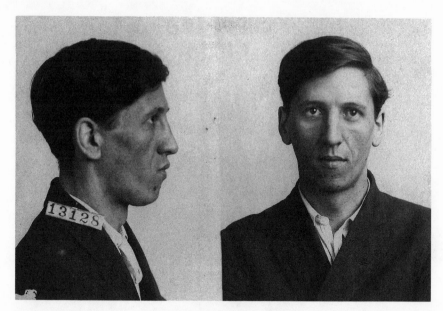

Leavenworth prison photo of Edward Hamilton, I.W.W. union leader sentenced to ten years in prison under the Espionage Act. At Leavenworth the Warden ordered Hamilton placed in segregation and branded him a "dangerous and irresponsible character." Department of Justice photo.

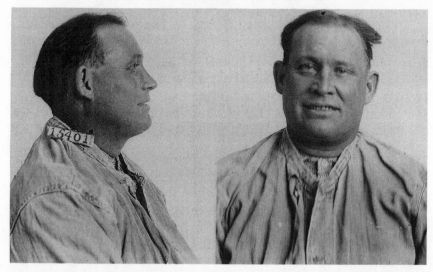

Orville Anderson prison photo. Anderson was the Socialist Party's candidate for governor from South Dakota. He served in Leavenworth from 1918–1921, convicted of calling President Wilson a "murder." Department of Justice photo.

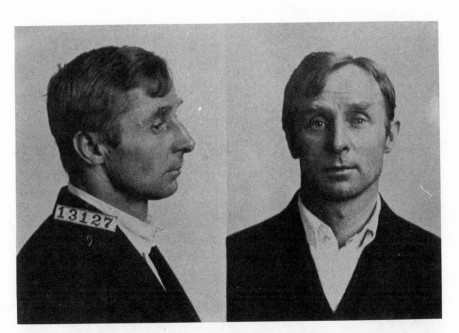

Peter Green, secretary of the I.W.W. Lumber Workers' Union served over six years in prison. In a private correspondence the Justice Department conceded that there was no evidence admitted into court which proved that Green had violated any law. Department of Justice photo.

Cornelius Lehane addressing an anti-war rally. Lehane was arrested and, according to FBI reports, died in prison in Bridgeport, Connecticut. Courtesy of the Library of Congress.

Part III

The Prisoners

Chapter 12

Federal Espionage and Sedition Act Prisoners

The following is a listing of the prisoners who served over one year in prison between 1917 and 1924 for violating federal conspiracy laws or the Espionage and Sedition Acts due to their opposition to World War I or their membership in various radical organizations.

George Adams was arrested in November 1917 in the roundup of IWW members in Omaha, Nebraska. After over 18 months in local jails, all charges against him were dropped.[1]

Jacob Abrams, an anarchist from New York, New York, was sentenced to twenty years in prison for circulating a leaflet critical of U.S. intervention in Russia in 1918. He served in Atlanta Penitentiary from 1919 to 1921 and was deported to Russia after his release.

While in prison Abrams sought advice from friends about whether he should accept a commutation of his sentence conditioned upon his agreeing to be deported to Russia. In one letter, confiscated by prison authorities, a friend of Abrams attempted to inform him of the difficulties he would face in Soviet Russia:

You want to know the truth about everything. This, however, is not an easy task. Not everything can be written, not only because others shall know it, but because others may not want you to know it and after all you are a prisoner and there is someone else who has "a say" about what you shall or shall not read.

... [A]ccording to latest there is practically no room in Russia now for one who cannot be under the most rigid discipline. In short Russia is now, as "Mother" [Emma Goldman] writes, a "big prison." ... [I]f one wants to be in Russia, the only work outside soviet work, that one can do, is to write and preach about the moon . . . and the question arises does it pay to suffer hunger and from other economical abnormalities prevailing in Russia now and after all have as much freedom as you have in Atlanta Prison?

Abrams' sentence was commuted on October 23, 1921, on the condition that he would be deported to Russia and never return to the United States. (See also the entry for Mollie Steimer, Abrams' codefendant.)[2]

Carl Ahlteen was editor of the IWW Swedish language newspaper *Alarm*. According to a Department of Justice memorandum, Ahlteen was convicted and sentenced to twenty years at Leavenworth merely for publishing an article in *Alarm* that opposed U.S. intervention in World War I. In relevant part Ahlteen wrote:

War, war, and again war, is the cry. What would a State with its brutal machinery do if the working class absolutely said that they would not transport one pound of food to such beings, who have taken as their business the murdering of others, whether it is our country's or other countries' soldiers.

After five years in jail Ahlteen and two other leading Swedish organizers for the IWW, Sigfrid Stenberg and Ragner Johannsen, accepted the commutation of their sentences conditioned upon their deportation from the United States. Each defendant had to swear that he would "never return" to this country.[3]

C. W. Anderson, secretary-treasurer of the Agricultural Workers Industrial Union, Local 450, in St. Paul, Minnesota, was convicted at the mass IWW trial in Wichita and was sentenced to nine years in prison. He served in Leavenworth Penitentiary. The Department of Justice described Anderson as "one of the leading officials and workers of the I.W.W. in the Middle West."[4]

Edward Anderson was originally sentenced to two years in prison. He served at Leavenworth Penitentiary from January 17, 1919, to September 2, 1920.[5]

Elmer Anderson, from Sacramento, California, was convicted at the mass IWW trial in Sacramento and sentenced to ten years in prison. He served in Leavenworth Penitentiary.[6]

Olin B. Anderson, a press agent for the IWW from Kallispell, Montana, was convicted at the mass IWW trial in Chicago, sentenced to five years in prison and fined $30,000. He served in Leavenworth Penitentiary from September 7, 1918, to June 30, 1922.

Anderson joined the IWW in 1917 and was hired as a press agent during the Fortina River drivers strike in Montana. After his arrest in Chicago, Anderson awaited trial in the Cook County (Illinois) Jail, where he suffered a physical breakdown and contracted tuberculosis.

After serving approximately four years at Leavenworth, Anderson petitioned for release. His spirit and health broken, Anderson wrote: "bitter experience and grim facts have brought a shocking disillusionment and convinced me of the utter futility of a continued sacrifice and suffering, shut away from life, liberty and love for what I once held dear as an ideal."

Anderson was paroled on June 30, 1992. According to an FBI report on his post-prison activities, Anderson never regained good health. His tuberculosis worsened, and, in 1924, he was committed to the Montana State Hospital for the Insane. Local authorities informed the FBI that he was "far gone with tuberculosis" and would die very soon. The FBI's reaction to Anderson's condition was blunt: "As this disposes of this IWW probably permanently, the matter will be considered closed."[7]

Orville Anderson, a farmer from Vermillia, South Dakota, was the Socialist Party's candidate for governor of South Dakota in 1918. He was sentenced to four years in prison and served in Leavenworth Penitentiary from October 5, 1918, to December 21, 1921.

Anderson was convicted for allegedly making the following statement:

President Wilson is a murderer in the first degree. He is murdering, not only Germans but his own people, the American people, as well, and he is violating the Constitution of the U.S. by drafting men and sending them to fight in Europe.

Anderson resumed political activities after his release from prison and was the subject of an investigation by the FBI in 1942. According to that investigation Anderson "continually gathered small groups of down and outers" and "exhorted them to stand up for their rights." During the Great Depression he led marches demanding more relief for the poor and demonstrations that "forcibly prevented foreclosures on farm mortgages."[8]

Charles Anding, from Winona, Minnesota, was arrested on May 25, 1918, for obstructing the draft.[9]

George Andreychine, the editor of the IWW's Bulgarian language newspaper in Chicago, Illinois, was convicted at the mass IWW trial in Chicago, sentenced to twenty years in prison and fined $20,000. He served in Leavenworth Penitentiary from September 7, 1918, to June 8, 1919. Andreychine jumped bail while his appeal was pending and became a fugitive from the law. He is said to have fled to Russia and to have been executed by Stalin's secret police.[10]

Gabriella (Ella) Antolini, an eighteen-year-old anarchist and Italian immigrant residing in New England, was convicted of anti-war activities. Antolini was confined in the Missouri State Prison in Jefferson City, Missouri. In prison she befriended Emma Goldman, who described Antolini:

She was a proletarian child, familiar with poverty and hardship, strong and socially conscious. Gentle and sympathetic, she was like a beam of sunshine, bringing cheer to her fellow prisoners and great joy to me.

Antolini served approximately two years in prison.[11]

Charles Ashleigh, a journalist and a poet from San Francisco, California, was convicted at the mass IWW trial in Chicago and sentenced to ten years in prison. He served in the Cook County Jail and Leavenworth Penitentiary from 1917 to 1921.

Alexander Lanier, a former captain of the Military Intelligence Division, General Staff, U.S. Army, reviewed the record in Ashleigh's case and wrote the following to President Woodrow Wilson:

> ... [T]here can be no question, in my opinion of the absolute innocence and wrongful conviction of Charles Ashleigh ... I defy anyone to show me one scintilla of evidence in the record of this trial that proves that [Ashleigh] conspired with anyone to violate any law, or that they did, in fact, violate any law. . . .
> ... I am of the opinion that these men were convicted contrary to the law and the evidence, solely because they were leaders of a revolutionary organization against which public sentiment was justly incensed; and that the verdict rendered was a foregone conclusion from the beginning in obedience to a public hysteria and popular demand, due to the psychology of the times.[12]

John Avila, from Lowell, Massachusetts, was convicted at the mass IWW trial in Chicago, sentenced to five years in prison and fined $20,000. He served in Leavenworth Penitentiary from September 30, 1917, to May 14, 1922, when his sentence expired. Avila had a wife and three children.[13]

Vincente A. Azuara, the editor of the IWW's *El Ribeldo* from Los Angeles, California, was convicted at the mass IWW trial in Chicago, sentenced to twenty years in prison and fined $20,000. He served in Leavenworth Penitentiary from September 1917 to December 20, 1922. Azuara's sentence was commuted when he agreed to be deported to Spain and to never return to the United States.[14]

William Bago, from Hamilton, Ohio, received a prison sentence of fifteen years, which was commuted to two years. He served in Atlanta Penitentiary from June 6, 1918, to March 3, 1920.[15]

John Baldazza, an organizer for the Italian Bakers Federation and manager of *Il Proletario*, the IWW's Italian language newspaper, from New York, New York, was convicted at the mass IWW trial in Chicago, sentenced to ten years in prison and fined $30,000. He served in Leavenworth Penitentiary from January 1918 to January 1920 and from April 1921 to December 26, 1921.

Baldazza was released on the condition that he would be deported to Italy. In his request for clemency, Baldazza stated:

> My sole purpose as organizer for the IWW was to better the conditions of the workmen of America so that they would possess better homes and be free from economic necessity, live under better hygienic conditions and be able to obtain

for themselves and their children higher education and realize the dignity of labor.[16]

Giovanni Baldazzi was sentenced to ten years in prison. He served in Leavenworth Penitentiary from August 30, 1918, to December 1921, when he was granted clemency and deported.[17]

Albert Barr, from Kansas, was sentenced to five years in prison. He served in Leavenworth Penitentiary from December 18, 1919, to June 17, 1921, when he was released on bond pending appeal.[18]

Joseph Basor, from Michigan, was sentenced to five years in prison. He served in Leavenworth Penitentiary.[19]

C. E. Bates was arrested in November 1917 in the roundup of IWW members in Omaha, Nebraska. After over 18 months in local jails, all charges against him were dropped.[20]

J. A. Beaumont, an electrician from Ocala, Florida, was sentenced to five years in prison. He served in Atlanta Penitentiary from March 4, 1918, to November 23, 1920, when he was paroled.[21]

Morris Becker, an anarchist and a vegetarian from New York, New York, was sentenced to a year and eight months in prison. He served in Atlanta Penitentiary from June 19, 1917, to July 25, 1917, and from September 12, 1917, to December 27, 1918. Becker was deported after being rearrested in December 1918 for failing to register for the draft.[22]

Roy Becker was arrested in November 1917 in the roundup of IWW members in Omaha, Nebraska. After over eighteen months in local jails, all charges against him were dropped.[23]

W. L. Bennefield, a farmer, a Socialist and a member of the Working Class Union from Oklahoma, was sentenced to ten years in prison. He began his imprisonment in Leavenworth Penitentiary on November 1, 1917. During Bennefield's incarceration his wife and seven children were left destitute.[24]

Charles Bennett, secretary of the Marine Transport Workers Industrial Union, Local 700, in Portland, Oregon, was convicted at the mass IWW trial in Chicago, sentenced to ten years in prison and fined $30,000. He served in the Cook County Jail and Leavenworth Penitentiary from September 1917 to May 1919 and from April 1921 to June 25, 1923.[25]

Jacob O. Bentall, from Minneapolis, Minnesota, was convicted for making a speech during his campaign as the Socialist Party's candidate for governor. He was sentenced to five years in prison and served in Leavenworth Penitentiary.[26]

A. F. W. Benzin, from Columbus, Ohio, was imprisoned July 10, 1918. He was sentenced to four and one-half years in prison.[27]

George P. Beohm, from Illinois, was sentenced to three years in prison. He served in Leavenworth Penitentiary.[28]

Alexander Berkman was born in Russia in 1870 and emigrated to the

United States at the age of eighteen. In the United States he became a leading figure in the international anarchist movement and edited the magazines *The Blast* and *Mother Earth*. Berkman was active in many radical causes, including labor rights campaigns and the early movement to legalize the distribution of birth control information. In New York City, he cofounded the Ferrer School (also known as the Modern School), which was dedicated to libertarian and humanistic educational principles.

Throughout his adult life Berkman worked closely with fellow anarchist Emma Goldman. Together, in 1917, they formed the No Conscription League to oppose World War I. In response to the anti-war activities of the league, the government moved swiftly to arrest Berkman and Goldman on June 15, 1917. They were jointly tried, convicted and sentenced to two years in prison.

Berkman served in Atlanta Penitentiary, where he was placed in solitary confinement for calling the warden a "hypocrite." In a letter to the superintendent of prisons, the warden stated that Berkman was placed in permanent isolation "for the peace and good order of the Institution." He accused Berkman of "carrying on revolutionary propaganda among the inmates" and becoming a "menace to the Institution."

After serving his full term in prison, Berkman, along with Goldman, was deported to Soviet Russia on the *S.S. Buford*. Although originally embraced by Lenin and the Bolshevik movement, Berkman strongly condemned the totalitarian nature of the Russian Revolution, and after the brutal crushing of the Kronstadt Rebellion in 1921, he and Goldman fled the Soviet Union for exile in Europe. He remained active in anarchist causes until his suicide in 1936. (See also the entry for Emma Goldman and Chapters 1 and 3 for details on the case against Berkman and Goldman and excerpts from Berkman's speech to the jury, respectively.)[29]

Charles Bernal was sentenced to two years in prison. He served in Leavenworth Penitentiary from October 10, 1918, to May 18, 1920.[30]

J. H. Beyer was convicted at the mass IWW trial in Chicago and served in Leavenworth Penitentiary. Beyer jumped bail pending the appeal of his conviction and became a fugitive from the law. He is said to have taken refuge in Soviet Russia.[31]

David T. Blodgett, from Des Moines, Iowa, was indicted for circulating a speech by Senator Thomas E. Watson of Georgia that criticized the conscription law. Convicted and sentenced to twenty years in prison for anti-war writings, Blodgett served in Atlanta and Leavenworth Penitentiaries from January 11, 1918, to January 7, 1922.

At Leavenworth Penitentiary he had a breakdown and was transferred to St. Elizabeth's Hospital for the Insane on January 4, 1919. On February 25, 1920, after being confined at St. Elizabeth's for over a year, Blodgett was transferred to Atlanta Penitentiary.

Outraged by the treatment meted out to Blodgett, Senator Watson introduced a bill in the Senate on October 20, 1921, calling for Blodgett's release. Blodgett's sentence was commuted on January 7, 1922.[32]

A. M. Blumberg, from Kansas, was convicted at the mass IWW trial in Wichita and sentenced to four years in prison. He served in Leavenworth Penitentiary from December 18, 1919, to June 17, 1921, when he was released on bond. He contracted tuberculosis while in prison.[33]

Leonard W. Bolhner served his sentence from November 9, 1918, to January 19, 1922.[34]

Arthur Boose, an IWW organizer from Abbotsford, Wisconsin, was convicted at the mass IWW trial in Chicago, sentenced to five years in prison and fined $30,000. He served in Leavenworth Penitentiary from September 1917 to May 14, 1922, when his sentence expired.[35]

Paul Bosko, a Socialist from Parkersburg, West Virginia, began serving a fifteen-year prison sentence on January 17, 1918.[36]

John Bosses, of Aberdeen, South Dakota, was convicted of seditious conspiracy and began serving his two and a half year sentence on May 16, 1918.[37]

G. W. Bouldin received a prison sentence of two years, which was commuted to a year and a day. He served in Leavenworth Penitentiary.[38]

G. J. Bourg, originally from Minneapolis, Minnesota, was secretary of the IWW's Kansas City (Missouri) local when arrested. He was convicted at the mass IWW trial in Chicago, sentenced to ten years in prison and fined $30,000. He served in Leavenworth Penitentiary from October 1917 to December 22, 1923.

Bourg was requested to take over the Kansas City, Missouri, local "after a bunch of drunken militiamen smashed up" the local union hall and "scared the former secretary into leaving town."

The Department of Justice admitted after Bourg's conviction that the "only written proof" of Bourg's making any statement against World War I was his statement that Kansas City had "gone crazy over patriotism."[39]

André Boutin, from Onondaga County, New York, was found guilty of disloyalty for circulating the pamphlet "Pure Common Sense," which stated, in part, "We need preparedness, not to kill one another, but to live peaceably, happily and equally." (See also Chapter 1.)[40]

E. M. Boyd, from Kansas, was sentenced to five years in prison. He served in Leavenworth Penitentiary from December 18, 1919, to June 17, 1921, when he was released on bond.[41]

Richard Brazier, an IWW officer from Spokane, Washington, was convicted at the mass IWW trial in Chicago, sentenced to twenty years in prison and fined $20,000. He served in Leavenworth Penitentiary from September 1917 to August 3, 1923, and was deported after his release. Brazier, who joined the IWW in 1908, became its national organizer and eventually was elected to its General Executive Board.[42]

Harry Brewer, a railroad man from Sacramento, California, was convicted at the mass IWW trial in Sacramento and sentenced to ten years in prison. He served in Leavenworth Penitentiary from August 1918 to December 22, 1923.[43]

Earl Browder was a trade union activist from Kansas City, Missouri. In 1917, Browder was convicted of failure to register for the draft and conspiracy to interfere with the draft. He served two years in prison at the Bates County Jail in Butler, Missouri, and at Leavenworth Penitentiary.

Soon after his release from prison in December 1920, Browder joined the Communist Party. He became a full member of the party's Executive Committee in 1922 and rose to its leadership in the 1930s during the party's most influential period in U.S. history. He served as general secretary from 1934 to 1945, but was stripped of his office in 1945. In 1946, Browder was expelled from the party and labelled a "renegade and revisionist."[44]

B. F. Bryant, a member of both the Socialist Party and the Universal Union from Maysville, Oklahoma, was sentenced to six years in prison. He served in Leavenworth Penitentiary from April 2, 1920, to September 1, 1922.[45]

G. T. Bryant, a twenty-year member of the Socialist Party at the time of his arrest and a state organizer for the Farmers and Laborers Protective Association of Texas, came from Ranger, Texas. He was sentenced to six years in prison and served in Leavenworth Penitentiary. His wife and two children suffered extreme poverty because of Bryant's imprisonment.[46]

Dan Buckley, the general secretary and treasurer of the IWW Construction Workers Industrial Union, Local 573, from San Francisco, was convicted at the mass IWW trial in Chicago, sentenced to ten years in prison and fined $30,000. He served in Leavenworth Penitentiary from September 1917 to February 1920 and from April 1921 to February 9, 1923.[47]

Lotta Burke, from Ohio, was sentenced to fifteen months in prison for circulating a leaflet urging men not to register for the draft. She served in the Missouri State Prison.[48]

J. H. Byers, from Flint, Michigan, was convicted at the mass IWW trial in Chicago, sentenced to ten years in prison and fined $30,000. Byers was imprisoned at Leavenworth from October 1917 to November 20, 1919, when he was released on bond pending appeal. He jumped bail and became a fugitive from the law. He had a wife and a child.[49]

Jack Caffray was convicted at the mass IWW trial in Wichita. He went insane in Shawnee County (Kansas) Jail.[50]

Vincente Balbas Capo, from San Juan, Puerto Rico, was convicted for writing an editorial against conscription in a Puerto Rican newspaper and sentenced to eight years in prison. He began serving his sentence on December 1, 1917.[51]

Edward S. Carey, from New York, New York, was convicted at the mass IWW trial in Sacramento and sentenced to five years in prison.[52]

Thomas Carey, from San Francisco, California, was convicted of conspiracy to violate the Selective Service Act and sentenced to two years in prison. A member of "American Patriots," he served his sentence at McNeil Island Penitentiary and was released in December, 1921, when his term was commuted by President Harding.[53]

Joseph Carroll, a laborer from Maryland, was convicted at the mass IWW trial in Sacramento and sentenced to three years in prison. He served in Leavenworth Penitentiary until his sentence expired on May 17, 1920. Carroll was repeatedly placed in "isolation on restricted diet" for "failing to break enough rock," "laziness," and "disobeying orders."[54]

Felix Cedene was sentenced to two years in prison. He served in Leavenworth Penitentiary from January 17, 1919, to September 2, 1920.[55]

Ralph Chaplin, from Chicago, Illinois, was sentenced to twenty years in prison at the IWW trial in Chicago. Chaplin was a songwriter and editor of the IWW's banner newspaper *Solidarity*. His most famous song, "Solidarity Forever," remains popular as the anthem of the trade union movement.

Chaplin served in Leavenworth Penitentiary from September 1918 to July 1919 and from April 1921 until the commutation of his sentence on June 25, 1923. The Department of Justice initially recommended against any reduction of sentence, calling Chaplin a "notorious agitator" who used "all his power and influence to belittle the government." At Leavenworth the warden criticized Chaplin as a "lazy," "sneaking" and "double dealing" prisoner:

Chaplin is more cunning than the average IWW prisoner and he tries sneaking ways to get others to make trouble for the prison officials . . . Chaplin poses as a poet and is a lazy loafer.

During his incarceration Chaplin's family and friends published a chapbook of prison poems.

Roger Baldwin, a close friend of Chaplin, reported that after his release from prison Chaplin cried for two weeks. Chaplin remained active in the labor movement until his death in 1961 at the age of seventy-four.[56]

Benton Claiborne served in Atlanta Penitentiary from September 10, 1918, to October 15, 1920.[57]

F. Clark, a Universal Union member from western Oklahoma, received a prison sentence of eight years, which was commuted to eighteen months. He served in Leavenworth Penitentiary.[58]

Stanley J. Clark, an attorney from Jacksonville, Texas, was convicted at the mass IWW trial in Chicago and sentenced to ten years in prison. He served in Leavenworth Penitentiary until July 21, 1922, when his sentence was commuted. He had two children. After prison, Clark left the IWW to join the U.S. Communist Party.[59]

Joseph M. Coldwell, from Providence, Rhode Island, was convicted under the Espionage and Sedition Acts for publicly stating that "war is organized murder." Coldwell served in Atlanta Penitentiary from October 27, 1919, until President Warren G. Harding commuted his sentence on December 25, 1921. Coldwell became active in labor and socialist politics in the 1890s. He rose to strike leader in Massachusetts, playing a major role in the Lawrence textile strike and the Hopedale strike (which he helped lead with Nicola Sacco). For strike-related activities he served a three-month sentence in the Worcester County (Massachusetts) Jail in 1912 (disorderly conduct) and a one-year sentence in the same jail for an alleged strike-related assault.

While jailed in Atlanta, Coldwell shared his cell with Eugene Debs and refused a pardon of sentence while "Comrade Debs" was still imprisoned.

For eight months after Coldwell's release his activities were monitored by the Department of Justice's Bureau of Investigations. The agents noted in their confidential report on Coldwell's activities that many of those who attended Coldwell's speeches were "Jews." Coldwell ran as the Socialist Party's candidate for governor and senator of Rhode Island in the 1930s and remained active in his party's activities until his death in 1949.[60]

Hubert Colley, from Oklahoma, served at Leavenworth Penitentiary.[61]

Robert Connellan, secretary of the IWW local in Stockton, California, was convicted at the mass IWW trial in Sacramento and sentenced to ten years in prison. He served in Leavenworth Penitentiary from July 1918 to December 22, 1923.[62]

Roy P. Connor, an organizer and delegate for the Agricultural Workers Industrial Union, Local 400, from Kennesaw, Georgia, was convicted at the mass IWW trial in Sacramento and sentenced to ten years in prison. Connor served in Leavenworth Penitentiary from September 5, 1917, to May 1918 and from August 23, 1918, to December 22, 1923. (See also Chapters 9 and 10 for detailed accounts of Connor's treatment and courage in prison.) Connor remained in segregation until his release.[63]

Thomas Cornell, a Socialist from St. Louis, Missouri, began serving a two-year prison sentence on October 31, 1917.[64]

Alexander Cournos, from Pittsburgh, Pennsylvania, was convicted at the mass IWW trial in Chicago, sentenced to ten years in prison and fined $30,000. He served in the Cook County Jail and Leavenworth Penitentiary from September 29, 1917, to October 21, 1919, and from April 25, 1921, to December 22, 1923.

At Leavenworth Penitentiary, Cournos was cited for twenty-one separate disciplinary infractions and was placed in "isolation on restricted diet" on numerous occasions. Grounds for discipline included "riotous conduct" (i.e., "rattl[ing] his dishes" to demand more rice), "loafing," improper possession of a "chocolate bar," participation in a work strike, "talking in mess hall" and "wasting food."[65]

Roy Crane, from Oklahoma, was sentenced to seven years in prison. He served in Leavenworth Penitentiary.[66]

Walter Crosby was released from prison on December 25, 1921.[67]

J. T. Cumbie, a seventy-four-year-old minister and a Socialist from Oklahoma, was sentenced to six years in prison. He served in Leavenworth Penitentiary from November 26, 1918, to June 23, 1921. Cumbie was an organizer for the Universal Union.[68]

Harry Daile served his sentence in Leavenworth Penitentiary.[69]

J. M. Danley, a farmer, a self-described "good Christian," a member of the Working Class Union and a fifteen-year member of the Socialist Party, came from Paragould, Arkansas. Danley was sentenced to ten years in prison. He served in Leavenworth Penitentiary from April 1918 to September 1, 1922. After Danley's arrest his wife died, and his five children (ages nineteen, seventeen, thirteen, nine and five) were "scattered" among friends and forced to survive on charity.[70]

Martin Darkow, from Easton, Pennsylvania, began serving a prison sentence on December 30, 1918.[71]

C. W. Davis, secretary of the Marine Transport Workers Industrial Union in Seattle, Washington, was convicted at the mass IWW trial in Chicago, sentenced to ten years in prison and fined $30,000. He served in Leavenworth Penitentiary from November 1917 to March 1918 and from September 1918 to June 25, 1923.[72]

A. M. Dean was released from prison on January 14, 1922.[73]

Peter De Bernardi, from Mountain View, California, was convicted at the mass IWW trial in Sacramento and sentenced to ten years in prison. He served in Leavenworth Penitentiary from August 1918 to December 1923.

De Bernardi was continuously placed in isolation and written up for offenses such as "refusing to break rock smaller," "loafing" and using "vulgar language," "stalling at work," and "calling an officer a 'dirty skunk.'" He was placed in permanent isolation and handcuffed to his cell for appearing to be "determined to prevent other men from working."

After his release his activities were monitored. FBI agents and informants investigating De Bernardi in the 1940s reported that he was an admirer of union leader Harry Bridges and knew "anti-fascist leaders" whom the FBI deemed "sympathetic to communism." According to the FBI, De Bernardi, who was an "ardent supporter of the working man," was terminated from at least three jobs because his employers "discovered" his prior Sedition Act conviction. (See Chapter 4 for disciplinary reports on De Bernardi in Leavenworth.)

The FBI reports stated that De Bernardi was "well liked by all of the neighbors and that he [was] never noticed [engaging] in suspicious activity around the house." In questioning his local letter carrier the FBI determined that De Bernardi only received "routine personal letters from friends."

In 1944, De Bernardi was personally interviewed by the FBI, and they noted that he "described himself as an ardent supporter of the working man and 'anti-Fascist.' "[74]

Eugene Victor Debs, from Terre Haute, Indiana, was the most influential socialist leader in U.S. history. In 1893, he organized the American Railway Union, which quickly grew to 150,000 members, becoming one of the largest industrial unions of its time. Debs led the famous Pullman strike and was jailed for six months for violating an injunction issued against the strikers.

In 1900, Debs helped form the Socialist Party of America and became its first candidate for president. In 1905, he helped create the IWW, but did not remain active in that union.

Debs was the Socialist Party's presidential candidate in 1904, 1908, and 1912. During this period the party grew into one of the largest third parties in U.S. history. By 1912, 1,039 Socialists held elected office, including 56 mayors, and, in 1914, the Socialist Party elected its first U.S. congressman (Meyer London of New York).

On April 6, 1917, when the United States entered World War I, the Socialist Party called an emergency convention in St. Louis. At the convention the party vigorously condemned the war. Initially, its anti-war stance substantially increased support from voters, notably in the municipal elections in the fall of 1917, when the Socialist Party collected record numbers of votes, including 24 percent of the vote in New York City, 34 percent of the vote in Chicago and 44 percent of the vote in Dayton, Ohio.

An alarmed federal government moved to "swiftly crack down" on the Socialist Party shortly after those elections. Its offices were raided, its newspapers were suppressed and hundreds of its leaders were arrested, Debs among them.

Debs was indicted for a speech he gave in Canton, Ohio, on June 16, 1918, in which he praised the anti-war activities of other socialists who were convicted of anti-war activities. At his trial Debs stated to the jury, "I have been accused of obstructing the war. I admit it. Gentlemen, I abhor war. I would oppose war if I stood alone."

Debs was found guilty under the Espionage Act and sentenced to ten years in prison. His conviction was sustained by a unanimous Supreme Court.

On April 12, 1919, he began serving his sentence in West Virginia Penitentiary at Moundsville, but was later transferred to Atlanta Penitentiary. In 1920, while Debs was in prison, the Socialist Party nominated him as its candidate for president. Although unable to campaign, Debs pulled over 900,000 votes, "the highest total of votes in the two decades of American socialism."

Due to the continuous public outcry over Debs' incarceration, the Department of Justice recommended that President Harding pardon him.

Despite his age and after nearly three years of incarceration, Debs continued to be viewed as a threat by the Department of Justice. (See Chapter
11.)

Debs was finally released from prison on Christmas Day, 1921. As he
left the prison, the more than two thousand remaining inmates sponta-
neously cheered his release. He remained active in socialist and labor
causes until his death in 1926.[75]

Giovanni De Cecca, from Brooklyn, New York, was sentenced to ten
years in prison. He began serving his sentence on July 10, 1918 in Leavenworth Penitentiary.

De Cecca, a member of the International Bible Students Association
(IBSA, also known as Jehovah's Witnesses), was tried along with seven
other members of that sect in New York for violating the Espionage Act.
The defendants included Joseph F. Rutherford, the spiritual leader of the
Jehovah's Witnesses; De Cecca; and others who were accused of circulating
Watch Tower, Kingdom News and "certain other literature" that could cause
"insubordination" or "disloyalty" in the military. This included the "dis-
tribution of an account of the trial by Italian Military authorities [of an
Italian citizen who] refus[ed] to put on his uniform and render [military]
service, setting forth his conscientious objection."

The IBSA members were found guilty and sentenced to varying terms
in prison.[76]

Edward F. Dicks was arrested in November 1917 in the roundup of IWW
members in Omaha, Nebraska. After over eighteen months in local jails,
all charges against him were dropped.[77]

Clark Dickson, of Cincinnati, Ohio, began serving a prison sentence on
August 7, 1918.[78]

William J. Dodge, a member of the Socialist Labor Party from Buffalo,
New York, received a prison sentence of six years, which was later commuted, for disloyal "utterances." He made the remarks in a speech "at
the corner of Main and Mohawk streets" in Buffalo. While Dodge was
addressing a crowd on the merits of socialism, a person took out his draft
card and showed it to Dodge. Dodge reportedly "scornfully" stated "some
honor" when he saw the card. The government charged that this statement was made "willfully and for the purpose of injuring the United
States." Dodge was convicted and served in Maryland Penitentiary from
September 18, 1918, to November 22, 1920.[79]

Perley Doe, from Denver, Colorado, began serving his sentence on January 11, 1918.[80]

J. T. Doran, an electrician from Seattle, Washington, was convicted at
the mass IWW trial in Chicago, sentenced to five years in prison and fined
$30,000. He served in Leavenworth Penitentiary from September 1917 to
March 1918, from September 1918 to October 1919 and from April 1921
to November 17, 1923.

The Department of Justice considered Doran "the most famous of IWW speakers." Doran was convicted despite the fact that the "record" in his case contained "no letter or article proven to have been written by him which referred disparagingly to the United States." There was "no proof that he made any reference to conscription, registration or the military" in any publication.[81]

Edward F. Doree, secretary of the IWW Textile Workers Union in Philadelphia, Pennsylvania, was convicted at the mass IWW trial in Chicago, sentenced to ten years in prison and fined $30,000. He served in Leavenworth Penitentiary until September 18, 1922, when his sentence was commuted. (See also the entry for Walter T. Neff.)[82]

John Douglas from Zanesville, Ohio, began serving a three-year prison sentence on June 26, 1918. He was convicted of sedition for "cursing the United States."[83]

Mortimer Downing, secretary of the IWW chapters in Oakland and Stockton, California, at the time of his arrest, was convicted at the mass IWW trial in Sacramento and sentenced to ten years in prison. He served in Leavenworth Penitentiary from November 1917 to December 22, 1923.

According to the Department of Justice, Downing was considered "a leader of the IWW on the Pacific coast." He had also been secretary of IWW chapters in Sacramento and Los Angeles. The Department of Justice described him as a "rabid anti-war agitator" with "misapplied intelligence." He was branded a "dangerous character" who had "a great influence over other men." After release from prison he was elected editor of the IWW paper *The Industrial Worker*.[84]

Harry Drew, from Kansas, was sentenced to four years in prison. He served in Leavenworth Penitentiary from December 18, 1919, to June 17, 1921, when he was released on bond.[85]

John T. Dunn, a Socialist from Providence, Rhode Island, was sentenced to twenty years in prison and served in Atlanta Penitentiary.[86]

Jesse Dunning, a member of the IWW from Bemidji, Minnesota, was arrested for possessing IWW literature. He received a two-year sentence.[87]

Phineas Eastman, from New Raymer, Colorado, was convicted at the mass IWW trial in Wichita and sentenced to seven years and six months in prison. He served in Leavenworth Penitentiary from June 23, 1919, to July 18, 1922.[88]

Godfrey Ebel, a laborer and an IWW member from San Francisco, California, was convicted at the mass IWW trial in Sacramento and sentenced to ten years in prison. He served in Leavenworth Penitentiary from April 1918 to June 6, 1923, when he was paroled.[89]

Albert Eberlie, a farmer from Sasakwa, Oklahoma, was sentenced to two years in prison. He served in Leavenworth Penitentiary from August 1917 to June 19, 1919.[90]

Forrest Edwards, from Louistown, Montana, was secretary-treasurer of the Agricultural Workers Industrial Union, Local 400, in Minneapolis at the time of his arrest. He was convicted at the mass IWW trial in Chicago, sentenced to twenty years in prison and fined $20,000. He served in Leavenworth Penitentiary from September 1917 to June 25, 1923.[91]

William Ehrhard, of St. Louis, Missouri, began serving a prison sentence on June 5, 1918.[92]

William Eimer was sentenced to five years in prison. He served in McNeil Island and Leavenworth Penitentiaries from September 10, 1918, to July 27, 1920.[93]

William Eliason began serving a prison sentence on May 17, 1918.[94]

Frank Elliott, from Fresno, California, was convicted at the mass IWW trial in Sacramento and sentenced to ten years in prison. He served in Leavenworth Penitentiary from September 1917 to December 22, 1923.[95]

James Elliott, from Fresno, California, was convicted at the mass IWW trial in Chicago, sentenced to five years in prison and fined $30,000. He served in Leavenworth Penitentiary from September 1917 to May 14, 1922, when his sentence expired.[96]

William P. Elmer, from Dent County, Missouri, was sentenced to five years in prison for writing a newspaper article. He served in McNeil Island Penitentiary from September 10, 1918, to July 27, 1920, when he was paroled.

According to the judge at his federal court trial, the portion of the article for which Elmer was convicted concerned the writer's impression of the facial expression of "a local soldier boy" who was "leaving home after a furlough." According to the court, the following excerpt from the article by Elmer was sufficient to find him guilty under the Espionage Act:

There is a look in the faces of these boys not there when they roamed like free Americans at home, but a look of resignation to fate, an utter helplessness for the future. They know they are to be manacled, and shackled, and marked for slaughter.[97]

Otto Elsner, from Chicago, Illinois, was convicted at the mass IWW trial in Sacramento and sentenced to three years in prison. He served in Leavenworth Penitentiary from January 25, 1919, to May 17, 1921.[98]

Orville Enfield, a Socialist from Oklahoma City, Oklahoma, was arrested on June 6, 1918. He was sentenced to twenty years in prison for seditious utterances.[99]

E. A. Engelin, of Minneapolis, Minnesota, began serving a five-year prison sentence on May 4, 1918.[100]

Dr. Marie D. Equi, a suffragist leader and IWW supporter from Portland, Oregon, was sentenced to three years in prison for making an antiwar speech on June 27, 1918, in an IWW union hall in Portland. She began serving her sentence on December 31, 1918.

In rejecting Dr. Equi's First Amendment argument, federal Judge Robert Sharp Bean stated that "some people" had a "misconception" that freedom of speech means a freedom that "everyone enjoys to say what he pleases," adding that "nothing [could be] further from the truth." The government has the "power" of "self-preservation," and "any man who speculates upon or trifles with this power does it at his own peril."[101]

Gustav Erdtmann, of St. Louis, Missouri, began serving a prison sentence on June 27, 1918.[102]

Pete Ervik, of Missoula, Montana, began serving a two- to four-year prison sentence on April 16, 1918.[103]

Frederick Esmond, an Oxford University graduate, was a newspaper and publicity agent for the IWW. Esmond headed the California Defense Committee for the Sacramento IWW Sedition Act defendants. After protesting the prison conditions endured by the Sacramento defendants to the U.S. attorney general, Esmond was himself arrested and charged with sedition. He was held in isolation for eight months and then tried along with the other "silent defendants" in Sacramento and sentenced to ten years.

Esmond responded to the announced convictions by shouting:

we, the outcasts, have been framed up, clubbed, beaten, slugged, martyred, and murdered. Is it any wonder that I do not consider myself bound to your procedures when this court and its proceedings are a disgrace to the United States?

Esmond never recovered from the weakened state of health caused by his pre-trial confinement in isolation. He entered Leavenworth Penitentiary on January 25, 1919. On April 7, 1921, he suffered a complete mental collapse—becoming "maniacal, noisy, destroying clothing and bedding." According to the prison physician, Esmond reportedly started to have "delirious hallucinations" and became "homicidal." The physician attributed Esmond's breakdown to "overwork of his mental facilities, accompanied by worry and depression."

Esmond was transferred to St. Elizabeth's Hospital where he slowly recuperated. He was pardoned and released from the asylum in February 1923.[104]

G. A. Fanning was sentenced to a year and six months in prison. He served in Leavenworth Penitentiary from March 4, 1919, to June 18, 1920.[105]

Theo Fedotoff, a Socialist from Bayonne, New Jersey, began serving a prison sentence for obstructing recruitment on May 15, 1918. He was sentenced to ten years for seditious remarks made in addressing a meeting of Russian workers for the purpose of starting a school.[106]

Franz J. Feinler was sentenced to four years in prison for making "seditious remarks." He served in McNeil Island Penitentiary from April 20, 1918, to May 8, 1920, when he was paroled.[107]

Henry Feltman, of Cincinnati, Ohio, began serving a sentence on September 6, 1918.[108]

Albert Feiron, from Detroit, Michigan, received a prison sentence of twenty years, which was commuted to five. He served in Leavenworth Penitentiary from August 7, 1918, to December 1921.[109]

George H. Fisher began serving a prison sentence on June 21, 1918. A member of the IBSA, Fisher was convicted in a mass trial in New York along with Giovanni De Cecca and seven other IBSA members. (See also the entry for Giovanni De Cecca.)[110]

Benjamin Fletcher, the leading African-American organizer for the IWW, organized over three thousand Philadelphia longshoremen into one of the IWW's largest and most effective units. Eventually, this local of the Marine Transport Workers Industrial Union controlled all the Philadelphia docks. His locals united both white and black workers into a single unit. To promote racial equality, the union established a monthly rotation system whereby the union's chairmanship was alternated between a black and a white worker.

Fletcher worked with other IWW leaders to eradicate racism within unions, Jim Crow laws, and lynchings.

At the Chicago sedition trial Fletcher was convicted despite the fact that his local had urged its members to register for the draft. He was sentenced to ten years in prison. After approximately four years at Leavenworth Penitentiary, Fletcher had his sentence commuted and was released on October 30, 1922.

While in prison Fletcher was punished for a variety of offenses, such as "loafing," "disobeying orders," "creating a disturbance" and "talking." (See also the entry for Walter T. Neff.)[111]

Sam Forbes was convicted at the mass IWW trial in Chicago and sentenced to five years in prison. He served a year and two months in Leavenworth Penitentiary. According to an FBI surveillance report, Forbes was chairman of the IWW General Executive Board and secretary in 1923.[112]

Mrs. Flora Foreman, a Socialist from Oregon, was sentenced to two to five years in prison. She served in the Women's Prison in McAllister, Oklahoma from October 16, 1918, to June 17, 1922. Foreman was a teacher. When her home in Oregon was burned down by "patriotic vigilantes," she left the state to "visit relatives in Texas," but was "arrested and held incommunicado" there in the summer of 1918. Convicted under the Espionage Act, she spent two years in the Women's Prison in McAllister, Oklahoma. At the time of her release she was described as a "physical wreck."[113]

John D. Ford was arrested in November 1917 in the roundup of IWW members in Omaha, Nebraska. After over eighteen months in local jails, all charges against him were dropped.[114]

John M. Foss, a steam fitter from Seattle, Washington, was convicted at the mass IWW trial in Chicago, sentenced to five years in prison and fined $30,000. He served in the Cook County Jail and Leavenworth Penitentiary from October 1917 to April 1918, from September 1918 to September 1919 and from April 1921 to June 25, 1923. He had a wife and three children.[115]

Wenzel Francik was convicted at the mass IWW trial in Wichita and sentenced to seven and a half years in prison.[116]

Ted Fraser, a meat cutter from Seattle, Washington, was convicted at the mass IWW trial in Chicago, sentenced to five years in prison and fined $30,000. He served in Leavenworth Penitentiary from September 1917 to July 1918 and from September 1918 to May 14, 1922.[117]

Robert Freehan, a Structural Iron Workers Industrial Union member from Chicago, Illinois, was convicted at the mass IWW trial in Sacramento and sentenced to four years in prison. He served in Leavenworth Penitentiary from September 1918 to February 22, 1922.[118]

Jacob Frohwerk, a newspaper editor from Kansas City, Missouri, was sentenced to ten years in prison. He began serving his sentence on June 29, 1918.[119]

Linn A. E. Gale was sentenced to seven years in prison. He served in Leavenworth Penitentiary. Gale published *Gale's International Monthly* and was associate editor of *La Lucha*, secretary of the Mexican Birth Control League and a member of the Executive Committee of the Communist Party of Mexico.[120]

F. J. Gallagher, an organizer and leader of the oil field strikes in the summer of 1917 from Chicago, Illinois, was convicted at the mass IWW trial in Wichita and sentenced to eight years in prison. He served in Leavenworth Penitentiary from December 1917 to December 22, 1923.[121]

Joe Garner was arrested in November 1917 in the roundup of IWW members in Omaha, Nebraska. After over eighteen months in local jails, all charges against him were dropped.[122]

John L. Geibel, from Sacramento, California, was sentenced to five years in prison. He served in McNeil Island Penitentiary. His wife was also convicted and sentenced to a year in the county jail. They were forced to leave their young son with a relative.[123]

Joseph Geier, from Ohio, was sentenced to fifteen months in prison and served in Atlanta Penitentiary.[124]

Frank Geizler, an IWW member from Fargo, North Dakota, began serving a two-year prison sentence on March 9, 1918.[125]

Rev. David Gerdes, a Dunkard from Chicago, Illinois, began serving a prison sentence on November 21, 1918. He was sentenced to ten years for giving a "seditious sermon."[126]

William Gessert, a farmer from Sheboygan County, Wisconsin, was sentenced to five years in prison for refusing to allow his son to be conscripted into the army. He served in Leavenworth Penitentiary from February 15, 1918, to September 24, 1919.[127]

Carl Glesser, a newspaper editor from Kansas City, Missouri, was a co-defendant with Jacob Frohwerk. He began serving his five-year sentence on April 30, 1918.[128]

Emma Goldman was born in Russia in 1869. She came to the United States at the age of seventeen (1886) and remained until her deportation in 1919. While in the United States she and her close friend and coworker Alexander Berkman became the leading spokespersons for the small, but influential, anarchist movement.

One of the most controversial public speakers in U.S. history, Goldman published the magazine *Mother Earth* and was a forceful exponent of free speech, women's rights, educational reform, anti-militarism and "free love." Her speeches were often banned. A pioneer in the earliest efforts to educate women about birth control, she directly challenged the laws against "disseminating birth control information" and gave the "first public instruction on the use of contraceptives." Goldman's speeches often led to her arrest.

Goldman strongly opposed the United States' entry into World War I. In 1917, she and Berkman founded the No Conscription League. The government moved quickly to crack down on Goldman and the league. On June 15, 1917, only eleven days after the passage of the Selective Service Act, Goldman's office was raided, and she was arrested for conspiring to obstruct conscription.

On June 27, 1917, she and codefendant Alexander Berkman were tried and found guilty of conspiracy.[129] Goldman was sentenced to two years' imprisonment and fined $10,000. Her conviction was upheld by the U.S. Supreme Court, and she served in Missouri State Prison in Jefferson City.

On September 28, 1919, after serving twenty-one months in prison, Goldman was released. But she was immediately subjected to deportation proceedings. In December 1919, Goldman, Berkman and 247 other radicals were expelled from the United States and deported to Russia in the transport ship the *S.S. Buford.*

When Goldman and Berkman arrived in Russia, they were warmly greeted by Lenin and urged to join the Bolshevik Party. Goldman and Berkman, however, declined. They remained committed to their anarchist principles, advocating free speech and civil liberties in Russia and strongly denouncing the repression they witnessed.

In March 1921, strikes broke out in Petrograd, which were soon supported by the local military unit in Kronstadt. Goldman and Berkman urged the government not to suppress the strike: "To remain silent now is impossible, even criminal. Recent events impel us anarchists to speak out." Goldman and Berkman urged mediation of the dispute between the strikers and the Soviet government. The government ignored their advice and crushed the strikers.

After the Kronstadt Rebellion Goldman and Berkman became open critics of the Soviet regime. They fled Russia on December 1, 1921, to permanent exile in Europe and Canada. Goldman died in Canada on May 14, 1940.[130]

Robert Goldstein, of Los Angeles, California, was sentenced to ten years in prison. He served in McNeil Island Penitentiary from May 9, 1918, to October 13, 1920, when his sentence was commuted.[131]

Joseph J. Gordon, from Chicago, Illinois, was convicted at the mass IWW trial in Chicago, sentenced to ten years in prison and fined $30,000. He served in the Cook County Jail and Leavenworth Penitentiary from September 7, 1918, to May 5, 1919, and from April 1921 to May 22, 1922.[132]

O. E. Gordon, a shoemaker from Columbus, Ohio, was convicted at the mass IWW trial in Wichita and sentenced to seven and a half years in prison. He served in the Cook County Jail and Leavenworth Penitentiary from November 1917 to December 23, 1922.[133]

Max Gorman was sentenced to ten years in prison. He served in McNeil Island Penitentiary from November 19, 1917, to April 7, 1920, when his sentence was commuted.[134]

Joe Graber, from Philadelphia, Pennsylvania, was convicted at the mass IWW trial in Chicago, sentenced to five years in prison and fined $30,000. He served in the Cook County Jail and Leavenworth Penitentiary from July 4, 1917, to October 18, 1919, and from April 21 to August 3, 1923.

Graber was a delegate and organizer for the Marine Transport Workers Industrial Union in Baltimore and for the Coal Mine Workers Industrial Union in Scranton, Pennsylvania. He was convicted despite the Department of Justice's admission that the "record" in his case "contains no proof that Graber did or said anything" to interfere with the war effort.[135]

Elias Graceley of Toledo, Ohio, began serving a sentence on April 5, 1918.[136]

Fred Grau, from Kansas, was sentenced to three years in prison. He served in Leavenworth Penitentiary from December 18, 1919, to January 21, 1921, when he was released on bond.[137]

John Grave, a laborer from Sacramento, California, was convicted at the mass IWW trial in Sacramento and sentenced to ten years in prison. He served in local county jails and Leavenworth Penitentiary from December 22, 1917, to March 1918 and from January 25, 1919, to December 22, 1923.

The Department of Justice classified him a "deliberate and bitterly radical man" because he "always closes his letters 'Yours for the Revolution.' "[138]

Harry Gray, a leader of the Agricultural Workers Industrial Union in

Sacramento, California, was convicted at the mass IWW trial in Sacramento and sentenced to ten years in prison. He served in Leavenworth Penitentiary from September 1917 to August 1918 and from January 1919 to December 22, 1923.[139]

Peter Green, secretary of the Lumber Workers Industrial Union, Local 500, in Portland, Oregon, was convicted at the mass IWW trial in Chicago, sentenced to ten years in prison and fined $30,000. He served in the Cook County Jail and Leavenworth Penitentiary from September 1917 to June 1918 and from September 1918 to August 1923.

Green was active in the lumber workers general strike in the Northwest during March 1917. The Department of Justice conceded that Green was convicted despite the absence of any "proof" that he "even said or did anything against our war."[140]

J. Gresbach, from Kansas, was sentenced to three and a half years in prison. He served in Leavenworth Penitentiary from December 18, 1919, to June 17, 1921, when he was released on bond.[141]

C. R. Griffin, a lumberjack from Bellingham, Washington, was convicted at the mass IWW trial in Chicago, sentenced to five years in prison and fined $30,000. He served in the Cook County Jail and Leavenworth Penitentiary from December 1917 to April 1918 and from September 7, 1918, to July 22, 1920.[142]

A. Gross, an IWW member in Centralia, Washington, was sentenced to twenty-eight months in prison. He served in McNeil Island Penitentiary from January 26, 1920, to December 1921, soon after which he was deported.[143]

Frank Grubl began serving a sentence in Leavenworth Penitentiary on October 5, 1918.[144]

Antonin Gualberti, an IWW member and a Socialist from Scranton, Pennsylvania, was sentenced to three years in prison for distributing literature against the draft. He served in Atlanta Penitentiary.[145]

Edward Hamilton, from Chicago, Illinois, was convicted at the mass IWW trial in Chicago, sentenced to ten years in prison and fined $30,000. He served in the Cook County Jail and Leavenworth Penitentiary from September 1917 to December 25, 1921.

At Leavenworth he was confined in segregation continuously, beginning on April 14, 1919, because he "broke dishes" and created disturbances in the dining room. The prison guards classified Hamilton as a "dangerous and irresponsible character." In a letter to the warden dated October 30, 1919, Hamilton reported that he and other IWW prisoners were "set upon with clubs, rocks and black-jacks" by guards and other prisoners assisting the guards.[146]

Edward C. Hamm was sentenced to three years in prison. He served in McNeil Island Penitentiary from July 31, 1918, to June 21, 1920.[147]

Henry Hammer, a teamster from Osseu, Minnesota, was convicted at the mass IWW trial in Sacramento and sentenced to ten years in prison. He served in Leavenworth Penitentiary from August 1918 to December 22, 1923.[148]

Thomas Hammerschmidt, from Ohio, was convicted for circulating a leaflet against registration and sentenced to fifteen months in prison. He served in Atlanta Penitentiary.[149]

Ralph S. Harald was sentenced to two years in prison. He served in McNeil Island and Leavenworth Penitentiaries beginning on September 8, 1920.[150]

Robert Harden, an IWW member from Duluth, Minnesota, was convicted of threatening the life of the president of the United States and sentenced to two years in prison. He served in Leavenworth Penitentiary from August 13, 1917, to October 14, 1919.[151]

Armin Von Harder was sentenced to three years in prison. He served in McNeil Island Penitentiary beginning on October 16, 1918.[152]

Ira Hardy, an African-American farmer from Rocky Point, Oklahoma, was sentenced to two years in prison. He served in Leavenworth Penitentiary from August 1, 1918, to June 10, 1919.[153]

Joseph Harper, from Winnfield, Louisiana, was convicted for circulating a pamphlet entitled "The Issue of the Day: Financial Slavery, Free Speech" and sentenced to two years in prison. He served in Leavenworth Penitentiary from January 17, 1919, to September 2, 1920.[154]

John Harrington, of Lewistown, Montana, began serving a prison sentence on April 20, 1918 for obstructing the draft.[155]

Henry Harris was arrested in November 1917 in the roundup of IWW members in Omaha, Nebraska. After over eighteen months in local jails, all charges against him were dropped.[156]

T. A. Harris, a member of the Universal Union from western Oklahoma, received a prison sentence of six years, later commuted to eighteen months. He served in Leavenworth Penitentiary beginning on April 17, 1920.[157]

George Harrison, a journalist for IWW newspapers from Chicago, Illinois, was convicted at the mass IWW trial in Chicago, sentenced to five years in prison and fined $30,000. He served in the Cook County Jail and Leavenworth Penitentiary from September 1917 to August 1920 and from April 1921 to February 1, 1923. The Department of Justice described Harrison as a "brilliant writer."[158]

J. E. Harvey, a farmer from Tyler, Texas, served in Atlanta Penitentiary from September 20, 1918, to October 15, 1920.[159]

John Hauer, of Fremont, Nebraska, began serving a twenty-year prison sentence for obstructing the draft on April 17, 1918.[160]

William D. ("Big Bill") Haywood was born in Salt Lake City, Utah. Haywood was a founding member and the general secretary of the IWW. One of the United States' most important union leaders, Haywood had served as the head of the Western Federation of Miners before founding the IWW. Between the late 1890s and 1917, Haywood helped lead some of the most important labor strikes in U.S. history, including the Telluride and Cripple Creek mine workers strikes in Colorado; the textile workers strike in Lawrence, Massachusetts; and the silk workers strike in Paterson, New Jersey. During 1906 and 1907, he spent over a year in jail, falsely accused of murdering a governor of Idaho. In that case he was successfully defended by Clarence Darrow.

According to a confidential FBI report, Haywood was described as a "daring and militant leader" and a "commanding figure" who "possessed the eloquence of speech and the ability to arouse and sway his listeners." However, because of his anti-war positions, the FBI concluded that "Haywood's career came to a necessary ending with America's entry into the World War."

On September 28, 1917, Haywood, along with ninety-six other suspected leaders of the IWW, was indicted in Chicago. On August 30, 1918, he was convicted of conspiracy, sentenced to twenty years in prison and fined $10,000. He entered Leavenworth Penitentiary on September 6, 1918, and served until July 15, 1919, when he was released on bond pending the appeal of his conviction.

Haywood, who was suffering from severe ulcers and diabetes, feared that he would die in prison if he complied with the terms of his bond and returned to prison after the appeals court upheld his conviction. Thus, on March 31, 1921, at the urging of the newly founded Communist Party, he fled the United States and obtained asylum in Soviet Russia. Seven other IWW defendants also jumped bail. The impact of this flight was devastating to the IWW:

Haywood's self-imposed exile, and his resultant forfeiture of bond, left the IWW financially shattered, lacking in experienced, competent leadership. . . . The amnesty campaign [for the other IWW defendants] . . . was dealt a severe blow.

According to the FBI file, Haywood was very unhappy in exile. He died on May 18, 1928, "a lonely and disillusioned old man."[161]

William G. Head, from Sioux Falls, South Dakota, was sentenced to three years in prison. He was the Secretary of the State Socialist Party and served in Leavenworth Penitentiary from November 2, 1917, to January 25, 1919, when he was released on bond. His sentence was thereafter commuted.[162]

Morris Hecht, from Kansas, was sentenced to five years in prison. He served in Leavenworth Penitentiary from December 18, 1919, to June 17, 1921, when he was released on bond.[163]

Edgar Held began serving a prison sentence on December 11, 1918, and was released on January 16, 1920, after his conviction was reversed by the federal court of appeals.[164]

Rev. H. M. Hendricksen of Lincoln, Nebraska, was convicted on April 18, 1918 of obstruction of the draft.[165]

Simon Hendrickson was arrested in November 1917 in the roundup of IWW members in Omaha, Nebraska. After over eighteen months in local jails, all charges against him were dropped.[166]

Ammon A. Hennesey, from Columbus, Ohio, was sentenced to nine months in prison for refusing to register for the draft. He served that prison term in a Delaware jail. He was also convicted of distributing literature against the draft and received a two-year prison sentence for this offense, serving between July 13, 1917, and February 18, 1919. He was an "Irish American Socialist." Hennesey remained a radical activist throughout his life.[167]

Ernest Henning was sentenced to three years in prison. He served in Leavenworth Penitentiary beginning on December 18, 1919.[168]

Emil Herman served his sentence in McNeil Island Penitentiary from June 6, 1918, to December 24, 1921. He was the former state secretary for the Socialist Party in Washington State.

In a speech given shortly after his release from jail, which was covertly transcribed by the FBI, Herman described the principles that resulted in his imprisonment:

I am opposed to war. I object to bloodshed. I would not take the life of a human being to save my own. I regard human life as infinitely sacred. I am opposed, therefore, to the system that ruthlessly sacrifices human life in the most barbarous manner possible.

Sixty thousand of our boys lie beneath the Flanders poppies. For what? Did not Lloyd George just the other day make the assertion that Europe was worse off than ever? That there were more men under arms than before the war?

The disarmament conference was a farce. To be true, they limit battleships, but laboratories in every country are occupied by those who work feverishly to perfect deadly and secret gas. The next war will be of airplanes and poison gas, and no one will be a non-combatant, not even the smallest infant.[169]

C. H. Herriage, a farmer from Tyler, Texas, was sentenced to three years in prison. He served in Atlanta Penitentiary from September 20, 1918, to December 2, 1920. Herriage had a wife and twelve children.[170]

Walter Heynacher, from Aberdeen, South Dakota, was sentenced to five years in prison. He served in Leavenworth Penitentiary.[171]

Edward Hibbard was arrested in November 1917 in the roundup of IWW members in Omaha, Nebraska. After over eighteen months in local jails, all charges against him were dropped.[172]

Rev. William Madison Hicks, a preacher, a lawyer, a pacifist and a Socialist Party member from Guthrie, Oklahoma, was sentenced to twenty years in prison. He served in Leavenworth Penitentiary. He had a wife and two children. His daughter Helen was born while he was in prison and was over three years old before she saw her father for the first time.[173]

S. B. Hicok was sentenced to four years and six months in prison. He served in Leavenworth Penitentiary from December 18, 1919, to June 17, 1921, when he was released on bond.[174]

P. J. Higgins, from Kansas, was sentenced to three and a half years in prison. He served in Leavenworth Penitentiary from December 18, 1919, to June 17, 1921, when he was released on bond.[175]

Theodore Hiller, a Socialist from Pawtucket, Rhode Island, was sentenced to twenty years in prison. He served in Atlanta Penitentiary.[176]

Amost L. Hitchcock, a Socialist from Sandusky, Ohio, began serving his ten-year prison sentence on June 28, 1918. Hitchcock was charged with publicly stating that "he did not believe in the Liberty loan" and that "every damn dollar goes into the pockets of the profiteers."[177]

R. R. Hoffman was sentenced to three years in prison. He served in McNeil Island Penitentiary.[178]

William Hood, a painter from San Francisco, California, was convicted at the mass IWW trial in Sacramento and sentenced to ten years in prison. He served in Leavenworth Penitentiary from December 1917 to December 22, 1923.[179]

Edgar Hoover, from Pittsburgh, Pennsylvania, was sentenced to three years in prison. He served in Leavenworth Penitentiary from July 1918 to July 16, 1921. In Leavenworth Penitentiary Hoover was placed in "isolation on restricted diet" for "disrespect toward officer," failing to "get up" in the morning, "talking in dining hall," "loafing," "talking in excess" and "mutinous conduct" for "shouting like a cat" when the guard attempted to speak with the prisoner. Hoover had over eighteen separate disciplinary write-ups.[180]

Clyde Hough, a machinist and IWW member from Rockford, Illinois, was convicted at the mass IWW trial in Chicago, sentenced to five years in prison and fined $30,000. He served in Leavenworth Penitentiary from April 1918 to July 1919 and from April 1921 to June 24, 1922. Hough was secretary of the Rockford chapter of the IWW.

Hough was serving a one-year sentence for refusing to register for the draft at the time he was indicted under the Espionage Act. He was convicted of "conspiracy" for conduct that purportedly occurred while he was in jail.[181]

Frank J. Howenstine received a sentence of ten years in prison, which was commuted to three. He served in McNeil Island Penitentiary from May 21, 1920, to September 20, 1922.[182]

E. J. Huber was sentenced to three years and six months in prison. He served in Leavenworth Penitentiary from December 18, 1919, to the end of his term.[183]

Dave Ingar, an ironworker from Detroit, Michigan, was convicted at the mass IWW trial in Chicago, sentenced to five years in prison and fined $20,000. He served in the Cook County Jail and Leavenworth Penitentiary from September 1917 to March 1918 and from September 1918 to May 14, 1922, when he was released at the expiration of his sentence.[184]

Otto Inglehardt, from Manchester, New Hampshire, was sentenced to a year in prison and began serving a sentence in Atlanta Penitentiary on October 7, 1918.[185]

Clure Isenhover, a Working Class Union member from western Oklahoma, was sentenced to six years in prison. He served in Leavenworth Penitentiary from October 6, 1917, to September 16, 1920, when he was paroled. He was convicted of "conspiracy to prevent and hinder" the Selective Service Act.[186]

Obe Isenhover, a Working Class Union member from Oklahoma, was sentenced to six years and four months in prison. He served in Leavenworth Penitentiary from October 20, 1917, to November 16, 1920, when he was paroled.[187]

Fred Jaakkola, from Detroit, Michigan, was convicted at the mass IWW trial in Chicago, sentenced to ten years in prison and fined $30,000. He served in Leavenworth Penitentiary from September 7, 1918, to May 9, 1919, when he was released on bail. Jaakkola jumped bail and became a fugitive from the law.[188]

Carl Jacobs was arrested in November 1917 in the roundup of IWW members in Omaha, Nebraska. After over eighteen months in local jails, all charges against him were dropped.[189]

Sam Jacobs, a teacher from Mobridge, South Dakota, was sentenced to two and a half years in prison. He served in Leavenworth Penitentiary from March 28, 1918, to January 18, 1919, and in St. Elizabeth's Hospital for the Insane from January 18, 1919, to the expiration of his sentence on May 20, 1920.

At Leavenworth Penitentiary Jacobs was placed into a straightjacket for "tearing up his bed clothes," "attempting to destroy" property and "yelling at the top of his lungs." St. Elizabeth's Hospital certified Jacobs' insanity and diagnosed his condition as "dementia praecox," adding that Jacobs was "hebephrenic" with "impulsive outbreaks of violence" and "hallucinations." The report from St. Elizabeth's notes that Jacobs had no history of insanity before he went to prison.[190]

Otto Janson, from Oakland, California, began serving a five-year prison sentence on May 10, 1918.[191]

Popp Janssen began serving a prison sentence in Leavenworth Penitentiary on November 13, 1918.[192]

Thomas A. Jenkins was arrested in November 1917 in the roundup of

IWW members in Omaha, Nebraska. After over eighteen months in local jails, all charges against him were dropped.[193]

Ragner Johannsen, a painter and IWW organizer from Chicago, Illinois, was convicted at the mass IWW trial in Chicago, sentenced to ten years in prison and fined $30,000. He served in Leavenworth Penitentiary from September 1917 to March 1918, from September 1918 to September 1919 and from April 1921 to November 1922. Johannsen worked as an organizer for the IWW in the Northwest and along the Pacific Coast and was responsible for organizing the Domestic Workers Industrial Union in Seattle. After his release from prison Johannsen was deported to Sweden.[194]

Edward Johnson, from Barronet, Wisconsin, began serving a prison sentence in Leavenworth Penitentiary on July 20, 1918. He was transferred to St. Elizabeth's Hospital for the Insane on January 18, 1919. Johnson had a wife and seven children. (See also Chapter 5.)[195]

Victor Johnson began serving a prison sentence on April 20, 1918. He served in Oahu Prison, Honolulu.[196]

C. H. Kamann, a teacher from Peoria, Illinois, began serving a prison sentence on May 9, 1918 for "alleged seditious remarks to children in his history class." [197]

Harry F. Kane, a printer and a member of the Executive Committee of the Globe-Miami District of the Western Federation of Miners in Phoenix, Arizona, was convicted at the mass IWW trial in Chicago, sentenced to five years in prison and fined $20,000. He served in the Cook County Jail and Leavenworth Penitentiary from October 1917 to February 19, 1920, and from April 1921 to July 22, 1923, when his sentence expired.

After his release from prison Kane became involved in the communist movement. During the Depression he was "active in organizing relief struggles of unemployed" workers.[198]

W. H. Kaufman, a "single taxer" from Olympia, Washington, began serving a five-year prison sentence on August 13, 1918. He served in McNeil Island Penitentiary. Kaufman was convicted for stating "Liberty bonds are a disgrace to America."[199]

Walter F. Keeler began serving a prison sentence on October 3, 1918.[200]

John Kidenowski was sentenced to three years in prison. He served in McNeil Island Penitentiary from July 20, 1918, to November 23, 1920.[201]

H. E. Kirchner, from Elizabeth, West Virginia, began serving a prison sentence in March 1918. He was convicted of publicly stating that "war was corrupt," the draft act was "unconstitutional" and the people should not purchase war bonds. Kirchner was state secretary of the West Virginia Socialist Party.[202]

Edward A. Kolbe, from Columbus, Ohio, began serving a five-year prison sentence on June 26, 1918.[203]

Conrad Kornman, from Sioux Falls, South Dakota, began serving a ten-year prison sentence on May 4, 1918, for "opposing the Liberty Loan in a letter to a friend." He served in Leavenworth Penitentiary.[204]

Frederick Krafft, an editor and a socialist politician from Ridgefield, New Jersey, was sentenced to five years in prison. He began serving his term in Atlanta Penitentiary on October 22, 1917. A "pro-war" Socialist, Krafft went to prison for making a speech in Newark, New Jersey. In upholding his sentence, the federal court of appeals noted that Krafft, an editor and a candidate for governor of New Jersey, was "a man of much public prominence." He received a full presidential pardon in 1919.[205]

L. Kramer, from New York, New York, was convicted of conspiracy to violate the Selective Service Act. Kramer was sentenced to two years in prison and served in Atlanta Penitentiary between June 1917 and May 1919. Kramer, an anarchist, had been active in the birth control movement prior to his arrest and had been fined in 1916 for speaking publicly on birth control. In prison the authorities considered Kramer "extremely abusive" and, at one point, ordered him manacled with handcuffs to his prison cell. He was confined in the "isolation building."[206]

Charles Krieger, an IWW organizer from Tulsa, Oklahoma, was held in jail awaiting trail under the Espionage Act from December 28, 1917, until at least May 1919. He was an organizer for the IWW in the Oklahoma oil fields.[207]

Conrad Kroschenski, of San Antonio, Texas, began serving a prison sentence on May 8, 1918. He was sentenced to twenty years in prison.[208]

J. Henry Kruse, of Cincinnati, Ohio, began serving a prison sentence on September 7, 1918. He served in Moundsville Penitentiary.[209]

William F. Kruse began serving a prison sentence on January 9, 1919.[210]

John Kunz of New Britain, Connecticut, was convicted on May 28, 1918.[211]

Hyman Lachowsky, an anarchist from New York, New York, was convicted under the Sedition Act for circulating a leaflet critical of U.S. intervention in Russia in 1918 and was sentenced to twenty years in prison. He served in Atlanta Penitentiary from 1919 to October 23, 1921, when he was released on the condition that he would be deported to Russia and never return to the United States. (See also the entries for Mollie Steimer and Jacob Abrams.)[212]

Jacques Lamaux was sentenced to two and a half years in prison. He served in Atlanta Penitentiary from July 26, 1919, to the end of his term.[213]

Charles L. Lambert, from Sacramento, California, was convicted at the mass IWW trial in Chicago, sentenced to twenty years in prison, and fined $20,000. He belonged to the IWW's General Executive Board. He served in the Cook County Jail and Leavenworth Penitentiary from September 1917 to January 31, 1923. Lambert was released on the condition that he would be deported and never to return to the United States.[214]

Artell Lancaster was arrested in November 1917 in the roundup of IWW members in Omaha, Nebraska. After over eighteen months in local jails, all charges against him were dropped.[215]

Lee Lang, a Socialist from Rock Island, Illinois, began serving a two-year prison sentence on May 9, 1918.[216]

James Larson, a brick maker from Barronet, Wisconsin, was sentenced to fifteen months in prison. He served in Leavenworth Penitentiary from May 1918 to May 1919. Larson had a wife and six children.[217]

E. W. Latchem was arrested in November 1917 in the roundup of IWW members in Omaha, Nebraska. After over eighteen months in local jails, all charges against him were dropped.[218]

Harry A. Latour was sentenced to two years in prison. He served in Leavenworth Penitentiary from January 17, 1919, to September 2, 1920.[219]

Leo Laukki, a university professor and editor of the IWW's Finnish language newspaper from Smithville, Minnesota, was convicted at the mass IWW trial in Chicago, sentenced to twenty years in prison and fined $20,000. He served in Leavenworth Penitentiary from September 7, 1918, to April 30, 1919, when bond was posted. Laukki jumped bail, became a fugitive from the law and fled to Russia.

Alexander S. Lanier, a former captain of the Military Intelligence Division of the Army General Staff, testified before the House Judiciary Committee to the "absolute innocence and wrongful conviction" of Laukki. Laukki had a wife and child.[220]

Jack Law, a machinist from Boston, Pennsylvania, was convicted at the mass IWW trial in Chicago, sentenced to five years in prison and fined $30,000. He served in Leavenworth Penitentiary from September 9, 1918, to September 28, 1919, and from April 25, 1921, to December 25, 1921. Law was convicted even though he had left the IWW two years before the indictments.[221]

Samuel Lefto began serving a prison sentence in Atlanta Penitentiary on April 6, 1918.[222]

L. N. Legendre, from Los Angeles, California, began serving a two-year prison sentence on July 20, 1918. He was convicted of sedition for stating "This is a war fostered by Morgan and the rich."[223]

Lehnemann, from LeMoore, California, was sentenced to five years in prison. He served in McNeil Island Penitentiary.[224]

Herman Lemke, from eastern Pennsylvania, served in Atlanta Penitentiary from December 30, 1918, to June 10, 1920.[225]

Morris Levine, a transient from Seattle, Washington, was convicted at the mass IWW trial in Chicago, sentenced to five years in prison and fined $30,000. He served in the Cook County Jail and Leavenworth Penitentiary from December 1917 to July 13, 1921. In 1954, Levine was reported to be a recipient of general relief from the county of Los Angeles.[226]

W. H. Lewis, a miner and secretary of the Metal Mine Workers Industrial Union, Local 800, in Miami, Arizona, was convicted at the mass IWW trial in Chicago, sentenced to five years in prison and fined $10,000. He served in the Cook County Jail and Leavenworth Penitentiary from September 1917 to March 1918, from September 1918 to June 1920 and from April 1921 to December 22, 1923.[227]

Gerard Liebisch, from San Juan, Puerto Rico, was sentenced to four years in prison. He served in Atlanta Penitentiary from December 15, 1917, to May 10, 1920. He had a wife and one child.

At the time of his arrest, Liebisch's wife was in "very bad health," and his three-and-a-half-year-old daughter was forced to "stay with strangers." Writing to a friend from prison almost two years after his arrest, Liebisch expressed worry about the child's welfare and his fear that she would not recognize her father when he went home from prison.[228]

Samuel Lippman, an anarchist from New York, New York, was sentenced along with Jacob Abrams and Mollie Steimer to twenty years in prison for circulating a leaflet critical of U.S. intervention in Russia during World War I. He served in Atlanta Penitentiary from 1919 to 1921.

After two and a half years in prison, Lippman's sentence was commuted on October 23, 1921, on the condition that he would be deported to Russia and never return to the United States. (See also the entry for Mollie Steimer.)[229]

Harry Lloyd, branch secretary of the Lumber Workers Industrial Union, Local 500, in Seattle, Washington, was convicted at the mass IWW trial in Chicago, sentenced to five years in prison and fined $30,000. He served in the Cook County Jail and Leavenworth Penitentiary from September 1917 to August 1919 and from April 1921 to December 24, 1923.[230]

Burt Lorton, a nine-year IWW member and secretary of its Chicago Recruiting Union, was convicted at the mass IWW trial in Chicago for seditious conspiracy and conspiracy to obstruct military service. He was sentenced on August 30, 1918, to ten years in prison and fined $30,000. He served in the Cook County Jail and Leavenworth Penitentiary from September 7, 1917, to December 24, 1923.

Although Lorton was arrested for obstructing enlistment, confidential Department of Justice documents admit that "[n]o evidence was adduced, either oral or otherwise showing that [he] had written, said or done anything against the war." Nevertheless, the Department of Justice urged against releasing Lorton because of his eminence in the trade union leadership: "The Metal Machinery Workers Union had gained a decided increase in members because of his agitation."

Lorton was placed in permanent segregation because of continuous conflicts with the prison administration. Among the pages of disciplinary write-ups, guards complained ferociously:

Yesterday [Lorton] said he knew several persons who did not have the nerve to steal but made their living standing over prisoners with a club. This was intended as an insult. . . . [Action taken:] Placed in isolation on restricted diet.

After being notified to break rock smaller, he just looked up and laughed. . . . [Action taken:] Reprimanded (already in isolation).

Throwing dishes and creating a general disturbance in dining room. . . . [Action taken:] Segregated indefinitely as a dangerous and irresponsible character.

Permanent segregation undermined Lorton's health. According to a letter to Leavenworth Warden A. V. Anderson from Carolina Lowe, an IWW Defense Committee official:

When he entered the penitentiary, he was strong and sturdy looking, a picture of robust health. When I saw him the other day, he looked like a different man, he looked so pale and has lost many pounds, I am sure, in weight.[231]

Vladimir Lossieff, an editor from New York, New York, was convicted at the mass IWW trial in Chicago, sentenced to twenty years in prison and fined $20,000. He served in the Cook County Jail and Leavenworth Penitentiary from September 1917 to April 1918 and from September 7, 1918, to June 30, 1919, when he was released on bond. Lossieff jumped bail and became a fugitive from the law. In 1925, Lossieff was reported to be in Russia.[232]

Chris A. Luber, head of the IWW's Sacramento office at the time of his arrest, was convicted at the mass IWW trial in Sacramento and sentenced to ten years in prison. He served in local county jails and Leavenworth Penitentiary from December 1917 to December 22, 1923. He had joined the IWW in 1912.[233]

Charles H. MacKinnon, an organizer for the Metal Mine Workers Industrial Union, Local 800, from Boston, Massachusetts, was convicted at the mass IWW trial in Chicago, sentenced to five years in prison and fined $30,000. He served in the Cook County Jail and Leavenworth Penitentiary from September 1917 to August 1919 and from April 1921 to December 22, 1923.

The brother-in-law of IWW General Secretary William Haywood, MacKinnon became an organizer with the IWW in 1906. In internal memoranda the Department of Justice conceded that no evidence of any kind was adduced at trial that demonstrated that MacKinnon had ever spoken or written anything critical about "the war, conscription, registration or military service."[234]

Harold G. Mackley, from Holland, Vermont, was convicted for "disloyalty to our country" and sentenced to fifteen years in prison. He served in Atlanta Penitentiary from March 21, 1918, to July 22, 1920.[235]

Sidney Wallace Mader, a Canadian citizen, was arrested in Berlin, New Hampshire, on September 1, 1917, under the Espionage Act. He was convicted and sentenced to three years. After serving in Atlanta Penitentiary his sentence was commuted, and he was released on April 1, 1919.

In the 1940s, Mader was the subject of an FBI investigation. He was "reported" to be a "suspected" member of the U.S. Communist Party who "distributed Communist propaganda" in Seattle, Washington. In 1940, his name was placed on a "custodial detention" list, which would have resulted in his arrest and detention "in the event of a national emergency." His name was removed from that list in 1945 when the FBI determined that the "subject is not actively engaged in un-American activities."[236]

Enrique Flores Magón, an anarchist publisher from Mexico City, Mexico, was convicted of "mailing non-mailable matter" (i.e., Mexican revolutionary material) and was sentenced to three years in prison. He served in McNeil Island and Leavenworth Penitentiaries from May 21, 1918, to September 10, 1920. His brother Ricardo Magón died in Leavenworth Penitentiary on November 21, 1922. (See also Chapters 6 and 14.) Magón published the newspaper *Regeneración* with his brother.

The FBI categorized the Magón brothers as "very prominent in the International Anarchist Movement" for having published articles "worldwide." They were both expelled from Mexico by General Porfirio Díaz for their opposition activities and settled in the United States. While in this country Enrique remained active in radical and Mexican revolutionary activities. The Magón brothers' newspaper *Regeneración* was suppressed by the government at the outbreak of World War I.

After Enrique Magón's release from Leavenworth the Department of Justice's Bureau of Investigation carefully monitored his activities. William Burns, the bureau's director, concluded that Magón was "responsible for the greater portion of anarchistic activities" in Los Angeles and instructed the bureau to "immediately" prepare materials to justify his deportation. The bureau was particularly upset with an "Open Letter" Magón published shortly after his release from prison, where he wrote:

[T]his ill called Country of Liberty has now converted into a crime punishable by twenty years in the Penitentiary anyone who preaches free thought and free speech. Thousands upon thousands of men and women have come under the law, merely for having sufficient valor to attack the ruling tyranny. . . . I must now ask you, must we remain indifferent before such outrages?

The Department of Justice continued to monitor Magón and on October 11, 1922, had him arrested on a deportation warrant. The court ruled that he was an "alien anarchist" who "knowingly distributes" "printed matter" "teaching opposition to all organized government." On March 21, 1923, Magón, his wife and four children were deported to Mexico.[237]

Ricardo Flores Magón, from Mexico City, Mexico, was sentenced to twenty-one years and one day in prison for publishing an anti-war editorial in his Los Angeles–based newspaper *Regeneración*. He was denied proper medical care in Leavenworth Penitentiary and died in that prison. (See chapters 6 and 14 for additional information on Mr. Magón.)[238]

Herbert Mahler, secretary of the IWW General Defense Committee and treasurer of the Everett Defense Committee, came from Seattle, Washington. He was convicted at the mass IWW trial in Chicago, sentenced to five years in prison and fined $30,000. He served in the Cook County Jail and Leavenworth Penitentiary from September 1917 to March 1918 and from September 1918 to May 14, 1922, when his sentence expired.[239]

Daniel Mahoney, of Peoria, Illinois, began serving a prison sentence on May 9, 1918. In 1919 his sentence was commuted to one year and one day.[240]

Paul Maihak, from Kansas, was sentenced to three years in prison. He served in Leavenworth Penitentiary from December 18, 1919, to June 6, 1921, when he was released on bond.[241]

J. H. Majors, from Bear, Oklahoma, was sentenced to two years in prison. He served in Leavenworth Penitentiary from August 1917 to June 10, 1918. Majors had a wife and four children.[242]

Albert E. Maken, of Townsend, Montana, was convicted of obstructing recruitment and began serving a four- to eight-year prison sentence in April 1918.[243]

James H. Manning, a laborer from Seattle, Washington, was convicted at the mass IWW trial in Chicago, sentenced to five years in prison and fined $30,000. He served in the Cook County Jail and Leavenworth Penitentiary.[244]

John D. Manus, of Chicago, Illinois, began serving a prison sentence on November 21, 1918. He was arrested due to the allegedly seditious content of letters he wrote to various newspapers.[245]

Herbert F. Mansol was convicted of obstructing recruitment and began serving a prison sentence May 26, 1918.[246]

J. Emma Martin began serving her prison sentence on July 31, 1918, in the Carson City (Nevada) Jail (DOJ Docket Entry).

John Martin, a lumberjack from Seattle, Washington, was convicted at the mass IWW trial in Chicago, sentenced to ten years in prison and fined $30,000. He served in Leavenworth Penitentiary from April 1918 to June 1920 and from May 1921 to November 13, 1922. Martin was released on the condition that he would be deported to Denmark.[247]

Robert J. Martin began serving a prison sentence on June 21, 1918. A member of the IBSA, Martin was convicted in a mass trial in New York along with Giovanni De Cecca and seven other IBSA members. (See also the entry on Giovanni De Cecca.)[248]

William E. Martin, a carpenter from Tennessee, was convicted of making "scurrilous and inflammatory statements" about the president of the United States and the Red Cross and was sentenced to two years and six months in prison. He served in Atlanta Penitentiary from October 4, 1918, to September 2, 1920. Martin had a wife and one child.[249]

William M. Martin, from Henrietta, Oklahoma, was sentenced to two years in prison. He served in Leavenworth Penitentiary from August 4, 1917, to June 11, 1919. In 1919, Martin participated in the anti-war "Green Corn" Rebellion in Oklahoma.[250]

Thomas Martínez, from Tucson, Arizona, began serving a three-year prison sentence on June 4, 1918.[251]

J. C. Masten, of Cincinnati, Ohio, began serving a prison sentence on September 6, 1918.[252]

Dr. Walter C. Matthey, from Davenport, Iowa, served his prison sentence in Leavenworth Penitentiary from October 18, 1918, to April 3, 1922. Matthey was convicted of aiding and abetting Daniel H. Wallace in giving a speech critical of war.[253]

J. A. Maxwell, a farmer from Broken Arrow, Oklahoma, was sentenced to two years in prison. He served in Leavenworth Penitentiary from August 6, 1917, to June 10, 1919. Maxwell had a wife and two children.[254]

W. H. Maxwell began serving a prison sentence on November 7, 1917, in Leavenworth Penitentiary.[255]

Harry McCarl, from Kansas, was sentenced to three years and six months. He served in Leavenworth Penitentiary from December 18, 1919, to June 17, 1921, when he was released on bond.[256]

Joe McCarthy, an organizer and delegate for the Lumber Workers Industrial Union in Minneapolis, Minnesota, was convicted at the mass IWW trial in Chicago, sentenced to five years in prison and fined $30,000. He served in the Cook County Jail and Leavenworth Penitentiary from December 1917 to August 1918 and from September 1918 to June 13, 1922.[257]

William V. McCoy, a "Virginia mountaineer" from Big Stone Gap, West Virginia, was convicted of conspiring to seize U.S. property and oppose the government and was sentenced to five years in prison. He served in Atlanta Penitentiary from August 17, 1917, to April 24, 1921. Although sixty-one years old when he went to prison, McCoy was confined in "the hole" from January to May 1918.[258]

Herbert McCutcheon, a former officer of the Western Federation of Miners, was convicted at the mass IWW trial in Chicago. He was imprisoned from August 30, 1918, to May 27, 1920, when he was freed on bond. McCutcheon jumped bail and became a fugitive from the law.[259]

John Alex MacDonald, editor of the *Industrial Worker*, received a ten-year sentence, of which he served over five years in Leavenworth Penitentiary. In prison he became a schoolteacher, but lost that position and was sent into isolation for "becoming sarcastic and ridiculing the laws and system of Government of the United States." He described his prison experience in harsh language:

Depicted by a Milton or a Dante, Hell had its flashes of sulphur, its massive pictures of damnation; here also is damnation, but it is a damnation sordid, soiled, small, unpicturesque and mouldy as a decaying corpse.

Although MacDonald was diagnosed as having a mild case of tuberculosis, the government refused to grant clemency because MacDonald published the poem entitled "A Patriot" in the *Industrial Worker*:

A Patriot

I love my country, yes, I do,
I love my Uncle Sam,
I also love my steak and eggs,

* * *

I guess I won't enlist.

I love my flag, I do, I do,
Which floats upon the breeze,
I also love my arms, and legs,

* * *

I guess I won't enlist.

I love my country, yes, I do,
I hope her folks do well;
Without our arms and legs and things
I think we'd look like Hell.
Yet men with faces half shot off
Are unfit to be seen;
I've read in books it spoils their looks,
I guess I won't enlist.

MacDonald's sentence was commuted in October 1923. He was deported to Canada where he remained active with the IWW.[260]

Pete McEvoy, an iron molder from San Jose, California, was convicted at the mass IWW trial in Chicago, sentenced to five years in prison and fined $30,000. He served in the Cook County Jail and Leavenworth Penitentiary from September 1917 to May 14, 1922.[261]

Phil McLaughlin, an IWW officer from Sacramento, California, was convicted at the mass IWW trial in Sacramento and sentenced to ten years in prison. He served in Leavenworth Penitentiary. The Department of Justice described McLaughlin as one of the main "leaders" of the IWW on the Pacific Coast.[262]

W. P. McLester, from Oklahoma, was sentenced to six years in prison. He served in Leavenworth Penitentiary from June 20, 1918, to August 15, 1920, when he was released on parole.[263]

A. W. McMasters began serving a prison sentence in Leavenworth Penitentiary on October 17, 1918.[264]

A. H. McMillan, from Brooklyn, New York, began serving a twenty-year prison sentence on June 21, 1918. He was convicted of sedition for distributing material of the International Bible Students Association.[265]

W. E. Mead, from Seattle, Washington, was sentenced to five years in prison, which he served in McNeil Island Penitentiary from June 10, 1918, to October 22, 1920, when his sentence was commuted.[266]

James Franklin Melton began serving a prison sentence on December 10, 1918, in McNeil Island Penitentiary.[267]

P. W. Meredith of Oregon City, Oregon, began serving a prison sentence on October 23, 1918.[268]

August A. Miller, from Deer Lodge, Montana, was arrested in April 1919 for "alleged seditious utterances." He received a two- to four-year sentence.[269]

Francis D. Miller, a member of the IWW's General Executive Board at the time of his arrest, came from Providence, Rhode Island. He was convicted at the mass IWW trial in Chicago, sentenced to ten years in prison and fined $30,000. He served in the Cook County Jail and Leavenworth Penitentiary from September 2, 1917, to March 1918, from September 1918 to July 1919, and from April 1921 to October 31, 1922. He had a wife and two children.[270]

Frank Miller, from Texas, was sentenced to five years. He served in Leavenworth Penitentiary from May 19, 1919, to the end of his term.[271]

J. A. Miller, from Denver, Colorado, began serving a two-year prison sentence in April 1918.[272]

Vallentine Mink began serving a prison sentence in McNeil Island Penitentiary on September 18, 1918.[273]

Pat Monahan was arrested in November 1917 in the roundup of IWW members in Omaha, Nebraska. After over eighteen months in local jails, all charges against him were dropped.[274]

Frank Monparler of Detroit, Michigan, began serving a prison sentence on July 17, 1918.[275]

T. A. Montgomery, from Tacoma, Washington, began serving a prison sentence on June 4, 1918, in the Pierre County Jail.[276]

Frank Moran was sentenced to two years in prison, which he served in Leavenworth Penitentiary from January 17, 1919, to September 2, 1920.[277]

William Moran, a seaman from Spokane, Washington, was convicted at the mass IWW trial in Chicago, sentenced to five years in prison and fined $20,000. He served in the Cook County Jail and Leavenworth Penitentiary from August 1917 to June 10, 1922.[278]

Bill Morgan, a farmer from Greenville, Alabama, was sentenced to two years in prison. He served in Atlanta Penitentiary from December 1919 to November 23, 1920, and refused parole.[279]

Tom Morgan was sentenced to two years in prison. He served in Atlanta Penitentiary from April 14, 1919, to November 23, 1920.[280]

C. W. Morris, a Working Class Union member from Oklahoma, was sentenced to six years in prison. He served in Leavenworth Penitentiary from October 6, 1918, to September 25, 1920, when he was paroled.[281]

James Mulrooney, a laborer from Seattle, Washington, was convicted at the mass IWW trial in Sacramento and sentenced to four years in prison. He served in local county jails and Leavenworth Penitentiary from December 1917 to February 22, 1922, and contracted tuberculosis in prison.[282]

H. H. Munson, a Socialist and president of the Working Class Union from Oklahoma, was arrested in May 1917 and held in jail until his trial. Sentenced to ten years in prison, Munson served in Leavenworth Penitentiary from November 1, 1917, to the end of his term. He had a wife and six children.[283]

John L. Murphy, a Socialist, a pacifist and an IWW member from Boston, Massachusetts, was convicted at the mass IWW trial in Sacramento and sentenced to five years in prison. He served in Leavenworth Penitentiary from January 17, 1919, to December 25, 1921, when he agreed to be "a law-abiding citizen" and had his sentence commuted.[284]

Walter T. Neff was a longshoreman and secretary-treasurer of the Marine Transport Workers Industrial Union, one of the most successful IWW locals, in Philadelphia. He was convicted at the mass IWW trial in Chicago, sentenced to twenty years in prison and fined $20,000. Neff served in Leavenworth Penitentiary from September 7, 1918, to August 18, 1919, and from April 25, 1921, to October 30, 1922.

According to Department of Justice records of the case against Neff and the other convicted leaders of the Marine Transport Workers Industrial Union (i.e., Benjamin Fletcher, Edward F. Doree and John Walsh), the pardon attorney investigating the case wrote that he was "having considerable difficulty" "ascertaining just what" the Marine Transport Workers Industrial Union defendants did "that constitute[d] the offense of which they were convicted." On April 8, 1922, the pardon attorney requested the Department of Justice's Bureau of Investigation to review the matter.

A week later the agent responsible for the raid on the office of the Marine Transport Workers Industrial Union and for the criminal investigation of Neff and the three other defendants responded to the pardon attorney. Incredibly, he reported that "it was only through Neff's influence that Philadelphia was saved from big labor trouble along the water front during the war." Not only was the agent unaware of any criminal activity Neff and the others engaged in, but also he spoke of Neff in glowing terms:

In conclusion, I wish to state that Walter Neff is a clean cut high class intelligent man and a perfect gentleman. He has a reputation of being able to get along

splendidly with his fellow employees. He is straightforward and mild mannered . . .
I personally do not know of any crime that he has ever committed against the
country.[285]

Mayer L. Nehring, a pharmacist and "Jewish anarchist" from Cleveland,
Ohio, was sentenced to nineteen years in prison. According to a Department of Justice Report, the federal judge who sentenced Nehring gave
him "the extreme sentence because it seemed to the judge that to allow
him liberty would be as foolish as 'to keep a rattlesnake as a pet without
removing its fangs.' " He served in Atlanta Penitentiary from February 24,
1919, to February 17, 1921. Nehring's sentence was commuted when he
agreed to be deported to Russia and never to return to the United States.
Nehring arrived in Russia, but the Soviet government refused him entry.
He was returned to the United States, where he eventually received a
presidential pardon.[286]

C. M. Nelson was sentenced to two years in prison. He served in
Moundsville Penitentiary from September 13, 1918, to April 2, 1920.[287]

John Nielson was arrested in November 1917 in the roundup of IWW
members in Omaha, Nebraska. After over eighteen months in local jails,
all charges against him were dropped.[288]

Pietro Nigra, a miner from Chicago, Illinois, was convicted at the mass
IWW trial in Chicago and sentenced to eighteen months in prison. He
served in the Cook County Jail and Leavenworth Penitentiary from October 1917 to April 1918, from March 1919 to April 1919 and from April
1921 to May 19, 1922.[289]

Joseph A. Oates, a miner from Globe, Arizona, was convicted at the
mass IWW trial in Chicago, sentenced to five years in prison and fined
$20,000. He served in the Cook County Jail and Leavenworth Penitentiary
from September 1917 to May 14, 1922.[290]

Daniel O'Connell, an attorney, a Socialist and an Irish Nationalist from
San Francisco, was convicted of giving "speeches." He was sentenced to
seven years in prison and served in McNeil Island Penitentiary. O'Connell
had formed an anti-draft organization called "American Patriots" to publish *The American Independent.* He was barred from practicing law in the
state of California because of his political activities.[291]

George O'Connell, from Imperial, California, was convicted at the mass
IWW trial in Sacramento and sentenced to ten years in prison. He served
in Leavenworth Penitentiary from August 1918 to December 22, 1923.[292]

Jack O'Connell was sentenced to two years in prison. He served in
McNeil Island Penitentiary from September 18, 1918, to December 29,
1919, when he was paroled.[293]

Kate Richards O'Hare, a popular speaker for the Socialist Party, was
born in Ottawa County, Kansas. Outspoken on social reforms concerning
child labor, the eight-hour work day and the rights of women workers,

O'Hare served as the Socialist Party's international secretary in 1913 and on the party's National Executive Committee in 1912 and 1913. O'Hare was also active in women's suffrage issues and was the first woman to run for the U.S. Senate (Missouri, 1916). She staunchly opposed World War I and was a member of the Socialist Party's Committee on War and Militarism, which drafted the party's April 1917 anti-war declaration in St. Louis.

O'Hare was convicted in December 1917 for what the government deemed were unlawful remarks in a speech delivered in Bowman, North Dakota. The prosecution alleged O'Hare stated that U.S. soldiers would be "used for fertilizer" in France. Sentenced to five years in prison, O'Hare served in Missouri State Penitentiary in Jefferson City from April 15, 1919, until her sentence was commuted by President Woodrow Wilson on May 29, 1920.

Prison was particularly hard on O'Hare, who was separated from her husband and four children. Emma Goldman, a fellow inmate in Jefferson City, described her condition:

Kate O'Hare is here two months and already looks as if she had spent half her time. She overestimated her power of endurance entirely. She has broken down twice and will never stand the [work]shop, never. To the everlasting shame of democracy be it said that political prisoners are given no other occupation except the terrible grind at the machines.

O'Hare's husband also expressed concern:

At the present moment I do not even know how long she will be able to hold herself together. This thing of ... men going to prison is one thing. Of mothers of young children is another. ... Her trial and conviction was a tremendous shock.

After release from prison O'Hare resumed an active role in reform efforts. In 1938, she was appointed assistant director of California's Department of Penology by Governor Culbert L. Olson. Although she served there for only a year, she is credited with instituting a number of important improvements. O'Hare died in January 1948.[294]

V. V. O'Hare, a miner from Los Angeles, California, was convicted at the mass IWW trial in Chicago, sentenced to five years in prison and fined $30,000. He served in the Cook County Jail and Leavenworth Penitentiary from March 1918 to July 22, 1920, when he was paroled.[295]

Charles Ohlsen of Newark, New Jersey, began serving a prison sentence on August 8, 1918.[296]

Louise Olivereau, a "philosophical anarchist" from Seattle, Washington, was sentenced to ten years in prison for circulating anti-war materials.

On December 13, 1917, she entered a jail in Canon City, Colorado, where she served two years.[297]

Theodore Olson, of Portland, Oregon, began serving a two-year prison sentence for "disloyalty" on September 25, 1918.[298]

Herman O'Rear, a farmer from Tyler, Texas, served in Atlanta Penitentiary.[299]

John O'Rear was sentenced to two years in prison. He served in Atlanta Penitentiary.[300]

Will O'Rear, from Tyler, Texas, was sentenced to three years in prison. He served in Atlanta Penitentiary from September 20, 1918, to February 11, 1921, when he was released on parole.[301]

John Pancner, from Chicago, Illinois, joined the IWW in 1905 and worked as a union organizer in Nevada, California, Minnesota, Michigan and Illinois. He was convicted at the mass IWW trial in Chicago, sentenced to ten years in prison and fined $30,000. He served in the Cook County Jail and Leavenworth Penitentiary from September 8, 1917, to May 19, 1919, and from April 30, 1921, to December 23, 1922.[302]

Louis Parenti, a laborer from San Francisco, California, was convicted at the mass IWW trial in Chicago, sentenced to five years in prison and fined $30,000. Parenti was imprisoned from September 1917 to June 1919 and from May 1921 to August 12, 1922, when his sentence was commuted on the condition that he would be deported. He had a wife and three children. He served in the Cook County Jail and Leavenworth Penitentiary.

During his first fifteen months in prison Parenti was unable to contact his wife, Marie. During that time she gave birth to a baby girl and wrote to the warden describing her condition:

Pardon me for taking the liberty to write. Days and nights I have had no rest. Since my husband has been in this prison I haven't received a single line from him. . . . I am a mother of three poor children and I have suffered all the tortures in the world. And also since my husband has been away we have born a baby girl that my husband has never seen. I had a big operation which I suffered a whole lot and I had to abandon for 4 weeks the children at home. I would beg you to allow my husband . . . to write a few lines to his wife.

At about the same time Parenti asked the warden to approve the following telegram to his wife: "I wish news my wife about you and little daughters. Tell me the truth. Kisses." On May 21, 1921, the Parentis were granted permission to communicate with each other.[303]

John Parson was arrested in November 1917 in the roundup of IWW members in Omaha, Nebraska. After over eighteen months in local jails, all charges against him were dropped.[304]

A. J. Partan was sentenced to two years in prison. He served in McNeil Island Penitentiary from May 6, 1919, to January 6, 1921.[305]

Walter Pasewalk was arrested in November 1917 in the roundup of IWW members in Omaha, Nebraska. After over 18 months in local jails, all charges against him were dropped.[306]

Joseph Pass, a writer from New York, New York, was arrested in New York City in October 1917 for "pro-peace" activity and sentenced to two years in prison. He served in McNeil Island Penitentiary.

After prison Pass served on the National Committee of the International Labor Defense and from 1936 to 1943 was editor of *Fight*, a newspaper published by the American League Against War and Fascism.

In the 1950s and 1960s Pass was subjected to surveillance by the FBI, which used agents and informants to keep tabs on him. After determining that the "subject" was a "writer by profession," they recommended against interviewing him because he "might cause embarrassment to the Bureau" in his publications.[307]

Morris Pass was the brother of Joseph Pass. An artist from Seattle, Washington, Morris Pass received a two-year prison sentence, which he served in McNeil Island Penitentiary.[308]

Frank Patton was sentenced to three years and six months in prison, which he served in Leavenworth Penitentiary from December 18, 1919, to June 17, 1921, when he was released on bond.[309]

Peter Perruchon, of Tucson, Arizona, began serving a three-year prison sentence on June 4, 1918.[310]

Grover H. Perry, an experienced organizer for the IWW and secretary-treasurer of the Metal Mine Workers Industrial Union in Salt Lake City, Utah, was convicted at the mass IWW trial in Chicago, sentenced to twelve years in prison and fined $20,000. He served in the Chicago House of Corrections from January 1 to September 6, 1918, and in Leavenworth Penitentiary from September 7, 1918, to September 13, 1919. He had a wife and a child.

In April 1917, just after the United States' entry into the war, Perry, an outspoken critic of U.S. involvement in the war, wrote an essay entitled "Why I Am a Patriot":

Patriotism to me means making this earth better to live upon, the bettering of conditions of men and women who toil and the setting free from toil all together the little children who now have to serve for gold.

Patriotism as I see it does not mean murder, it does not mean rapine. It does not mean pillage and destruction, yet war means all of these things. The ordinary conception of patriotism is to shoulder a gun and shoot some other "patriot" of some other country for no other reason at all except that you have been ordered to do so. My sense of patriotism revolts at such slaughter and such deeds.

At Leavenworth Perry was diagnosed with pulmonary tuberculosis and confined in the prison hospital. The prison physician described Perry's condition as "not promising." After being released on bond on September 13, 1919, Perry jumped bail and became a fugitive from the law.[311]

James A. Peterson, of Minneapolis, Minnesota, began serving a four-year prison sentence in Leavenworth Penitentiary on April 19, 1918. A Republican candidate for governor, he was arrested for making anti-war speeches during the election campaign.[312]

Rudolph Peterson, a laborer from Yakima, Washington, was sentenced to three years in prison. He served in McNeil Island Penitentiary.

According to the Department of Justice, Peterson was convicted because he was "sitting around . . . with his fellow workmen and, in the course of a discussion about liberty bonds, advised against their purchase." Peterson went to trial within eighteen hours of his arrest and had no time to obtain witnesses in his defense.[313]

Tony Petnoshki, a Socialist from Norwich, Connecticut, was sentenced to twenty years in prison. He served in Atlanta Penitentiary.[314]

James Phillips, a seaman from Boston, Massachusetts, was convicted at the mass IWW trial in Chicago, sentenced to five years in prison and fined $30,000. He served in the Cook County Jail and Leavenworth Penitentiary from March 1918 to June 18, 1922. Phillips was deported after his release from prison.[315]

Walter Phillips, a Working Class Union member from Oklahoma, was sentenced to four years in prison. He served in Leavenworth Penitentiary from October 6, 1917, to January 6, 1921.[316]

John Phipps was convicted of "conspiring to seize U.S. property and oppose the government" and was sentenced to five years in prison. He served in Atlanta Penitentiary from August 18, 1918, to the end of his term.[317]

Clinton H. Pierce, a Socialist Party member from Albany, New York, began serving a prison sentence on November 17, 1917. He served in the Albany County Jail.[318]

John Piergres began serving a prison sentence in Leavenworth Penitentiary on May 15, 1918.[319]

Edgecomb Pincho was sentenced to two years in prison, which he served in McNeil Island Penitentiary from August 3, 1918, to November 29, 1919.[320]

Charles Plann, a farmer from Louverne, Minnesota, was convicted at the mass IWW trial in Chicago, sentenced to five years in prison and fined $30,000. He served in the Cook County Jail and Leavenworth Penitentiary from September 1917 to October 1919 and from April 1921 to June 28, 1922.[321]

Robert Poe was sentenced to three years and six months in prison. He served in Leavenworth Penitentiary from December 18, 1919, to June 17, 1920, when he was released on bond.[322]

Earl Potter, a barber from Konawa, Oklahoma, was sentenced to two years in prison. He served in Leavenworth Penitentiary from August 5, 1917, to June 10, 1919.[323]

John Potthast, a laborer from Baltimore, Maryland, was convicted at the mass IWW trial in Sacramento and sentenced to ten years in prison. He served in local jails and Leavenworth Penitentiary from August 17, 1918, to December 22, 1923.[324]

S. J. Powell, secretary-treasurer of the Texas Farmers and Laborers Protective Association, part of the Working Class Union, in Anson, Texas, was sentenced to six years in prison. He served in Leavenworth Penitentiary from December 13, 1919, to August 1, 1922.[325]

William Powell, of Detroit, Michigan, received a prison sentence of twenty years, which was commuted to two years, and served in Leavenworth Penitentiary from July 24, 1918, to April 22, 1919.[326]

Albert B. Prashner, from Scranton, Pennsylvania, was convicted at the mass IWW trial in Chicago, sentenced to ten years in prison and fined $30,000. He served in the Cook County Jail and Leavenworth Penitentiary from September 1917 to March 1918, from September 1918 to September 1919 and from April 1921 to December 23, 1921. The Department of Justice commuted his sentence after Prashner "denounced in all sincerity his former IWW associates and all radical affiliation" and declared that he "no longer [held] the ideas which led him to join" the IWW.[327]

James Price was sentenced to four years in prison. He served in Leavenworth Penitentiary from January 17, 1919, to August 20, 1920, when he was released on bond. He was subsequently arrested under the California Criminal Syndicalism Act. (See also Chapter 13).[328]

Benedict Prieth, a newspaper editor from New Jersey, was convicted under the Espionage Act.[329]

Victor Privat, from Ketchum, Oklahoma, was sentenced to two years in prison. He served in Leavenworth Penitentiary from November 1917 to May 8, 1919.[330]

Edward Quigley was convicted at the mass IWW trial in Sacramento and sentenced to ten years in prison. He contracted an especially serious case of tuberculosis at Leavenworth Penitentiary, but was denied adequate medical care and was forced to protest the unsanitary prison hospital conditions. These were so deplorable that even the guards acknowledged them in Quigley's official prison record: "Other men state that the nurse is filthy and handles the thermometer with filthy hands. This is corroborated by practically all patients in the annex."

A Department of Justice memorandum stated that Quigley was dying from tuberculosis and both lungs were infected: "An outside physician of high standing states that Quigley will probably not live more than three or four years at the most." Consequently, the pardon attorney recommended a commutation of sentence: "This prisoner is no longer defiant but is *subdued and appears to be improved by reason of his imprisonment.* He promises to be law abiding in the future" (emphasis supplied). The prison doctor concurred with these opinions, noting that the likelihood of Quigley's recovery was "very doubtful" and that between January and October 1923 Quigley's condition had "appreciably failed."

Nevertheless, Quigley was kept in prison for two more months, until December 23, 1923, when his sentence was commuted.[331]

James Quinlan, a laborer from Sacramento, California, was convicted at the mass IWW trial in Sacramento and sentenced to ten years in prison. He served in Leavenworth Penitentiary from August 16, 1918, to December 22, 1923.

Quinlan was continuously placed in "isolation" on a "restricted diet" for offenses such as "loafing," telling a guard to "f—k himself" and fighting. He was "cuffed to a grated wall" because he was "defiant" and had "no regard for the rules or the institution."[332]

Floyd Ramp, a founder of the U.S. Communist Party from Roseburg, Oregon, was sentenced to two years in prison for conspiracy to obstruct the draft. He served in McNeil Island and Leavenworth Penitentiaries from February 1918 to December 1919. In 1921, the FBI described Ramp as "one of the most notorious radicals in the entire country."[333]

William Randall, secretary of the IWW local in Tacoma, Washington, was sentenced to three years in prison. He served in McNeil Island Penitentiary from January 29, 1920, to the end of his term.[334]

John F. Randolph, a Socialist from Auburn, New York, received a sentence of ten years, which was commuted on November 21, 1918.

Randolph was convicted solely for stating in a "lunch room" conversation that the U.S. government was "rotten," that he "never bought a liberty bond" and that he did not "believe in conscription." After being found guilty, he told the U.S. district court judge that his trial and conviction were "a joke."

The prosecuting U.S. attorney recommended against Randolph's release, stating that the "defendant had no use for civilization and is better off in confinement."[335]

Peter Randolph, a cook from Auburn, New York, was sentenced to ten years in prison. He served in Atlanta Penitentiary from December 5, 1918, to May 7, 1920.[336]

Joseph J. Ratti was arrested in November 1917 in the roundup of IWW members in Omaha, Nebraska. After over eighteen months in local jails, all charges against him were dropped.[337]

Julius Reck began serving a prison sentence on December 12, 1918, in the Richland County Jail.[338]

Walter M. Reeder, a Universal Union member from Wilson, Oklahoma, was sentenced to six years in prison and served in Leavenworth Penitentiary.[339]

Otto B. Reichelt, from New Jersey, received "a severe sentence" despite Department of Justice "skepticism as to the proof against Reichelt."[340]

Frank Reilly was sentenced to two years. He served in Leavenworth Penitentiary from January 17, 1919, to September 2, 1920.[341]

Edwin S. Reitz, from Aberdeen, South Dakota, began serving a five-year prison sentence on May 16, 1918. He was convicted of making "statements tending to obstruct the draft."[342]

W. M. Reivo was sentenced to two years in prison, which he served in McNeil Island Penitentiary from May 6, 1919, to January 26, 1921.[343]

Manuel Rey, a seaman and an organizer for the Transport Workers Industrial Union, Local 100, from Niagara Falls, New York, was convicted at the mass IWW trial in Chicago and sentenced to twenty years in prison. He served in the Cook County Jail and Leavenworth Penitentiary from June 26, 1917, to December 15, 1922. Rey was released on the condition that he would be deported to Spain and never return to the United States.[344]

Julius Rhuberg, of Sherman County, Oregon, was sentenced to fifteen months in prison. He served in McNeil Island Penitentiary.[345]

C. H. Rice, a lumberjack from Owenton, Kentucky, was convicted at the mass IWW trial in Chicago, sentenced to ten years in prison and fined $30,000. He served in the Cook County Jail and Leavenworth Penitentiary from January 1918 to April 1918 and from September 1918 until his parole on July 21, 1922.[346]

Z. L. Risley, from Stanford, Texas, was president of the Texas Farmers and Laborers Protective Association (part of the Working Class Union). He was sentenced to six years in prison, which he served in Leavenworth Penitentiary from December 13, 1919, to August 1, 1922.[347]

Librado Rivera, an anarchist and copublisher with the Magón brothers of *Regeneración*, was sentenced to fifteen years in prison. He served in McNeil Island and Leavenworth Penitentiaries. After five years in prison Rivera developed rheumatism, pyorrhea and other ailments. He was released from prison and deported to Mexico in October 1923.[348]

John Robbins, from Miami, Arizona, was sentenced to two years in prison, which he served in Leavenworth Penitentiary from March 1918 to January 18, 1920.[349]

Walter Roberts was sentenced to three years in prison and served in Atlanta Penitentiary from October 2, 1918, to October 25, 1920.[350]

Fred H. Robison, an IBSA member (i.e., a Jehovah's Witness), began serving a prison sentence on June 21, 1918. (See also the entry for Giovanni De Cecca.)[351]

Billie Rogers, from Oklahoma, was sentenced to ten years in prison and served in Leavenworth Penitentiary from March 1, 1919, to July 24, 1922, when he was paroled.[352]

Florencio Romero, of San Juan, Puerto Rico, began serving a prison sentence on May 6, 1918. He was sentenced to four years in prison for "attempting to form an anti-militarist league."[353]

Tom Ross was arrested in November 1917 in the roundup of IWW members in Omaha, Nebraska. After over eighteen months in local jails, all charges against him were dropped.[354]

Arthur Roth, from New York, New York, began serving a five-year prison sentence on July 18, 1918.[355]

Charles Rothfiser, the editor of the IWW's Hungarian language newspaper, from Chicago, Illinois, was convicted at the mass IWW trial in Chicago, sentenced to twenty years in prison and fined $20,000. He served in Leavenworth Penitentiary from September 7, 1918, to April 28, 1919, when bond was posted. Rothfiser jumped bail and became a fugitive from the law.[356]

James Rowan, the secretary-treasurer of the Lumber Workers Industrial Union, Local 500, from Spokane, Washington, was convicted at the mass IWW trial in Chicago, sentenced to twenty years in prison and fined $20,000. He served in the Cook County Jail and Leavenworth Penitentiary from August 1917 to September 1919 and from April 1921 to December 22, 1923.

The Department of Justice deemed Rowan "the most dangerous man in the entire IWW movement" for having been the "guiding spirit" of the lumber workers general strike in the Northwest.[357]

Joe Ruby was arrested in November 1917 in the roundup of IWW members in Omaha, Nebraska. After over eighteen months in local jails, all charges against him were dropped.[358]

John Ruck, from Helena, Montana, began serving a three- to six-year prison sentence on April 16, 1918.[359]

Fred J. Saal, from Cleveland, Ohio, began serving a ten-year prison sentence for "seditious utterances" on August 17, 1918.[360]

Sam Sadler, from Seattle, Washington, received a prison sentence which was commuted to two years. He served in McNeil Island Penitentiary from March 18, 1918, to October 27, 1920.[361]

Vincent St. John is credited as the shaping force of the early IWW. A founder of the IWW, St. John was its general secretary from 1908 to 1914. According to his contemporaries, St. John was canonized by every member who knew him.

At age twenty-four St. John became an Executive Board member and president of the Telluride, Colorado, local of the Western Federation of Miners. In Telluride he organized one of the first sit-down strikes in U.S. history—instead of going out on strike, the mine workers took "peaceful possession of their mines." As an officer of that union, St. John helped lead some of the most controversial strikes of his day, including those in Coeur d'Alenes, Colorado, and Goldfield, Nevada. To mine operators, St. John was a notorious troublemaker with the potential to destroy their businesses. One of the mine operators' private detectives told the *Rocky Mountain News* that St. John had given the mine owners of Colorado "more trouble in the past years than twenty other men. If left undisturbed, he would have the entire district organized in another year."

St. John guided the development of the IWW in its early years: "[I]n the years 1906–1914, the years when the character of the IWW was fixed, and its basic cadres assembled, it was St. John who led the movement." In 1914, however, St. John refused to run for reelection as general secretary and turned the post over to William ("Big Bill") Haywood. Shortly thereafter he left the IWW and prospected for gold in New Mexico.

Despite the fact that he had dropped his union membership in 1915 and no longer was actively involved in any political movement, St. John was indicted under the Espionage Act in the Chicago mass trial of IWW members. Although the FBI described St. John as a "notorious agitator" with a "voluminous file" of radical union activity, internal Department of Justice documents conceded that the government had absolutely no evidence against him. One memorandum summed up his case: "The trial against him was a farce. There was absolutely no evidence against him, and yet he was convicted and the Circuit Court of Appeals confirmed his conviction." St. John was sentenced to ten years in prison. On June 24, 1922, after four years in Leavenworth Penitentiary, St. John's sentence was commuted.[362]

Monserrate Sánchez, from Rio Piedras, Puerto Rico, received a sentence of four years in prison, which was commuted to two years. He served in Atlanta Penitentiary from July 25, 1918, to April 15, 1920.[363]

Paul Sandargos, a coal miner from Scranton, Pennsylvania, was convicted for distributing literature against the draft and sentenced to three years in prison. He served in Atlanta Penitentiary from October 17, 1917, to February 21, 1920. Sandargos had a wife and two children.

In a letter to his brother, Sandargos described his meeting with Eugene Debs in prison:

I see E. V. Debs on Saturday and Sunday afternoons when we are in the yard. I find him a splendid fellow and full of spirit. He will always fight for the workers, no matter where or when. All of the poor fellows here run to him for help. It is pitiful, yet funny to see men from up in the mountains who never saw or heard of him before, going to him for advice. He pats them on the shoulder and cheers them up. Says all will come out all right. That they must not worry but keep their spirits and a cool head and before long they are satisfied that being in prison with him is just as good as being outside without him. It is truly wonderful.[364]

August Sandberg, from Tucson, Arizona, began serving his two-year sentence for "seditious remarks" on June 4, 1918.[365]

Vincent Santilli, a miner from Sacramento, California, was convicted at the mass IWW trial in Sacramento and sentenced to ten years in prison. He served in local county jails and Leavenworth Penitentiary from December 1917 to September 1, 1923.[366]

Michael Sapper, an IWW delegate and organizer of oil field workers, from New York, New York, was convicted at the mass IWW trial in Wichita and sentenced to seven and a half years in prison, which he served in Leavenworth Penitentiary. The Department of Justice wrote that Sapper "should be permanently segregated from society" because of his political beliefs.[367]

Torazo Sato was convicted of "entering the United States without a passport" and sentenced to thirteen months in prison. He began serving his sentence in McNeil Island Penitentiary on October 4, 1920.[368]

Silas Saylor, an ordained preacher of the Pentecostal Church from Beverly, Kentucky, was convicted because he told his congregation that he was "personally . . . dedicated . . . to the service of the Lord . . . and therefore cannot kill." He was sentenced to three years in prison and served in Atlanta Penitentiary. He had a wife and seven children.[369]

Sam Scarlett, a machinist and IWW lecturer from Chicago, Illinois, was convicted at the mass IWW trial in Chicago, sentenced to twenty years in prison and fined $20,000. He served in Leavenworth Penitentiary from September 7, 1918, to January 31, 1923. Scarlett's sentence was commuted when he agreed to be deported to England and swore never to return to the United States.

In 1939, the FBI reopened its files on Scarlett when it was rumored that he had been arrested in Canada for helping to publish certain articles in *The Clarion*, a pro-communist newspaper in Toronto. Incredibly, the FBI continued its search for Scarlett from 1940, when he was rumored to have died, until 1959, simply to confirm his death. Scarlett's FBI record, released in 1990, was riddled with withheld and deleted pages.[370]

Peter Schellbach, of Jersey City, New Jersey, began serving a prison sentence on June 14, 1918. He was given a three–ten year term for "reviling president Wilson."[371]

August Schening began serving a prison sentence on March 12, 1918.[372]

Francis X. Schilling, from Marathon City, Wisconsin, was sentenced to eighteen months in prison and served in Leavenworth Penitentiary from December 5, 1918, to February 17, 1920. He had a wife and nine children.[373]

Carl Schilter, from Sacramento, California, began serving a two and a half year prison sentence on June 30, 1918.[374]

John G. Schlechter was convicted for libelous and slanderous writings against the government. He began serving a prison sentence on November 2, 1918.[375]

Carl Schnell, from Kansas, was sentenced to three years in prison. He served in Leavenworth Penitentiary from December 18, 1919, to the end of his term.[376]

C. B. Schoberg, from Covington, Kentucky, was convicted of making disloyal statements and began serving his sentence in Moundsville Penitentiary on September 13, 1918.[377]

Charles G. Schulze, from San Diego, California, served in McNeil Island Penitentiary from September 27, 1918, to November 27, 1919. Schulze, who was sixty years old at the time of his incarceration, suffered a breakdown in health.[378]

Wilhelm Schumann, a Lutheran pastor from Fort Dodge, Iowa, was convicted of preaching "disloyalty among his congregation" and was sentenced to five years in prison. He served in Leavenworth Penitentiary from July 11, 1918, to December 25, 1921.[379]

Erwin Schwaer of Milwaukee, Wisconsin, began serving a prison sentence on May 3, 1918.[380]

John L. Seebach, from Minneapolis, Minnesota, was convicted for writing three letters against the war. He served in Leavenworth Penitentiary from September 2, 1918, to February 14, 1920.

In upholding the conviction, the appeals court held that the Constitution does not include an "invitation to destroy the fundamental structure of government."[381]

Christian Seeger was sentenced to two years in prison and served in Leavenworth Penitentiary from October 31, 1918, until November 17, 1919, when he was paroled.[382]

Frank Shaffer, of Everett, Washington, was sentenced to two and a half years in prison and served in McNeil Island Penitentiary from July 10, 1918, until January 23, 1920, when he was pardoned.

Shaffer was convicted of mailing a book published by the IBSA entitled *The Finished Mystery*. One of the passages the government found offensive stated:

The war itself is wrong. Its prosecution will be a crime. There is not a question raised, an issue involved, a cause at stake, which is worth the life of one [soldier].[383]

Don Sheridan, a plumber and the secretary of the Agricultural Workers Industrial Union, Local 400, in Spokane, Washington, was convicted at the mass IWW trial in Chicago, sentenced to ten years in prison and fined $30,000. He served in the Cook County Jail and Leavenworth Penitentiary from September 1917 to August 3, 1923.[384]

Al Shidler, a Socialist from Tonopah, Nevada, began serving a two-year prison sentence on July 15, 1918, in McNeil Island Penitentiary.[385]

John Shirey, a Working Class Union member from Oklahoma, was sentenced to six years in prison. He served in Leavenworth Penitentiary from October 6, 1917, to November 16, 1920.[386]

Stephen Shuren was arrested in Kansas and scheduled to be tried in the mass IWW trial in Wichita. While awaiting trial Shuren attempted suicide at the Shawnee County Jail in Kansas.

The attempted suicide occurred after Shuren had spent approximately a year in jail. After having been forced to share a cell with a seriously syphilitic inmate, Shuren "snapped," using his shaving razor "to cut a deep wound in his neck from ear to ear, and fell to the floor." Nearly dead he was rushed to the hospital. While recuperating he wrote: "Life has denied me everything. What have I to live for? Why should I live?" Within two weeks of the attempt, he was transferred back to the Shawnee County Jail.

His fellow IWW inmates watched over Shuren continuously after his return. A reporter commissioned by the National Civil Liberties Union and *Survey* magazine visited Shuren and wrote that "the expression in his eyes was not normal and he looked at me from his clouded face. The men said that little of his mind seemed to remain."

Shuren was transferred to the state insane asylum at Osawattomie. Soon thereafter the government dropped its indictment of these Wichita IWW defendants.[387]

Tobe Simons, a Working Class Union member from Oklahoma, was sentenced to four to six years in prison. He served in Leavenworth Penitentiary from October 6, 1917, until October 19, 1921, when he was paroled.[388]

Archie Sinclair, a laborer and a writer for *Solidarity* and *The Industrial Worker*, from Bemidji, Minnesota, was convicted at the mass IWW trial in Chicago and sentenced to ten years in prison. He served eleven months in the Cook County Jail and four years and five months in Leavenworth Penitentiary. He was released on the condition that he would be deported. Sinclair had joined the IWW in 1914.[389]

Charlie Slom began serving a prison sentence on September 13, 1918, in Moundsville Penitentiary.[390]

James Slovik, secretary of the Marine Transport Workers Industrial Union, Local 200, from Cleveland, Ohio, was convicted at the mass IWW trial in Chicago, sentenced to ten years in prison and fined $30,000. He served in the Cook County Jail and Leavenworth Penitentiary from September 1917 to March 1918 and from September 1918 to August 13, 1923.[391]

C. L. Smith was arrested in November 1917 in the roundup of IWW members in Omaha, Nebraska. After over eighteen months in local jails, all charges against him were dropped.[392]

George W. Snell, a farmer from Tyler, Texas, served a prison sentence in Atlanta Penitentiary from September 20, 1918, to October 15, 1920.[393]

Maurice L. Snitken, a lawyer from Indianapolis, Indiana, was sentenced to six years in prison. He served in Atlanta Penitentiary from June 23, 1918, until August 25, 1920, when he was paroled. Snitken had a wife and a child.[394]

E. J. Sonnenburg served a prison sentence in McNeil Island Penitentiary from July 31, 1918, to June 21, 1920.[395]

J. R. Sparkman, a Working Class Union member from Oklahoma, was sentenced to six years in prison and served in Leavenworth Penitentiary from October 6, 1917, to September 16, 1920.[396]

H. C. Spence, from Wewoka, Oklahoma, was sentenced to ten years in prison and served in Leavenworth Penitentiary from November 1, 1917, to May 5, 1921. Spence had a wife and three small children.[397]

Myron Sprague, a laborer and a delegate for Local 573 of the Construction Workers Industrial Union from Stockton, California, was convicted at the mass IWW trial in Sacramento and sentenced to ten years in prison. He served in Leavenworth Penitentiary from April 1918 to December 22, 1923.[398]

Leo Stark was sentenced to four years and six months in prison and served from December 18, 1919, until he was released on bond.[399]

E. V. Starr, from Montana, was convicted for refusing to kiss the flag and sentenced to ten to twenty years in prison.[400]

M. Staurt, a participant in the Oklahoma "Green Corn" Rebellion, received a prison sentence of six years, which was commuted to eighteen months, and served in Leavenworth Penitentiary beginning on April 17, 1920.[401]

Fred Steadman, of Concord, New Hampshire, began serving a prison sentence on October 4, 1918.[402]

Mollie Steimer and six fellow anarchists from New York City (Jacob Abrams, Samuel Lipman, Hyman Lachowsky, Gabriel Probes, Jacob Schwartz and Hyman Rosansky) were arrested in August 1918 and charged with violating the Espionage Act of 1917, as amended May 16, 1918. The sole basis of the indictment was the distribution of two leaflets condemning the allied intervention in Russia shortly after the Bolshevik Revolution. An FBI report referred to Steimer as a "Jewess" and a "free lover" who was "inciting sedition." The twenty-one-year-old Steimer was convicted, sentenced to fifteen years in prison and fined $5,000.

Her case was appealed to the U.S. Supreme Court, and in the landmark decision of *Abrams v. United States*, the Court upheld her conviction, with Justices Oliver Wendell Holmes and Louis D. Brandeis dissenting. She served six months on Blackwell's Island in the East River of New York and then was sent to the Jefferson City, Missouri, penitentiary.

On November 24, 1921, after serving two and a half years of her sentence, Steimer, along with three of her codefendants, was deported to the Soviet Union. In addition to being deported, Steimer was prohibited from ever returning to the United States. Steimer's attorney, Harry Weinberger, lamented her expulsion from America:

Three boys and one little girl, four deportees, will sail out of New York harbor to Russia, a land of hunger and disease, sent [away] from relatives and friends, the worst form of human punishment, for the crime of having an honest opinion. . . . [They] raised their voice of protest by leaflets against the illegal and unconstitutional use of U.S. troops in Russia.

In Russia Steimer fought with the Communist government over political liberties and the rights of labor. On November 1, 1922, she was arrested by the Russian secret police and forced to go on a hunger strike to obtain release three weeks later. Arrested again by the secret police on July 9, 1923, Steimer was expelled from the Soviet Union on September 27, 1923.

Steimer remained active in anarchist politics during her exile. She was in Germany when Hitler seized power and was forced to flee to France. In 1940, after Germany occupied France, Steimer was sent to a concentration camp, but she escaped after six months of confinement. From there she fled to Mexico where she lived out the rest of her life committed to anarchist ideals.[403]

Sigfrid Stenberg, the manager of the IWW paper *Alarm*, from Minneapolis, Minnesota, was convicted at the mass IWW trial in Chicago, sentenced to ten years in prison and fined $30,000. He served in the Cook County Jail and Leavenworth Penitentiary from September 1917 to November 1919 and from April 1921 to November 1922. Stenberg had a wife and one child. Stenberg was released on the condition that he would be deported to Sweden and never return to the United States.[404]

Bernard Stenzel, from Dubuque, Iowa, began serving a prison sentence in Leavenworth Penitentiary on May 2, 1918.[405]

Fritz Stepanovitch, a Socialist from Mattapan, Massachusetts, was sentenced to twenty years in prison and served in Atlanta Penitentiary.[406]

Ernest A. Stephens served a prison sentence from July 30, 1918, to June 21, 1920, in McNeil Island Penitentiary.[407]

Joseph V. Stilson, publisher of the newspaper *Kova* and a member of the Lithuanian Socialist Federation in Pennsylvania, was sentenced to three years in prison. He began his sentence in Maryland Penitentiary on December 6, 1918. His case was appealed to and upheld by the U.S. Supreme Court in *Stilson v. United States*, 250 U.S. 583 (1919).[408]

Anthony J. Stopa, from Detroit, Michigan, was convicted for saying "young men are fools if they join the Army to be shot down like dogs" and was originally sentenced to twenty years in prison. Stopa served in Leavenworth Penitentiary from August 7, 1918, to December 1921. Stopa denied making the statements attributed to him, and claimed to be loyal to the government.[409]

Frank Strand began serving a prison sentence on May 17, 1918.[410]

Herbert Stredwick, a leader of the IWW's San Pedro, California, office and a Construction Workers and Marine Transport Workers delegate from Seattle, Washington, was convicted at the mass IWW trial in Sacramento and sentenced to five years in prison. He served in Leavenworth Penitentiary. He had a wife and one child.[411]

George V. Strode, from Jills, Arizona, was sentenced to two years in prison. He served in Leavenworth Penitentiary from May 1, 1918, to the end of his term.[412]

Charles A. Stuart, a Socialist and a Universal Union member from western Oklahoma, served time in Leavenworth Penitentiary.[413]

Abraham L. Sugarman, from Mankato, Minnesota, was convicted of "obstructing military service" and sentenced to three years in prison. The State Secretary of the Socialist Party, he served in Leavenworth Penitentiary from April 25, 1919, to November 22, 1920. Sugarman contracted pulmonary tuberculosis and a "psoas abscess" in prison. Although the abscess was "incised and drained through the right groin," it was "still discharging" pus after the operation.[414]

Thomas R. Sullivan, a Socialist and Christian Scientist from New York, New York, was sentenced to two years in prison for obstructing the draft. He served in Leavenworth Penitentiary from July 14, 1919, to February 19, 1921.

According to FBI reports, Sullivan was arrested at the Bridgman, Michigan, Workers Party convention in 1922. He remained active in radical labor activities and became an organizer for the Harlem Trade Union Council and the United Office and Professional Workers of America, Congress of Industrial Organizations. After prison Sullivan helped found the American Communist Party.

He was continuously investigated by the FBI between 1949 and 1972 as a Communist. The bureau noted his participation in demonstrations against the Vietnam War during the 1960s and continued to classify him as "potentially dangerous" to the interests of the government in 1972, when he was at the advanced age of eighty-one.[415]

Oscar Swanson was arrested in November 1917 in the roundup of IWW members in Omaha, Nebraska. After over eighteen months in local jails, all charges against him were dropped.[416]

Pink Swindle served a sentence in Atlanta Penitentiary from September 20, 1918, until October 15, 1920, when his sentence was commuted.[417]

Joshua Sykes, a pastor in the Church of the Living God from Berkeley, California, served a prison term in McNeil Island Penitentiary from January 21, 1919, to June 10, 1922. Sykes' religion forbade the purchase of Liberty Bonds and standing for the National Anthem.[418]

Caesar Tabib, from New York, New York, was convicted at the mass IWW trial in Sacramento and sentenced to ten years in prison. He served in

Leavenworth Penitentiary from August 1918 to September 1920 and from May 1921 to December 23, 1923. Tabib developed chronic pulmonary tuberculosis in prison. (See Chapters 4 and 7 for excerpts of his prison record.)[419]

A. O. Taichin, a Socialist from Bayonne, New Jersey, was convicted along with Theo Fedotoft of "seditious remarks" at a meeting to set up a school. He began serving his ten-year sentence on May 15, 1918.[420]

John A. Talishus of Syracuse, New York, began serving a prison sentence in Maryland Penitentiary on September 18, 1918.[421]

William Tanner, from Chicago, Illinois, was convicted at the mass IWW trial in Chicago, sentenced to five years in prison and fined $30,000. He served in the Cook County Jail and Leavenworth Penitentiary from December 1917 to May 1919 and from April 1921 to October 27, 1922. Tanner's sentence was commuted on the condition that he would be deported and never return to the United States.[422]

Gustave H. Taubert, from Concord, New Hampshire, began serving a three-year prison sentence on June 4, 1918.[423]

James P. Thompson, one of the founders of the IWW, from Seattle, Washington, was convicted at the mass IWW trial in Chicago, sentenced to ten years in prison and fined $30,000. He served in the Cook County Jail and Leavenworth Penitentiary from September 1917 to March 1918 and from September 1918 to December 22, 1923. He had a wife and two children.

While in Leavenworth Penitentiary, Thompson learned that his wife was "sick and broke," and he pleaded with the IWW Defense Committee to help her. Thompson helped write the IWW's constitution and also served as an organizer and a lecturer.[424]

Jacob Tori, an IWW delegate and organizer from San Francisco, California, was indicted by the Department of Justice for his "rantings" against the war and his urging young men "not to register" for the draft. He was convicted at the mass IWW trial in Sacramento and sentenced to ten years in prison, which he served in local county jails and Leavenworth Penitentiary from December 1917 to December 24, 1923. An organizer and a delegate for the IWW since 1913, Tori helped organize the fruit-packing industry.

Tori's lack of cooperation in prison caused prison officials to declare him the "most worthless man" at Leavenworth. His twenty written reprimands included offenses such as "killing time," "indolence and defiance," "getting up from the supper table without permission," "wasting food at dinner" and "talking in the mess hall." Twice he was placed in isolation on a restricted diet for being "worthless and insolent." On four occasions he was reprimanded for "refusing to break enough rock."

Tori was among the last of the IWW prisoners released on December 24, 1923.[425]

Placido Torres received a prison sentence of two years and served in McNeil Island Penitentiary from April 24, 1919, until his sentence was commuted on October 29, 1920.[426]

Harry E. Townsley, a Socialist from Columbus, Ohio, was convicted for distributing literature against the draft and sentenced to two years in prison. He served in Atlanta Penitentiary.[427]

H. L. Trelease, a Socialist from Fargo, North Dakota, was sentenced on February 23, 1919, to two years in prison and served the term in Leavenworth Penitentiary until he was released and deported in December of 1921.[428]

R. Trumble was sentenced to two years in prison and served in Atlanta Penitentiary from September 20, 1918, until his parole on December 4, 1920.[429]

Isadore Trzeliakiewicz was sentenced to three years in prison and served in Atlanta Penitentiary from June 3, 1918, to September 25, 1920.[430]

Norris Tucker served a prison term in Atlanta Penitentiary.[431]

John I. Turner, a lumberjack and an organizer and a delegate for the Lumber Workers Industrial Union, Local 500, from Spokane, Washington, was convicted at the mass IWW trial in Chicago, sentenced to ten years in prison and fined $30,000. He served in the Cook County Jail and Leavenworth Penitentiary from December 1917 to June 25, 1923.[432]

William E. van Amburgh, an IBSA member, began serving his sentence on June 21, 1918. (See also the entry for Giovanni De Cecca.)[433]

George F. Voetter, a blacksmith from Pittsburgh, Pennsylvania, was convicted at the mass IWW trial in Sacramento and sentenced to ten years in prison. He served in local county jails and Leavenworth Penitentiary from December 22, 1917, to December 22, 1923.[434]

Paul Vogel, from eastern Pennsylvania, began serving his prison sentence on December 18, 1918, in the Mercer County Jail in East Trenton, New Jersey.[435]

Curt Von Einen, from Tucson, Arizona, was sentenced to two years in prison and served in Leavenworth Penitentiary from June 18, 1918, to March 10, 1920.[436]

Carl J. E. Wacher was sentenced to eighteen months in prison and served in McNeil Island Penitentiary from September 29, 1917, to the end of his term.[437]

Clarence W. Waldron, a Pentecostal preacher from Windsor, Vermont, was convicted in part for distributing a pamphlet entitled "The Word of the Cross" and in part for stating that "A Christian ought not and should not fight." He received a fifteen-year prison sentence and served in Atlanta Penitentiary from April 1, 1918, until his sentence was commuted on April 1, 1919. Waldron had one child.[438]

W. T. Walker, a Choctaw Indian from Taft, New Mexico, received a prison sentence of two years, which was commuted to a year and a day. He served in Leavenworth Penitentiary.[439]

John Wallberg, from Kansas, was sentenced to three years and six months in prison and served in Leavenworth Penitentiary from December 18, 1919, until his release on bond on June 17, 1921.[440]

John Walsh, an IWW leader in the early years of the movement from New York, New York, was convicted at the mass IWW trial in Chicago and sentenced to ten years in prison. He served in the Cook County Jail and Leavenworth Penitentiary from December 1917 to January 1920 and from April 1921 to October 30, 1922.

While in prison Walsh accumulated sixteen disciplinary reports for infractions ranging from "conspiring to have other inmates strike" to "wasting food." (See also the entry for Walter T. Neff.)[441]

Maukt Wand, from Houston, Texas, was sentenced to fifteen months in prison and served in Atlanta Penitentiary from November 2, 1918, to November 3, 1919.[442]

Jim Ward was arrested in November 1917 in the roundup of IWW members in Omaha, Nebraska. After over eighteen months in local jails, all charges against him were dropped.[443]

Elizabeth Watkins began serving a prison term on September 13, 1918, in Missouri State Penitentiary.[444]

August Weissenfels, of Chicago, Illinois, began serving a prison sentence on November 1, 1918. He was sentenced to ten years for "opposing his son's enlistment" into the armed services.[445]

Robert Weir was arrested in November 1917 in the roundup of IWW members in Omaha, Nebraska. After over eighteen months in local jails, all charges against him were dropped.[446]

William Wiertola was arrested in November 1917 in the roundup of IWW members in Omaha, Nebraska. After over eighteen months in local jails, all charges against him were dropped.[447]

Nathan L. Welch, the editor of the *Michigan Socialist*, from Detroit, Michigan, served eighteen months of a two-year prison sentence at Leavenworth Penitentiary for activities undertaken while working as an editor.[448]

Hulet M. Wells, from Seattle, Washington, was tried jointly with Joseph Pass and sentenced on March 18, 1918. He served in McNeil Island Penitentiary from March 19, 1918, until his sentence was commuted to two years on November 13, 1920.[449]

George Wenger was sentenced to three years in prison and served in Leavenworth Penitentiary from December 18, 1919, until his release on bond on June 17, 1920.[450]

Frank Wensil, an IWW organizer and a delegate from Cedar Rapids, Iowa, was convicted at the mass IWW trial in Wichita and sentenced to seven and a half years in prison. He served in Leavenworth Penitentiary from November 19, 1917, to December 22, 1923. Wensil had joined the IWW in 1909.[451]

Louis Werner, from eastern Pennsylvania, served in Atlanta Penitentiary from December 30, 1918, to June 10, 1920.[452]

Rev. Walter A. Werth, a Lutheran pastor from Winesburg, Ohio, was sentenced to two years in prison. He served in Atlanta Penitentiary from August 7, 1918, to March 31, 1920.[453]

Frank Westerlund, an IWW organizer from Duluth, Minnesota, was convicted at the mass IWW trial in Chicago, sentenced to five years in prison and fined $30,000. He served in the Cook County Jail and Leavenworth Penitentiary from January 23, 1918, to April 28, 1919, and from April 26, 1921, until his parole on October 20, 1922. Westerlund had a wife and one child.[454]

Pierce C. Wetter was convicted at the mass IWW trial in Chicago, sentenced to five years in prison and fined $20,000. He served in the Cook County Jail and Leavenworth Penitentiary from November 1917 to July 13, 1922.[455]

William Weyh, an IWW leader, was convicted of seditious conspiracy at the mass IWW trial in Chicago, sentenced to five years and fined $20,000. He began his term in Leavenworth Penitentiary on September 7, 1918. Weyh contracted tuberculosis at Leavenworth. Despite his tuberculin condition, he was forced to perform hard labor (breaking rocks) until he suffered twelve hemorrhages in a single day. On December 27, 1921, the prison physician notified Warden W. I. Biddle that Weyh's condition was terminal: "He has had several very severe pulmonary hemorrhages in the past few days and the case is very liable to terminate fatally at any time."

Even this did not persuade the Department of Justice, which refused to pardon Weyh. According to IWW prisoners:

[After his December hemorrhages] he was so emaciated as to be scarcely recognizable. It was at this point that a prison official said to him: "I don't believe you have another ten hours to live if you stay in this place. Drop your I.W.W. affiliations, and you can be out of here." Weyh's answer was: "No, I'll die first."

Weyh continued to suffer in jail for another year until he agreed to the Department of Justice's demand that he be deported if his tuberculosis was cured. Weyh was released on January 25, 1922, but never recuperated and died from tuberculosis two years later, on March 22, 1924.[456]

John White, from Ohio, began serving a 21-month prison sentence on October 28, 1918, in Moundsville Penitentiary.[457]

Albert Whitehead was arrested with IWW members in Sacramento and held in the San Francisco County Jail for a year, during which time he contracted tuberculosis.[458]

Earl Whitten, a Working Class Union member from Oklahoma, was sentenced to six years in prison and served from October 6, 1917, until his parole on September 16, 1920.[459]

J. E. Wiggins, from Oklahoma, was sentenced to four years in prison and served in Leavenworth Penitentiary from April 18, 1919, to May 20, 1922.[460]

G. Williams was sentenced to two years in prison and served in Leavenworth Penitentiary from November 26, 1918, to July 4, 1920.[461]

John Williams, of Charleston, South Carolina, was convicted of making "seditious utterances" on May 7, 1918. He served in Atlanta Penitentiary.[462]

George Winski was arrested in November 1917 in the roundup of IWW members in Omaha, Nebraska. After over eighteen months in local jails, all charges against him were dropped.[463]

John H. Wolf, from Sioux Falls, South Dakota, began serving a five-year prison sentence in Leavenworth Penitentiary on May 4, 1918.[464]

Walter Wolski was arrested in November 1917 in the roundup of IWW members in Omaha, Nebraska. After over eighteen months in local jails, all charges against him were dropped.[465]

James Woods, from Wheeling, West Virginia, was sentenced to three years in prison and served in Atlanta Penitentiary from July 6, 1918, to October 26, 1920.[466]

C. J. Woodworth, an IBSA member, began serving a prison sentence on June 21, 1918. (See also the entry for Giovanni De Cecca.)[467]

Thomas Yarkineas, of Jersey City, New Jersey, began serving a four- to ten-year prison sentence on June 14, 1918.[468]

George P. Yarlott, from Kansas, was sentenced to two years and ten months in prison and served in Leavenworth Penitentiary.[469]

Christian Yearous, a sixty-one-year-old farmer from Wisconsin, alleged he was "framed up" under the Espionage Act. After serving a year at Leavenworth Penitentiary, Yearous was bitter. In a letter to the Department of Justice demanding that his name be cleared, Yearous wrote: "I am an old man that the lawyers have robbed of my home and family and the law will not protect me. . . . All I ask is justice."[470]

Adolph F. Younger, a Socialist from Providence, Rhode Island, was sentenced to twenty years in prison and served in Atlanta Penitentiary.[471]

Charles F. Zademack, from Cleveland, Ohio, was sentenced to five years, which was commuted to eighteen months in prison. He served in Atlanta Penitentiary from August 9, 1918, to October 27, 1919.[472]

Nicholas S. Zogg, a civil engineer and an anarchist, was convicted in Los Angeles of violating the Espionage Act and was sentenced to ten years in prison. First confined in McNeil Island Penitentiary, Zogg was transferred to Atlanta Penitentiary because he was in an "advanced stage" of tuberculosis. Although they recognized that Zogg's health was rapidly deteriorating, his jailers continuously denied him proper meals and placed him in isolation. The Department of Justice classified Zogg as "a very dangerous anarchist" who was "absolutely defiant." He was incarcerated from October 15, 1918, to June 1924.[473]

Morris Zucker, a Socialist from Brooklyn, New York, was sentenced to fifteen years in prison for giving a seditious speech.[474]

NOTES

1. National Civil Liberties Bureau, *War Time Prosecutions and Mob Violence* (New York: NCLB, March, 1919), 69: 58, Archives of the American Civil Liberties Union, Princeton University [hereafter NCLB]

2. *Abrams v. United States*, 250 U.S. 616 (1919); U.S. Pardon Attorney, "List of Men Convicted of Violations of the Espionage Act," obtained from the U.S. Pardon Attorney under the Freedom of Information and Privacy Act (FOIPA); Loula D. Lasker, "America and Her Political Prisoners," *Survey*, August 2, 1920, p. 578; "Clemency/Pardon List" [hereafter CLM], National Endowment for the Humanities Youthgrant #AY-20064–81–113 Files and Materials (Washington, DC); Atlanta Penitentiary Record [hereafter Atlanta Record] #10421.

3. Leavenworth Penitentiary Record [hereafter Leavenworth Record] #13100; Department of Justice [hereafter DOJ], memorandum of January 31, 1921.

4. House of Representatives Committee on the Judiciary, *Hearings on Amnesty for Political Prisoners*, 67th Cong., 2nd Session (March 16, 1922) [hereafter HCJ], 32; DOJ Espionage Act Docket Entry, DOJ Files, National Archives [hereafter DOJ Docket Entry]; Leavenworth Record #14801.

5. U.S. Pardon Attorney, "List."

6. Leavenworth Record #13561.

7. Leavenworth Record #13149; Federal Bureau of Investigation [hereafter FBI] Report File #5908 (62–993); Statement of Olin B. Anderson, July 31, 1921, Archives of the American Civil Liberties Union, Princeton University [hereafter ACLU Archives].

8. *Anderson v. United States*, 264 F. 75 (8th Cir. 1920); Leavenworth Record #15401; U.S. Pardon Attorney, "List of So-Called Political Prisoners to Whom the President Has Granted Clemency," December 1921, vol. 267: 80–81, ACLU Archives [hereafter PPL]; CLM; Political Amnesty Committee to U.S. Pardon Attorney, November 27, 1921, with attached "Tenant Farmer Prisoners Confined at Leavenworth, Convicted Under the Espionage Act"; FBI File on Anderson, declassified and released in FBI Freedom of Information and Privacy Act [hereafter FOIPA] #263,824.

9. NCLB.

10. Leavenworth Record #13101.

11. Emma Goldman, *Living My Life* (1931; reprint, New York: Dover, 1970), 671; Philip S. Foner and Sally M. Miller, eds., *Kate Richards O'Hare: Selected Writings and Speeches* (Baton Rouge: Louisiana State University Press, 1982), 207–208; Elizabeth G. Flynn, *The Rebel Girl: An Autobiography* (New York: International Publishers, 1955), 250.

12. U.S. Pardon Attorney, "List"; PPL; CLM; American Civil Liberties Union [hereafter ACLU], "The Truth About the IWW Prisoners" [Pamphlet] (New York: ACLU, 1922); HCJ, 22–26.

13. Leavenworth Record #13148.

14. Leavenworth Record #13102.

15. CLM; NCLB; Loula D. Lasker, "America and Her Political Prisoners," *Survey*, August 2, 1920, pp. 578–592.

16. ACLU, "The Truth"; Leavenworth Record #13116.

17. PPL; CLM.

18. U.S. Pardon Attorney, "List"; U.S. Attorney General, *Letter of March 9, 1922, re Government Prosecutions Under the Espionage Act*, 67th Cong., 2d Sess., 1922, Senate Doc. No. 159.

19. U.S. Attorney General, *Government Prosecutions.*

20. NCLB.

21. U.S. Pardon Attorney, "List"; Atlanta Record #9195; U.S. Attorney General, *Government Prosecutions.*

22. Atlanta Record #7378; NCLB.

23. NCLB.

24. U.S. Pardon Attorney, "List"; DOJ Docket Entry; ACLU leaflet, Political Prisoners in Federal Prison (Feb. 22, 1922) [hereafter PPFP]; Political Amnesty Committee, "Tenant Farmer Prisoners," Vol. 196, ACLU Archives.

25. U.S. Attorney General, Pardon Application (1923); Leavenworth Record #13117.

26. "Political Prisoners in Federal Prisons," February 22, 1922, ACLU Archives [hereafter PPFP]; in miscellaneous files of the author collected under NEH Youthgrant #AY-20064–81–113 [hereafter M]; NCLB; DOJ Memorandum (undated), M; U.S. Attorney General, *Government Prosecutions*; DOJ, "Interpretation of War Statutes," #180 [bulletins issued by DOJ during World War I].

27. NCLB.

28. U.S. Attorney General, *Government Prosecutions.*

29. Atlanta Record #7422; Alexander Berkman, *The Russian Tragedy* (Orkney, England: Cienfuegos Press, 1976) [a collection of reprints of Berkman pamphlets originally published in Germany in 1922]. *Prison Memoirs of an Anarchist* (New York: Mother Earth Publishing, 1912) is Berkman's brilliantly written memoir about his imprisonment for attempting to shoot Henry Clay Frick during the Homestead strike in Pennsylvania; Goldman, *Living My Life.*

30. U.S. Pardon Attorney, "List"; CLM.

31. FBI File on Herbert McCutcheon; declassified and released in FBI FOIPA #271,377; Leavenworth Record #13120.

32. U.S. Pardon Attorney, "List"; PPL; CLM; NCLB; Atlanta Record #10707.

33. U.S. Pardon Attorney, "List"; Winthrop D. Lane, "Uncle Sam: Jailer," *Survey*, September 6, 1919, pp. 800–834; U.S. Attorney General, *Government Prosecutions.*

34. NCLB; U.S. Attorney General, *Government Prosecutions.*

35. Leavenworth Record #13150.

36. NCLB.

37. NCLB.

38. U.S. Pardon Attorney, "List"; CLM.

39. Leavenworth Record #13118.

40. *United States v. Boutin*, 251 F. 313 (N.D.N.Y. 1918).

41. U.S. Pardon Attorney, "List"; U.S. Attorney General, *Government Prosecutions*.

42. Leavenworth Record #13103; Richard Brazier, "A Letter from Ellis Island," *Solidarity*, October 27, 1923.

43. Leavenworth Record #13562.

44. Philip J. Jaffe, *The Rise and Fall of American Communism* (New York: Horizon Press, 1975); *Kansas City Journal*, November 6, 1917; *Kansas City Times*, November 6, 1917; *Kansas City Star*, December 3, 1917.

45. U.S. Pardon Attorney, "List"; CLM; PPFP; Political Amnesty Committee, "Tenant Farmer Prisoners"; Vol. 196, ACLU Archives; DOJ, "Interpretation," #161; HCJ, 70.

46. PPFP; Political Amnesty Committee, "Tenant Farmer Prisoners."

47. CLM; Leavenworth Record #13119; FBI File on Buckley, declassified and released in FOIPA #271,525.

48. U.S. Attorney General, *Government Prosecutions*.

49. Leavenworth Record #13120.

50. Winthrop Lane, "Uncle Sam: Jailer," *Survey*, September 6, 1919, pp. 800–812.

51. NCLB; Lasker, "America and Her Political Prisoners."

52. Leavenworth Record #13585.

53. FBI File on William Hicks, declassified and released in FOIPA #271,504; PPL.

54. Leavenworth Record #13591.

55. U.S. Pardon Attorney, "List."

56. Leavenworth Record #13104; Ralph Chaplin, *Bars and Shadows: The Prison Poems of Ralph Chaplin* (Ridgewood, N.J.: Nellie Seeds Nearing, 1922); Ralph Chaplin, *The Centralia Conspiracy* (Chicago: Charles H. Kerr & Co., 1972); FBI File No. 61–5 and 61–2631; Ralph Chaplin, *Wobbly: The Rough-and-Tumble Story of an American Radical* (Chicago: University of Chicago Press, 1948); Roger Baldwin, interview with author, New Jersey, summer of 1980.

57. U.S. Pardon Attorney, "List"; CLM.

58. U.S. Pardon Attorney, "List."

59. Leavenworth Record #13121; FBI File on Clark, declassified and released in FBI FOIPA #230,301.

60. FBI Files #61–747 and #100–227403; Atlanta Record #10057; Winfield Scott Townley, "Portrait of a Free Man," in *Exiles and Fabrication* (Garden City, N.Y.: Doubleday, 1961); M; Winston Phelps, "Joseph Coldwell, Apostle of Socialism," *Providence Sunday Journal*, September 1, 1946; Obituary, *New York Times*, June 16, 1949; DOJ, "Interpretation," #158.

61. Political Amnesty Committee, "Tenant Farmer Prisoners."

62. Leavenworth Record #13563.

63. Leavenworth Record #13564.

64. NCLB.

65. Leavenworth Record #13123.

66. U.S. Attorney General, *Government Prosecutions*; U.S. Pardon Attorney, "List"; PPFP; Political Amnesty Committee, "Tenant Farmer Prisoners."

67. U.S. Attorney General, *Government Prosecutions*.

68. PPL; CLM; Political Amnesty Committee, "Tenant Farmer Prisoners"; FBI File on Hicks, declassified and released in FBI FOIPA #271,504; DOJ, "Interpretation," #3161.

69. Political Amnesty Committee, "Tenant Farmer Prisoners."

70. DOJ Docket Entry; PPFP; Political Amnesty Committee, "Tenant Farmer Prisoners"; Leavenworth Record #12941.

71. *Schaefer v. United States*, 251 U.S. 466 (1920); NCLB; DOJ, "Interpretation," #181.

72. Leavenworth Record #13124.

73. U.S. Attorney General, *Government Prosecutions.*

74. Leavenworth Record #13565; FBI File on De Bernardi, declassified and released in FBI FOIPA #232,304.

75. Eugene V. Debs, *Walls and Bars* (Chicago: Kerr Publishing, 1927); Daniel Bell, *Marxian Socialism in the United States* (Princeton, N.J.: Princeton University Press, 1967); DOJ, U.S. Pardon Attorney files obtained under FOIPA; U.S. Department of Justice, Attorney General H. M. Daugherty to President Warren G. Harding, "In the Matter of the Application for Pardon in Behalf of Eugene V. Debs," DOJ Memorandum 35–386–3336, December 23, 1921, Yale University Library; *Debs v. United States*, 249 U.S. 211 (1919).

76. Atlanta Record #8764.

77. NCLB.

78. NCLB.

79. Lasker, "America and Her Political Prisoners"; U.S. Pardon Attorney, "List"; CLM; NCLB; DOJ, "Interpretation," #202.

80. NCLB; DOJ, "Interpretation," #167.

81. Leavenworth Record #13151.

82. Leavenworth Record #13125; FBI File #61–1489.

83. NCLB.

84. Leavenworth Record #13566; *Industrial Worker*, May 17, 1924.

85. U.S. Pardon Attorney, "List"; U.S. Attorney General, *Government Prosecutions.*

86. Ammon A. Hennesey, letter of March 24, 1918, on political prisoners in Atlanta, Georgia, ACLU Archives [hereafter PPA].

87. NCLB.

88. U.S. Pardon Attorney, "List"; Leavenworth Record #14803.

89. Leavenworth Record #13567.

90. DOJ Docket Entry; Leavenworth Record #12031.

91. Leavenworth Record #13105.

92. NCLB.

93. U.S. Pardon Attorney, "List."

94. NCLB.

95. Leavenworth Record #13568.

96. Leavenworth Record #13152.

97. U.S. Attorney General, *Government Prosecutions;* DOJ, "Interpretation," #170.

98. Leavenworth Record #13592.

99. NCLB.

100. NCLB.

101. NCLB; Flynn, *Rebel Girl,* 240, 252; DOJ, "Interpretation," #172.

102. NCLB.

103. NCLB.

104. Department of Interior Medical Certificate (Government Hospital for the Insane); Leavenworth Record #13569; B. Salmon to R. Baldwin, letter of August 29, 1921, ACLU Archives; *Labor Unity*, February 8, 1923; Joyce Kornbluh, *Rebel Voices: An IWW Anthology* (Ann Arbor: University of Michigan Press, 1968).

105. U.S. Pardon Attorney, "List."

106. NCLB.

107. U.S. Pardon Attorney, "List."

108. NCLB.

109. U.S. Pardon Attorney, "List"; PPL; Loula D. Lasker, "America and Her Political Prisoners," *Survey*, August 2, 1920, pp. 578–582; DOJ Docket Entry; CLM; NCLB.

110. NCLB; DOJ, "Interpretation," #119.

111. Leavenworth Record #13126; *New York Times*, July 11, 1949; FBI File #61–1489.

112. U.S. Pardon Attorney, "List"; FBI File on Sam Forbes, declassified and released in FBI FOIPA #271,434.

113. U.S. Pardon Attorney, "List"; NCLB; Flynn, *Rebel Girl*, 254.

114. NCLB.

115. Leavenworth Record #13154.

116. ACLU, "The Truth."

117. Leavenworth Record #13155.

118. Leavenworth Record #13588.

119. *Frohwerk v. United States*, 249 U.S. 204 (1919); NCLB; DOJ, "Interpretation," #128.

120. S. Reid Spencer, "Get Gale Out of Prison," Socialist Party Collection, Duke University.

121. Leavenworth Record #14802.

122. NCLB.

123. U.S. Pardon Attorney, Application for Executive Clemency, March 13, 1919, Files of Pardon Attorney, National Archives.

124. U.S. Attorney General, *Government Prosecutions.*

125. NCLB.

126. NCLB.

127. Leavenworth Record #12419; DOJ Docket Entry; CLM; DOJ Memorandum, February 13, 1919.

128. NCLB; DOJ, "Interpretation," #128.

129. See Chapter 3 for Alexander Berkman's closing remarks to the jury.

130. Goldman, *Living My Life*; Alix Kates Shulman, ed., *Red Emma Speaks: Selected Writings and Speeches by Emma Goldman* (New York: Vintage Books, 1972); Obituary, *New York Times*, May 14, 1940.

131. U.S. Pardon Attorney, "List"; Loula D. Lasker, "America and Her Political Prisoners," *Survey*, August 2, 1920, pp. 578–582; CLM.

132. CLM; Leavenworth Record #13122.

133. Leavenworth Record #14805.

134. U.S. Pardon Attorney, "List"; CLM.

135. Leavenworth Record #13156.

136. NCLB.
137. U.S. Pardon Attorney, "List."
138. Leavenworth Record #13570.
139. Leavenworth Record #13571; FBI File on Harry Gray, declassified and released in FBI FOIPA #232,326
140. Leavenworth Record #13127.
141. M.
142. Leavenworth Record #13157; U.S. Pardon Attorney, "List."
143. U.S. Pardon Attorney, "List"; FBI File on A. Gross released in FOIPA #271,504.
144. DOJ Docket Entry.
145. PPA.
146. Leavenworth Record #13128; PPL; U.S. Pardon Attorney, "List"; CLM.
147. DOJ Docket Entry; CLM.
148. Leavenworth Record #13572.
149. U.S. Attorney General, *Government Prosecutions.*
150. U.S. Pardon Attorney, "List."
151. DOJ Docket Entry; NCLB; Leavenworth Record #12496.
152. U.S. Pardon Attorney, "List."
153. DOJ Docket Entry; Leavenworth Record #12032.
154. DOJ, "Interpretation," #76; U.S. Pardon Attorney, "List."
155. NCLB.
156. NCLB.
157. U.S. Pardon Attorney, "List"; CLM; DOJ, "Interpretation," #161.
158. Leavenworth Record #13158.
159. U.S. Pardon Attorney, "List"; CLM; Atlanta Record #10608.
160. NCLB.
161. Leavenworth Record #13106; FBI File #61–2494; Bryan D. Palmer, "Big Bill Haywood's Defection to Russia and the IWW: Two Letters," *Labor History* 17 (Spring 1976): 271; William D. Haywood, *Bill Haywood's Book: The Autobiography of William D. Haywood* (New York: International Publishers, 1929).
162. U.S. Pardon Attorney, "List"; PPL; NCLB; DOJ Docket Entry; FBI File on William Hicks, declassified and released in FBI FOIPA #271,504.
163. U.S. Pardon Attorney, "List."
164. NCLB; FBI File on Edgar Held, declassified and released in FBI FOIPA #271,495.
165. NCLB.
166. NCLB.
167. NCLB; PPA; Ammon Hennesey, *The Book of Ammon* (Salt Lake City: Ammon Hennesey, 1965).
168. U.S. Pardon Attorney, "List."
169. DOJ Docket Entry; CLM; NCLB; FBI File on E. Herman, declassified and released in FBI FOIPA #271,347.
170. U.S. Pardon Attorney, "List"; CLM; Atlanta Record #10601.
171. U.S. Pardon Attorney, "List"; CLM; NCLB; FBI File on W. Heynachner, declassified and released in FBI FOIPA #271,507.
172. NCLB.

173. *New York Call*, April 27, 1922; U.S. Pardon Attorney, "List"; PPFP; NCLB; Vol. 196, ACLU Archives; DOJ, "Interpretation," #160; FBI FOIPA #271,504.

174. U.S. Pardon Attorney, "List"; U.S. Attorney General, *Government Prosecutions.*

175. U.S. Attorney General, *Government Prosecutions.*

176. PPA.

177. NCLB; DOJ, "Interpretation," #122.

178. U.S. Pardon Attorney, "List."

179. Leavenworth Record #13573.

180. Political Amnesty Committee, "Tenant Farmer Prisoners"; Leavenworth Record #13834.

181. Leavenworth Record #13159; ACLU, "The Truth"; FBI File on C. Hough, declassified and released in FBI FOIPA #232,330.

182. U.S. Pardon Attorney, "List"; DOJ Docket Entry; CLM; U.S. Attorney General, *Government Prosecutions.*

183. U.S. Pardon Attorney, "List."

184. Leavenworth Record #13160.

185. DOJ Docket Entry; Atlanta Record #8907.

186. DOJ, "Interpretation," #23 (1917); U.S. Pardon Attorney, "List"; DOJ Docket Entry; CLM; DOJ, *Attorney General's Annual Report* (1920).

187. U.S. Pardon Attorney, "List"; DOJ Docket Entry; CLM; U.S. Attorney General, *Government Prosecutions*; DOJ, "Interpretation," #23.

188. Leavenworth Record #13129.

189. NCLB.

190. DOJ Docket Entry; CLM; NCLB; Leavenworth Record #12735; U.S. Attorney General, *Government Prosecutions.*

191. NCLB.

192. DOJ Docket Entry.

193. NCLB.

194. Leavenworth #13130; U.S. Pardon Attorney to U.S. Attorney General, memorandum of January 31, 1921, National Archives.

195. DOJ Docket Entry; Leavenworth Record #13076.

196. DOJ Docket Entry.

197. NCLB.

198. Leavenworth Record #13161; FBI Report #100–12358–3.

199. DOJ Docket Entry; NCLB; DOJ, "Interpretation," #134.

200. DOJ Docket Entry.

201. U.S. Pardon Attorney, "List"; CLM.

202. NCLB; DOJ, "Interpretation," #174.

203. NCLB.

204. DOJ Docket Entry; NCLB.

205. *Krafft v. United States*, 249 F. 919 (3d Cir. 1918); NCLB.

206. Atlanta Record #7379; NCLB.

207. *Solidarity*, March 8, 1919, and May 3, 1919.

208. NCLB.

209. DOJ Docket Entry; NCLB.

210. NCLB.

211. NCLB.

212. U.S. Pardon Attorney, "List"; Loula D. Lasker, "America and Her Political Prisoners," *Survey*, August 2, 1910, pp. 578–582; CLM.

213. U.S. Pardon Attorney, "List."

214. Leavenworth Record #13107.

215. NCLB.

216. NCLB.

217. DOJ Docket Entry; Leavenworth Record #13074.

218. NCLB.

219. U.S. Pardon Attorney, "List."

220. U.S. Pardon Attorney, "List"; Leavenworth Record #13108; U.S. Attorney General, *Government Prosecutions*, HCJ, 26.

221. Leavenworth Record #13131; Jack Law, "Statement," April 20, 1921, Special Collections, Yale University Library.

222. DOJ Docket Entry.

223. NCLB.

224. U.S. Pardon Attorney, Application for Executive Clemency, Files of the U.S. Pardon Attorney, National Archives, [hereafter AEC].

225. *Schaefer v. United States*, 251 U.S. 466 (1920); DOJ Docket Entry; CLM; NCLB; DOJ, "Interpretation," #181.

226. Leavenworth Record #13162.

227. Leavenworth Record #13163.

228. AEC, September 15, 1919; U.S. Pardon Attorney, "List"; CLM; NCLB; Atlanta Record #8858.

229. Atlanta Record #10420; U.S. Pardon Attorney, "List"; Loula D. Lasker, "America and Her Political Prisoners," *Survey*, August 2, 1920, pp. 578–582; CLM; NCLB.

230. Leavenworth Record #13164.

231. Leavenworth Record #13132.

232. Leavenworth Record #13109.

233. Leavenworth Record #13574.

234. Leavenworth Record #13165.

235. U.S. Pardon Attorney, "List"; CLM; NCLB; AEC, October 28, 1919.

236. FBI File #100–2754; NCLB.

237. Leavenworth Record #14596.

238. *Magón v. United States*, 260 F. 811 (9th Cir. 1919); Leavenworth Record #12839; FBI Report #190–27627.

239. Leavenworth Record #13166.

240. NCLB.

241. U.S. Pardon Attorney, "List"; U.S. Attorney General, *Government Prosecutions*.

242. DOJ Docket Entry; Leavenworth Record #12033.

243. NCLB.

244. Leavenworth Record #13167.

245. NCLB.

246. NCLB.

247. Leavenworth Record #13134; HCJ, 10.

248. NCLB; DOJ, "Interpretation," #119.

249. U.S. Pardon Attorney, "List"; Atlanta Record #8916; DOJ, "Interpretation," #157.

250. DOJ Docket Entry; CLM; Leavenworth Record #12319.

251. NCLB.

252. NCLB.

253. DOJ Docket Entry; CLM; NCLB; FBI File on Walter Mattbey, declassified and released in FBI FOIPA #271,312; U.S. Attorney General, *Government Prosecutions.*

254. DOJ Docket Entry; Leavenworth Record #12034.

255. DOJ Docket Entry.

256. U.S. Pardon Attorney, "List"; U.S. Attorney General, *Government Prosecutions.*

257. Leavenworth Record #13168; ACLU, *The Truth about the IWW Prisoners* (New York: ACLU, 1922).

258. Atlanta Record #7510; U.S. Pardon Attorney, "List"; Letter from Hennesey to *The Call,* March 24, 1918, 26: 143, ACLU Archives.

259. U.S. Pardon Attorney, "List"; FBI File on H. McCutcheon, declassified and released in FBI FOIPA #271,377.

260. Leavenworth Record #13133.

261. Leavenworth Record #13170, DOJ Docket Entry.

262. U.S. Attorney General, *Government Prosecutions;* DOJ Report #35–438; Leavenworth Record #13575.

263. U.S. Pardon Attorney, "List"; U.S. Attorney General, *Government Prosecutions.*

264. DOJ Docket Entry.

265. NCLB.

266. U.S. Pardon Attorney, "List"; DOJ Docket Entry; CLM; NCLB; DOJ, "Interpretation," #103.

267. DOJ Docket Entry.

268. NCLB.

269. NCLB.

270. Leavenworth Record #13135; Vol. 217, ACLU Archives.

271. U.S. Pardon Attorney, "List"; U.S. Attorney General, *Government Prosecutions.*

272. NCLB; DOJ, "Interpretation," #104.

273. DOJ Docket Entry.

274. NCLB.

275. NCLB.

276. DOJ Docket Entry.

277. U.S. Pardon Attorney, "List."

278. Leavenworth Record #13171.

279. U.S. Pardon Attorney, "List"; Atlanta Record #9427.

280. U.S. Pardon Attorney, "List."

281. U.S. Pardon Attorney, "List"; DOJ Docket Entry; DOJ, "Interpretation," #23; CLM.

282. U.S. Pardon Attorney, "List"; Leavenworth Record #13589.

283. U.S. Pardon Attorney, "List"; DOJ Docket Entry; PPFP; Political Amnesty Committee, "Tenant Farmer Prisoners."

284. U.S. Pardon Attorney, "List"; PPL; CLM; Vol. 165, ACLU Archives; HCJ, 45.

285. Leavenworth Record #13110; FBI File #61–1489.

286. U.S. Pardon Attorney, "List"; DOJ Docket Entry; CLM; Atlanta Record #9272; FBI File on M. Nehring, declassified and released in FBI FOIPA #271,285.

287. U.S. Pardon Attorney, "List"; CLM.

288. NCLB.

289. Leavenworth Record #13704.

290. Leavenworth Record #13172.

291. "Political Prisoners in Federal Prisons," January 13, 1922, Socialist Party Collection, Duke University, *O'Connell v. United States*, 253 U.S. 142 (1920); HCJ, 2, 18–20, 61–64.

292. Leavenworth Record #13576.

293. U.S. Pardon Attorney, "List"; CLM.

294. Foner and Miller, *Kate Richards O'Hare*, Emma Goldman, "Kate Richards O'Hare," address at testimonial dinner, November 17, 1919, Tamiment Collection, New York University; Goldman to "H. W.," June 29, 1919, Alexander Berkman's Atlanta Prison Record; W. E. Zeuch, "The Truth About the O'Hare Case" [Pamphlet] (St. Louis: Frank P. O'Hare, undated); FBI File #61–1215; O'Hare Letters, Socialist Party Collection, Duke University.

295. Leavenworth Record #13173.

296. NCLB.

297. NCLB; Scott Nearing, *The Making of a Radical* (New York: Harper Colophon Books, 1972).

298. NCLB.

299. U.S. Pardon Attorney, "List"; Atlanta Record #10604.

300. U.S. Pardon Attorney, "List."

301. U.S. Pardon Attorney, "List"; U.S. Attorney General, *Government Prosecutions.*

302. Leavenworth Record #13136.

303. Leavenworth Record #13174; FBI Report #190–27627.

304. NCLB.

305. U.S. Pardon Attorney, "List."

306. NCLB.

307. U.S. Pardon Attorney, "List"; NCLB; Lasker, "America and Her Political Prisoners"; FBI File on Joseph Pass, declassified and released in FBI FOIPA #271,426.

308. U.S. Pardon Attorney, "List"; NCLB; Lasker, "America and Her Political Prisoners."

309. U.S. Pardon Attorney, "List"; U.S. Attorney General, *Government Prosecutions.*

310. NCLB.

311. U.S. Pardon Attorney, "List"; Leavenworth Record #13137.

312. DOJ Docket Entry; NCLB.

313. AEC, April 4, 1919; DOJ Memorandum #198934.

314. PPA.

315. Leavenworth Record #13175.

316. DOJ, "Interpretation," #23; U.S. Pardon Attorney, "List"; PPL; DOJ Docket Entry; CLM.

317. U.S. Pardon Attorney, "List."

318. DOJ Docket Entry; NCLB; Lasker, "America and Her Political Prisoners."

319. DOJ Docket Entry.

320. U.S. Pardon Attorney, "List"; DOJ Docket Entry.

321. Leavenworth Record #13176.

322. U.S. Pardon Attorney, "List"; U.S. Attorney General, *Government Prosecutions.*

323. DOJ Docket Entry; Leavenworth Record #12036.

324. Leavenworth Record #13577.

325. S. J. Powell, "In the Bryant Case et al.," 1919, Socialist Party Collection, Duke University; PPFP; Political Amnesty Committee, "Tenant Farmer Prisoners," Leavenworth Record #14765.

326. Loula D. Lasker, "America and Her Political Prisoners," *Survey,* August 2, 1920, pp. 578–582; CLM; NCLB.

327. Leavenworth Record #13138; U.S. Pardon Attorney, "List."

328. U.S. Pardon Attorney, "List"; U.S. Attorney General, *Government Prosecutions.*

329. *United States v. Prieth,* 254 F. 946 (D.N.J. 1918); NCLB; DOJ, "Interpretation," #130, #156.

330. DOJ Docket Entry; CLM; Leavenworth Record #12320.

331. Leavenworth Record #13578.

332. Leavenworth Record #13579.

333. DOJ Docket Entry; NCLB; FBI File on F. Ramp, #61–342.

334. U.S. Pardon Attorney, "List"; PPFP; Socialist Party, "Political Prisoners in Federal Prisons," January 15, 1922, Socialist Party Collection, Duke University.

335. NCLB; DOJ Memorandum #193941, February 4, 1919.

336. Atlanta Record #8999; U.S. Pardon Attorney, "List"; DOJ Docket Entry; CLM.

337. NCLB.

338. DOJ Docket Entry.

339. U.S. Pardon Attorney, "List"; CLM; PPFP; Political Amnesty Committee, "Tenant Farmer Prisoners"; Vol. 196, ACLU Archives; DOJ, "Interpretation," #161; HCJ, 70.

340. DOJ Memorandum, March 14, 1919.

341. U.S. Pardon Attorney, "List."

342. NCLB.

343. U.S. Pardon Attorney, "List"; CLM.

344. Leavenworth Record #13111; Rey statement, Yale University Library.

345. U.S. Pardon Attorney, "List"; DOJ Docket Entry; DOJ, "Interpretation," #107.

346. Leavenworth Record #13139.

347. "In the Case of G. T. Bryant, et al.," Socialist Party Collection, Duke University; Leavenworth Record #14766.

348. *New York Leader,* October 6, 1923; Fred Leighton, "Vindictive Action of U.S. Officials," *Federated Press,* August 25, 1923; DOJ Report #35–473; *Magón v. United*

States, 260 Fed. 811 (9th Cir. 1919); U.S. Pardon Attorney, "List"; DOJ Docket Entry; PPFP; NCLB.

349. DOJ Docket Entry; Leavenworth Record #12903.

350. U.S. Pardon Attorney, "List"; DOJ Docket Entry; CLM.

351. NCLB; DOJ, "Interpretation," #119.

352. U.S. Attorney General, *Government Prosecutions.*

353. NCLB.

354. NCLB.

355. NCLB.

356. Leavenworth Record #13112.

357. Leavenworth Record #13113.

358. NCLB.

359. NCLB.

360. NCLB.

361. CLM; NCLB.

362. U.S. Pardon Attorney, memorandum for U.S. Attorney General, December 10, 1923; FBI File #61–1181; Leavenworth Record #13144; James P. Cannon, *The First Ten Years of American Communism* (New York: Pathfinder Press, 1973); Melvyn Dubofsky, *We Shall Be All: A History of the IWW* (New York: Quadrangle, 1969); Flynn, *Rebel Girl.*

363. U.S. Pardon Attorney, "List"; CLM; Atlanta Record #8859.

364. DOJ Docket Entry; Atlanta Record #7635; PPA.

365. NCLB.

366. Leavenworth Record #13580.

367. Leavenworth Record #14806.

368. U.S. Pardon Attorney, "List."

369. AEC, February 10, 1919.

370. Leavenworth Record #13114; FBI File on Sam Scarlett, declassified and released in FBI FOIPA #232,358.

371. NCLB.

372. NCLB.

373. DOJ Docket Entry; Leavenworth Record #13366; AEC, November 22, 1917.

374. NCLB.

375. DOJ Docket Entry.

376. U.S. Attorney General, *Government Prosecutions;* U.S. Pardon Attorney, "List."

377. DOJ Docket Entry; NCLB; DOJ, "Interpretation," #149.

378. DOJ Docket Entry; CLM; Morganstern to Wilson, August 12, 1919, ACLU Archives.

379. U.S. Pardon Attorney, "List"; PPL; DOJ Docket Entry; CLM; FBI File on William Hicks, declassified and released in FBI FOIPA #271,504.

380. NCLB.

381. DOJ Docket Entry; CLM; NCLB; *Seebach v. United States,* 262 F. 885 (8th Cir. 1919).

382. U.S. Pardon Attorney, "List"; CLM.

383. U.S. Pardon Attorney, "List"; CLM; NCLB; DOJ, "Interpretation," #125, #190.

384. Leavenworth Record #13140.

385. DOJ Docket Entry; NCLB.

386. U.S. Pardon Attorney, "List"; DOJ Docket Entry; CLM; DOJ, "Interpretation," #23.

387. Lane, "Uncle Sam: Jailer."

388. DOJ, "Interpretation," #23; U.S. Pardon Attorney, "List"; DOJ Docket Entry; CLM; Political Amnesty Committee, "Tenant Farmer Prisoners"; U.S. Attorney General, *Government Prosecutions.*

389. *Industrial Worker,* October 27, 1923, and December 18, 1923; Leavenworth Prison #13141; FBI File on A. Sinclair, declassified and released in FBI FOIPA #232,360.

390. DOJ Docket Entry.

391. Leavenworth Record #13142.

392. NCLB.

393. U.S. Pardon Attorney, "List"; CLM; Atlanta Record #10615.

394. U.S. Pardon Attorney, "List"; PPL; CLM; Atlanta Record #8590.

395. DOJ Docket Entry; CLM.

396. DOJ, "Interpretation," #23; U.S. Pardon Attorney, "List"; DOJ Docket Entry; CLM.

397. U.S. Pardon Attorney, "List"; DOJ Docket Entry; Political Amnesty Committee, "Tenant Farmer Prisoners"; U.S. Attorney General, *Government Prosecutions.*

398. Leavenworth Record #13581.

399. U.S. Pardon Attorney, "List"; U.S. Attorney General, *Government Prosecutions.*

400. Howard Zinn, *A People's History of the United States* (New York: Harper & Row, 1980), 59.

401. U.S. Pardon Attorney, "List"; Political Amnesty Committee, "Tenant Farmer Prisoners."

402. NCLB.

403. *Abrams v. United States,* 250 U.S. 616 (1919); Zosa Szajkowski, "Double Jeopardy—the Abrams Case of 1919," April 1971, American Jewish Archives; Margaret S. Marsh, *Anarchist Women, 1870–1920* (Philadelphia: Temple University Press, 1981); FBI File #94–1–19363-X.

404. Leavenworth Record #13143; Memorandum to U.S. Attorney General, January 31, 1921, National Archives and Record Service File on Ahlteen.

405. DOJ Docket Entry; NCLB.

406. PPA.

407. DOJ Docket Entry; CLM.

408. DOJ Docket Entry; NCLB.

409. U.S. Pardon Attorney, "List"; Loula D. Lasker, "America and Her Political Prisoners"; PPL *Survey,* August 2, 1920, pp. 578–582; DOJ Docket Entry; CLM; FBI File on Hicks, declassified and released in FBI FOIPA #271,504.

410. NCLB.

411. Leavenworth Record #13587.

412. AEC, April 8, 1919; NCLB.

413. Political Amnesty Committee, "Tenant Farmer Prisoners."

414. DOJ Docket Entry; NCLB; Leavenworth Record #13847; *United States v. Sugarman,* 245 F. 604 (D. Minn. 1917); DOJ, "Interpretation," #195.

415. Political Amnesty Committee, "Tenant Farmer Prisoners"; Leavenworth

Record #14320; Labor Defense Council, "Nine Questions and Eight Answers About the Michigan 'Red Raid' Cases," [Undated pamphlet], M; FBI FOIPA #271,273.

416. NCLB.

417. U.S. Pardon Attorney, "List"; CLM.

418. "Political Prisoners in Federal Prisons," January 13, 1922, Socialist Party Collection, Duke University; PPFP; HCJ, 2.

419. Leavenworth Record #13582.

420. NCLB.

421. DOJ Docket Entry.

422. Leavenworth Prison Record #13177.

423. NCLB; DOJ, "Interpretation," #108.

424. Leavenworth Record #13145.

425. Leavenworth Record #13583.

426. U.S. Pardon Attorney, "List"; CLM.

427. NCLB; PPA.

428. PPL; FBI File on Hicks, declassified and released in FBI FOIPA #271,504.

429. U.S. Pardon Attorney, "List."

430. U.S. Pardon Attorney, "List"; DOJ Docket Entry.

431. DOJ Docket Entry.

432. Leavenworth Record #13146.

433. NCLB; DOJ, "Interpretation," #119.

434. Leavenworth Record #13584; DOJ Docket Entry.

435. Judgment reversal, *Schaefer v. United States*, 251 U.S. 466 (1920); DOJ Docket Entry; DOJ, "Interpretation," #181.

436. Leavenworth Record #13048; DOJ Docket Entry; NCLB.

437. U.S. Pardon Attorney, "List."

438. Atlanta Record #8187; NCLB; Loula D. Lasker, "America and Her Political Prisoners," *Survey*, August 2, 1920, pp. 578–582; DOJ, "Interpretation," #79.

439. DOJ Docket Entry; Letter from U.S. Attorney to U.S. Attorney General, July 14, 1919, National Archives and Records Service.

440. U.S. Pardon Attorney, "List."

441. Leavenworth Record #13147; FBI File #61–1489.

442. Atlanta Record #8974.

443. NCLB.

444. DOJ Docket Entry.

445. NCLB.

446. NCLB.

447. NCLB.

448. Nathan L. Welch, "Iron Heel in Leavenworth Prison," *New Solidarity* (February 1919); *New York Call*, April 29, 1918.

449. U.S. Pardon Attorney, "List"; CLM; NCLB; FBI File on J. Pass, declassified and released in FBI FOIPA #271,426.

450. U.S. Pardon Attorney, "List"; U.S. Attorney General, *Government Prosecutions*.

451. Leavenworth Record #14804.

452. DOJ Docket Entry; CLM; NCLB; *Schaefer v. United States*, 251 U.S. 466 (1920).

453. Atlanta Record #8824; DOJ Docket Entry; NCLB.

454. Leavenworth Record #13178.

455. Leavenworth Record #13179; FBI Report #190–27627.

456. Leavenworth Record #1318; *Industrial Worker*, March 22, 1924; Pierce C. Wetter, "The Men I Left at Leavenworth," *Survey*, October 1922.

457. *White v. United States*, 263 F. 17 (6th Cir. 1920); DOJ Docket Entry.

458. IWW, "The Silent Defense" [Pamphlet] (Chicago: IWW, undated), 7.

459. U.S. Pardon Attorney, "List"; DOJ Docket Entry; CLM; DOJ, "Interpretation," #23.

460. U.S. Pardon Attorney, "List"; PPFP; Political Amnesty Committee, "Tenant Farmer Prisoners"; U.S. Attorney General, *Government Prosecutions.*

461. U.S. Pardon Attorney, "List"; DOJ Docket Entry.

462. DOJ Docket Entry; NCLB.

463. NCLB.

464. DOJ, "Interpretation," #81; DOJ Docket Entry; NCLB.

465. NCLB.

466. U.S. Pardon Attorney, "List"; Atlanta Record #8740.

467. NCLB; DOJ, "Interpretation," #119.

468. NCLB.

469. U.S. Attorney General, *Government Prosecutions.*

470. DOJ Docket Entry; FBI File on C. Yearous, declassified and released in FBI FOIPA #271,273.

471. PPA.

472. DOJ Docket Entry; CLM; Atlanta Record #8823.

473. Atlanta Record #9657; U.S. Pardon Attorney, "List"; DOJ Docket Entry; FBI File on N. Zogg, declassified and released in FBI FOIPA #271,268; HCJ, 2, 59.

474. NCLB.

Chapter 13

State Anti-Sedition and Criminal Syndicalism Prisoners

The following is a list of persons incarcerated for at least one year under various state criminal syndicalism, anti-anarchy or other sedition laws.

CALIFORNIA CRIMINAL SYNDICALISM ACT PRISONERS

J. C. Allen, from Eureka, received a three-year prison sentence for having an IWW membership card and served in San Quentin from April 27, 1924, until his term expired.[1]

Louis Allen, an IWW member from Los Angeles, received a one- to fourteen-year prison sentence and served in Folsom from December 1921 to September 11, 1925. At Folsom guards placed a blanket over Allen's head and beat him until he became "insensible."[2]

A. E. Anderson received a four-year prison sentence for giving testimony in court on behalf of a fellow member of the IWW and served in San Quentin from September 20, 1923, to 1926. (See also the entry for J. A. Casdorf.)[3]

Charles Andrews, an IWW member from Los Angeles, received a three-year prison sentence, which he served in San Quentin.[4]

Frank Bailey, an IWW member from Sacramento, received a four-year prison sentence, which he served in San Quentin from March 1923 until his term expired.[5]

William Baker, an IWW member from Los Angeles, received a one- to fourteen-year prison sentence, which he served in San Quentin from December 1921 to March 11, 1925.[6]

Fred Bamman, an IWW member from Portola, received a four-year prison sentence, which he served in San Quentin from October 29, 1923, until his term expired.[7]

Ivan Barnes, from Portola, received a four-year prison sentence, which he served in San Quentin from October 29, 1923, until his term expired.[8]

Jack Beavert, from Eureka, received a three-year prison sentence, which he served in San Quentin from April 27, 1924, until his term expired.[9]

Richard Bendig, an IWW member from Los Angeles, received a one- to fourteen-year prison sentence, which he served in San Quentin from December 1921 to June 9, 1923.[10]

C. F. Bentley, an IWW member from Stockton, received a one- to fourteen-year prison sentence.[11]

Harold Bird, an IWW member from Portola, received a four-year prison sentence, which he served in San Quentin from October 29, 1923, until his parole.[12]

Albin Bratland, from Sacramento, received a four-year prison sentence, which he served in San Quentin from September 17, 1923, to 1926.[13]

John Bruns, an IWW member from Lasco, received a four-year prison sentence, which he served in San Quentin from November 12, 1924, until his term expired.[14]

William Bryan, from Eureka, received a four-year prison sentence for having an IWW membership card and served in San Quentin from April 27, 1924, until his term expired.[15]

William Burns was arrested in Yosemite National Park for violating the California criminal syndicalism law by organizing for the IWW and "knowingly" becoming a member of the union. He was arrested in April 1923 and served approximately seventeen months in the county jail while awaiting trial. Because he was arrested in a federal park, Burns was tried in federal court. His jury consisted of a bank president, a "real estate shark," a deputy sheriff, the superintendent of a bonding company and other persons with admitted prejudice against the IWW. Burns received a fifteen-month prison sentence, which he served in Leavenworth Penitentiary from November 1927 until May 14, 1928, when his sentence was commuted by President Calvin Coolidge.[16]

Roy A. Carter, an IWW member from Portola, received a four-year prison sentence, which he served in San Quentin from October 29, 1923, until his term expired.[17]

J. A. Casdorf, an IWW member from Sacramento, received a five-year prison sentence, which he served in San Quentin from May 6, 1922, to December 5, 1923.

Along with codefendant Earl Firey, Casdorf was charged with the crime of being a member of the IWW, an organization that illegally advocated "criminal syndicalism."

After the defendants' first two witnesses (P. Beasley and Charles B. La Rue) testified, the witnesses were promptly arrested under the California criminal syndicalism law. Thereafter the prosecuting state attorney declared in the presence of other potential witnesses that "all witnesses who would thereafter take the stand in this case and admit they were paid up members of the IWW in good standing, would be arrested."

The defense pleaded that such statements by the prosecution were prejudicial, that "other witnesses" were "intimidated and terrorized so as to render them less efficient as witnesses" and that other prospective witnesses were "scared away." The trial judge overruled these objections, and eventually eight other IWW members who took the stand were arrested.

On appeal, the California District Court of Appeals affirmed Casdorf's conviction. The court held that the "propriety" of the district attorney's action was "debatable," but that he "acted in good faith" merely to "warn" witnesses of the "consequence[s]" of their testimony. The court held that there was "no prejudice to the substantial rights of the defendants."

After the Casdorf conviction, the ten witnesses who took the stand on his behalf were all tried and convicted under the criminal syndicalism law. These convictions were also upheld in *People v. LaRue*, 216 P. 627 (Cal. App. 1923).[18]

Pat Casey, an IWW member from Oakland, received a five-year prison sentence, which he served in San Quentin from November 1921 to January 1926.[19]

Hugo Cederholm, an IWW member from Los Angeles, received a four-year prison sentence, which he served in San Quentin from July 12, 1923, until his term expired.[20]

J. B. Childs, from Los Angeles, received a four-year prison sentence, which he served in San Quentin from July 12, 1923, until his term expired. Four months into his term at San Quentin, on November 16, Childs was beaten by a guard so severely that his head required four stitches; both his arms were "discolored," and one of them bore a "deep cut." To protest the guard's brutality toward Childs, seventy-one IWW prisoners launched a work strike. They were all subsequently put "in solitary confinement on bread and water."[21]

Joseph Clohessy, an IWW member from Los Angeles, received a five-year prison sentence, which he served in Folsom from July 12, 1923, until his term expired.[22]

Tom Connors, an IWW officer, served a prison sentence in San Quentin from June 2, 1925, to February 1927.

Connors was secretary of the IWW General Defense Committee in California. During his criminal syndicalism trial in Maryville, a prospective juror obtained a copy of literature printed by the General Defense Committee. The state of California dropped the criminal syndicalism charge against Connors and tried him for "corruptly attempting to influence a juror." Connors went through three trials on this charge. The first trial resulted in a hung jury; the second resulted in a conviction that was reversed by an appellate court. At the third trial Connors was found guilty and sentenced to three years of imprisonment.[23]

Frank Cox, an IWW member from Eureka, received a four-year prison sentence for attending an IWW meeting and "taking minutes" and served in San Quentin from April 10, 1923, until his term expired.[24]

John Craig, an IWW member from Sacramento, received a one- to fourteen-year prison sentence, which he served in San Quentin from June 6, 1920, to March 1922.[25]

Charles Crowley, an IWW member from Portola, received a three-year prison sentence, which he served in San Quentin from October 29, 1923, until his parole.[26]

Ed Dawe, an IWW member from Maryville, received a four-year prison sentence, which he served in San Quentin from November 7, 1923, until his term expired.[27]

C. A. Drew, an IWW member from Susanville, received a four-year prison sentence, which he served in San Quentin from March 31, 1923, until his term expired.[28]

Daniel Duffy, an IWW member, received a one- to fourteen-year prison sentence on December 9, 1921, and became a fugitive from the law.[29]

H. C. Duke, an IWW member from Los Angeles, received a five-year prison sentence, which he served in Folsom from July 12, 1923, until his term expired.[30]

Mickey J. Dunn, an IWW member from Oakland, received a five-year prison sentence, which he served in San Quentin from November 1921 to January 1926.[31]

Omar J. Eaton, an IWW member from Eureka, received a five-year prison sentence, which he served in San Quentin from July 8, 1922, to April 1926.[32]

H. M. Edwards, from Sacramento, received a four-year prison sentence for giving testimony in court on behalf of a fellow member of the IWW and served in San Quentin from August 25, 1923, to 1926. (See also the entry for J. A. Casdorf.)[33]

Leo Ellis was arrested in San Francisco in November 1919 and convicted under the California Criminal Syndicalism Act for taking part in IWW activities. He escaped from a county jail in May 1920 and became a fugitive from the law. Ellis was captured in Texas in 1926 and returned to California to serve his three-year sentence in San Quentin. In 1928, Ellis was the last member of the IWW to be released from San Quentin.[34]

Lawrence Emery, from Sacramento, was convicted of violating the California Criminal Syndicalism Act because of his role in the Imperial Valley farmer workers strike. He was sentenced to three to forty-two years in prison and served in San Quentin from June 1930 to February 1933. Emery was an organizer for the Marine Transport Workers Industrial Union and a member of the Communist Party.

In early 1930, Emery traveled to Imperial Valley as an organizer for the Trade Union Unity League and began organizing a farm worker strike. The 1930 strike was not successful. Among the demands pushed by the union were an eight-hour work day, abolition of child labor, equal pay for equal work and an end to race segregation among the employees.

Because of the strike activities, Emery, along with thirty-two others, was indicted under the California Criminal Syndicalism Act. Eventually, eight defendants stood trial and were convicted.

The judge presiding at the trial was extremely hostile to the defendants. In a letter to the parole board the judge wrote: "The Court considers the defendants . . . a decided menace and detriment to society and civilization."[35]

Ernest Erickson, an IWW member from Los Angeles, received a four-year prison sentence, which he served in San Quentin from July 12, 1923, until his term expired.[36]

Oscar Erickson, an IWW officer and a leader of the Imperial Valley farm workers strike, received a three- to forty-two-year prison sentence for violating the California Criminal Syndicalism Act and served in San Quentin. He was national secretary of the Agricultural Workers Industrial League. (See also the entry for Lawrence Emery.)[37]

C. Erwin, an IWW member, served a prison sentence in San Quentin.[38]

Earl Firey, an IWW member from Sacramento, received a five-year prison sentence, which he served in Folsom from February 17, 1922, to 1925. (See also the entry for J. A. Casdorf.)[39]

William Flanagan, an IWW member, received a one- to fourteen-year prison sentence, which he served in San Quentin. When guards put Flanagan in the "dungeon" for failing to work hard enough, thirty-six IWW inmates launched a work strike.[40]

F. Franklin, an IWW member, received a five-year sentence, which he served in San Quentin from March 1923 until his term expired.[41]

L. V. French, from Eureka, received a three-year prison sentence for having an IWW membership card and served in San Quentin from April 27, 1924, until his term expired.[42]

W. I. Fruit, an IWW member from Los Angeles, received a one- to fourteen-year prison sentence, which he served in San Quentin from December 1921 to March 11, 1925.[43]

J. Gaveel, an IWW member, served a prison sentence in San Quentin.[44]

R. A. Gibson, an IWW member, served a prison sentence in San Quentin. In June 1924, the IWW criminal syndicalism prisoners struck in San Quentin to protest Gibson's detention in solitary confinement.[45]

John Golden, an IWW member from Eureka, received a one- to fourteen-year prison sentence, which he served in San Quentin from January

23, 1920, to May 23, 1924. Prison officials, riled by Golden's refusal to "accept the status and tasks of a convict" because he considered himself a "political prisoner who had committed no crime," punished him by keeping him in solitary confinement for over a year until he physically collapsed.[46]

James P. Gordon, from Los Angeles, received a five-year prison sentence, which he served in Folsom from July 12, 1923, until his term expired.[47]

Jack Gravel was mistreated by prison officials in 1922, provoking fellow IWW inmates to strike.[48]

L. Gross, an IWW member, served a prison sentence in San Quentin.[49]

John Hannon, an IWW member from Oakland, received a five-year prison sentence, which he served in San Quentin from November 9, 1921, to March 2, 1925. During his prison term Hannon lost vision in one eye and became "nearly blind" in the second.[50]

H. R. Hanson, an IWW member from Los Angeles, received a four-year prison sentence, which he served in San Quentin from July 12, 1923, until his term expired.[51]

Frances Hart, an IWW member from Los Angeles, received a four-year prison sentence, which he served in San Quentin from July 12, 1923, until his term expired.[52]

Eduardo Herera, an activist in the Imperial Valley farm workers strike, received a two- to twenty-eight-year prison sentence for violating the California Criminal Syndicalism Act and served in San Quentin from June 1930 to April 28, 1932. After prison, he was deported to Mexico. (See also the entry for Lawrence Emery.)[53]

John Hiza, an IWW member, received a seven-year prison sentence, which he served in Folsom from March 1923 until his term expired.[54]

J. L. Hollis, an IWW member from Los Angeles, received a three-year sentence, which he served in San Quentin from July 12, 1923, until his term expired.[55]

Thomas Hooker, an IWW member from Stockton, received a one- to fourteen-year prison sentence, which he served in San Quentin from March 19, 1920, to January 12, 1922.[56]

Tetsuji Horiuchi, a Trade Union Unity League organizer and leader of Japanese workers in the Imperial Valley farm workers strike, received a three- to thirty-three-year prison sentence for violating the California Criminal Syndicalism Act and served in Folsom State Prison from June 1930 to January 1932. (Also see the entry for Lawrence Emery.) Upon Horiuchi's release from prison the U.S. Department of Labor withdrew its deportation order and allowed him to depart "voluntarily" for the Soviet Union. He left the United States on August 17, 1932.[57]

Roy House, an IWW member from Portola, received a four-year prison sentence, which he served in San Quentin from October 29, 1923, until his term expired.[58]

Pierre Jans, an IWW member from Los Angeles, received a four-year prison sentence, which he served in San Quentin from July 12, 1923, until his term expired.[59]

B. Johansen, an IWW member from Sacramento, received a four-year prison sentence, which he served in San Quentin from September 17, 1923, to 1926.[60]

J. J. Johnson, an IWW member from Los Angeles, received a four-year prison sentence, which he served in San Quentin beginning on July 12, 1923.[61]

William Joozdeff, an IWW member from Sacramento, received a four-year prison sentence, which he served in San Quentin from March 1923 until his term expired.[62]

T. O. Kleiberg, an IWW member from Los Angeles, received a four-year prison sentence, which he served in San Quentin from July 12, 1923, until his term expired.[63]

Walter Kohrs, an IWW member from Los Angeles, received a four-year prison sentence, which he served in San Quentin beginning on July 12, 1923.[64]

R. Kuilmen, from Eureka, received a four-year prison sentence, which he served in San Quentin from April 10, 1923, until his term expired for attending a meeting of the IWW local in Eureka. In June 1924, IWW inmates struck to protest Kuilmen's detention in solitary confinement.[65]

Bert Kyler, from Sacramento, received a three-year prison sentence for giving testimony in court on behalf of a fellow member of the IWW and served in San Quentin from August 28, 1923, to January 31, 1926. (See also the entry for J. A. Casdorf.)[66]

James La Londe, an IWW member from Sacramento, received a four-year prison sentence, which he served in San Quentin from July 12, 1923, until his term expired.[67]

R. Leonard, an IWW member, served a prison sentence in San Quentin.[68]

Charles Lesse, an IWW member, received a one- to fourteen-year sentence, which he served in San Quentin from January 23, 1920, to May 1922. After his release, Lesse was deported to Finland.[69]

R. V. Lewis received a one- to fourteen-year prison sentence for violating the California Criminal Syndicalism Act by taking part in IWW activities and served in a county jail and San Quentin from May 1920 to June 1922. San Quentin prison officials refused to provide medical attention to Lewis when he developed an abscess on his leg, resulting in the amputation of that leg.[70]

G. Lindfors, from Los Angeles, received a three-year prison sentence, which he served in San Quentin from July 12, 1923, until his term expired.[71]

William Longstreth, an IWW member from Eureka, received a three-year prison sentence, which he served in San Quentin from April 27, 1924, until his term expired.[72]

Thomas Lyons, an IWW member from Los Angeles, received a three-year prison sentence, which he served in San Quentin from July 12, 1923, until his term expired.[73]

James P. Malley, an IWW officer from San Francisco, received a five-year prison sentence, which he served in San Quentin from December 23, 1919, to December 24, 1921. Malley was secretary of the IWW local in San Francisco.[74]

Laurri Mammi, an IWW member, was convicted on April 5, 1923, served a prison sentence in San Quentin and was released after a year in prison when a higher court reversed his conviction.[75]

James Martin, an IWW member, received a five-year prison sentence, which he served in San Quentin from March 1923 until his term expired.[76]

Henry Matlin, an IWW member, served a prison sentence in San Quentin.[77]

F. E. McClennigan, from Los Angeles, served a prison sentence in San Quentin.[78]

Thomas McDermott was charged with "feloniously circulating and publicly displaying certain books" in violation of the California Criminal Syndicalism Act.[79]

C. F. McGrath, an IWW member from Eureka, received a four-year prison sentence, which he served in San Quentin from April 10, 1923, until his term expired.[80]

James McHugo, an IWW officer from Oakland, received a one- to fourteen-year prison sentence, which he served in San Quentin from December 22, 1919, until his parole on December 25, 1921. McHugo was secretary of the IWW local in Oakland.[81]

James McLaughlin, from Oakland, received a five-year prison sentence, which he served in Folsom from November 9, 1921, to August 9, 1925.[82]

E. D. McNassor, an IWW member from Portola, received a four-year prison sentence, which he served in San Quentin from October 29, 1923, until his term expired.[83]

John McRae, an IWW member from Eureka, received a three-year prison sentence for having an IWW membership card and served in San Quentin from April 27, 1924, until his term expired.[84]

Phillip Mellman, an IWW member from Sacramento, received a four-year prison sentence, which he served in San Quentin from March 1923 until his term expired.[85]

Robert W. Minton, an IWW member from Sacramento, received a five-year prison sentence, which he served in San Quentin from February 5, 1925, until his term expired.[86]

William Minton, an IWW member from Los Angeles, received a four-year prison sentence, which he served in San Quentin from July 12, 1923, until his term expired.[87]

Francis J. Nash, an IWW member from Sacramento, received a four-year prison sentence for giving testimony in court on behalf of a fellow member of the IWW and served in San Quentin from August 25, 1923, to 1926. (See also the entry for J. A. Casdorf.)[88]

Alex Nicholson, an IWW member from Eureka, received a four-year prison sentence, which he served in San Quentin from April 27, 1924, until his term expired.[89]

J. Nolan, an IWW member, served a prison sentence in San Quentin.[90]

James Olson, an IWW member from Los Angeles, received a one- to fourteen-year prison sentence, which he served in San Quentin from December 1921 to February 11, 1926.[91]

Thomas O'Mara, an IWW member from Sacramento, received a four-year sentence for giving testimony in court on behalf of a fellow member of the IWW and served a prison sentence in San Quentin from August 25, 1923, to 1926. (See also the entry for J. A. Casdorf.)[92]

John Orlando, an IWW member from Sacramento, received a four-year prison sentence, which he served in San Quentin from March 1923 until his term expired.[93]

Braulio Orosco, an activist in the Imperial Valley farm workers strike, received a two- to twenty-eight-year prison sentence for violating the California Criminal Syndicalism Act and served in San Quentin from June 1930 to November 28, 1931. (See also the entry for Lawrence Emery.) Orosco was deported to Mexico after his release from prison.[94]

Cris Pedersen, an IWW member from Sacramento, received a five-year prison sentence, which he served in San Quentin from September 17, 1923, to 1926.[95]

Edward R. Peters, an IWW member from Los Angeles, received a one- to fourteen-year prison sentence, which he served in San Quentin from December 1921 to January 10, 1924.[96]

Henry Powell, from Eureka, received a three-year prison sentence, which he served in San Quentin from April 27, 1924, until his term expired.[97]

James Price, an IWW member from Los Angeles, received a one- to fourteen-year prison sentence, which he served in Folsom from 1921 to 1926. Price was the only prisoner to serve time under both federal and state sedition laws. As a defendant at the mass IWW trial in Sacramento, Price spent one year in jail awaiting trial and was then sentenced to four years in prison under the Espionage Act, which he served in Leavenworth Penitentiary from January 25, 1919, to August 20, 1920, when he was released on bond. In May 1921, while out on bond, Price was arrested under the California criminal syndicalism law.[98]

John Pugh, an IWW member from Los Angeles, received a four-year prison sentence, which he served in San Quentin from July 12, 1923, until his term expired.[99]

J. C. Robinson, an IWW member from Los Angeles, served a prison sentence in San Quentin until his conviction was reversed (1925).[100]

Jim Roe, from Sacramento, received a one- to fourteen-year prison sentence, which he served in San Quentin from December 26, 1921, to December 26, 1924. Roe was over seventy years old and crippled when arrested for selling copies of an IWW paper. After his conviction Roe declined an appeal, telling the General Defense Committee not to "waste" money on his case because he was "too old to be of much use if I were out. Keep the money for the defense of the young fellows."[101]

George Roeschlau, an IWW member from Los Angeles, received a four-year prison sentence, which he served in San Quentin from July 12, 1923, until his term expired.[102]

Arthur G. Ross, an IWW member from Sacramento, received a four-year prison sentence, which he served in San Quentin from September 17, 1923, to 1926.[103]

Danny Roxas, a farm worker activist and IWW officer, received a three- to forty-two-year prison sentence for violating the California Criminal Syndicalism Act and served in San Quentin from June 1930 to July 1932. He was secretary of the Agricultural Workers Industrial League and a leader of the Imperial Valley farm workers strike of 1930. (See also the entry for Lawrence Emery.[104]

D. C. Russell, an IWW member from Sacramento, received a three-year prison sentence, which he served in the Sacramento County Jail from April 1924 until his term expired.[105]

William Rutherford, an IWW member from Sacramento, received a four-year sentence for giving testimony in court on behalf of a fellow member of the IWW and served a prison sentence in San Quentin from August 25, 1923, to March 31, 1927. (See also the entry for J. A. Casdorf.)[106]

George Ryan, an IWW member, received a five-year prison sentence, which he served in San Quentin from November 1921 to January 1926.[107]

R. J. Sánchez served a prison sentence in San Quentin, where he contracted tuberculosis. He was released in June 1924 on the condition that he would be deported.[108]

Frank Sherman, from Woodland, served a prison sentence in San Quentin from December 21, 1921, to February 21, 1926.[109]

Carl Sklar, a Communist Party organizer and a leader of the Imperial Valley farm workers strike, from Los Angeles, received a three- to thirty-three-year prison sentence for violating the California Criminal Syndicalism Act and served in Folsom State Prison from June 1930 to October 3, 1932. (See also the entry for Lawrence Emery.)[110]

C. J. Smith, an IWW member from Los Angeles, received a four-year prison sentence, which he served in San Quentin beginning on July 12, 1923.[111]

Frank Spector, a district organizer for the International Labor Defense and a farm worker activist, received a three- to forty-two-year prison sentence for violating the California Criminal Syndicalism Act and served in Folsom State Prison from June 1930 to 1932. Spector played an active role in the Imperial Valley farm workers strike of 1930. (See also the entry for Lawrence Emery.)[112]

Leo Stark, from Los Angeles, received a five-year prison sentence, which he served in Folsom from July 12, 1923, until his term expired.[113]

Nick Steelik, an IWW organizer from Los Angeles, was arrested on September 19, 1919, for "willfully" advocating, teaching, aiding and abetting criminal syndicalism by "spoken and written word." He was sentenced to five years in prison and served in San Quentin from April 1920 to June 1922. As in other criminal syndicalism cases, there was "no evidence" of the "consummation of any crime" except the fact that Steelik was an "authorized organizer" of the IWW and "advocated revolution."[114]

William Stein, an IWW member from Los Angeles, received a one- to fourteen-year prison sentence, which he served in San Quentin from April 1920 to June 1922.[115]

Homer B. Stewart, an IWW member from Sacramento, received a four-year prison sentence, which he served in San Quentin from December 24, 1923, to March 24, 1927.[116]

A. Strangeland, an IWW member, served a prison sentence in Folsom.[117]

C. J. Sullivan, from Los Angeles, received a five-year prison sentence, which he served in Folsom from July 12, 1923, until his term expired.[118]

H. V. Taylor, an IWW member from Eureka, received a four-year prison sentence, which he served in San Quentin from April 27, 1924, until his term expired.[119]

John C. Taylor, a Communist Labor Party member from Oakland, received a one- to fourteen-year prison sentence, which he served in San Quentin from June 1920 to December 20, 1921.[120]

C. J. Terrill, an IWW member from Los Angeles, received a four-year prison sentence, which he served in San Quentin from July 12, 1923, until his term expired.[121]

G. Terrill, an IWW member, served a prison sentence in San Quentin.[122]

Fred W. Thompson, an IWW member from Maryville, received a four-year prison sentence, which he served in San Quentin from November 7, 1923, to March 7, 1927.

In a 1981 letter to the author, Thompson described the experience of the California IWW criminal syndicalism inmates:

In San Quentin we wobs went on strike several times (not asking non-wobs to join us) in protest against what we considered unjust discipline to some of our members. Punishment was solitary confinemen꞉, not actually solitary—sometimes in the "hole," underground completely dark but because of our number, putting us two to a cell. Sure that situation was uncomfortable—we had nothing to sit on but the floor, for they took our blanket away at daybreak, and the diet [of] bread and water, and we combatted the sense of isolation—imperfect there because of our numbers—by singing or inventing games. (I recall our efforts for example to list the rivers of North America, starting with the McKenzie and going clockwise, or seeing how far we could go in the dark with the series, 2X3 is 6, 4X6 is 24, 5X24 is 120, 6 times 120 is 720, etc.) Sometimes we were confined on bread and water in a row in the new prison, with daylight, but nothing to read for a month. We had some forbidden pencils and tried making crossword puzzles for each other, sneaking them down the line. Most of us had got in because we stuck our heads out in life outside, and we were an innovative lot of people, better able than most to cope with daily problems. We got along well with the prisoners in on ordinary offenses. I judge that prison conditions have much deteriorated since my days in San Quentin. The food I hear is not as terrible as it was then—weevils in the oatmeal, beans almost every meal, often half cooked—but crowding is worse; radios have worsened life instead of improving it, for one can't get quiet; I heard of no homosexual rape when I was in San Quentin, and I don't believe the prisoners would have permitted it. In general prisoners of all sorts acted with consideration for each other.

Thompson remained active in the IWW for his entire adult life and, in 1955, published *The I.W.W., Its First Fifty Years*.[123]

F. Varella, from Los Angeles, received a four-year prison sentence, which he served in San Quentin beginning on July 12, 1923.[124]

Joseph Vargo, an IWW member from Sacramento, received a four-year prison sentence, which he served in San Quentin from April 1923 until his term expired.[125]

Joseph Wagner, from Sacramento, received a four-year prison sentence, which he served in Folsom from April 1923 until his term expired.[126]

Arthur C. Ward, an IWW member, served a prison sentence in Preston Reform School from July 1, 1922, to October 1923.[127]

P. Ware, an IWW member, served a prison sentence in San Quentin.[128]

John G. Weiler, a Communist Labor Party member, received a one- to fourteen-year prison sentence for violating California's criminal syndicalism law and served in San Quentin from February 1921 until his parole in May 1923.[129]

Howard Welton, an IWW member from Oakland, received a three-year prison sentence, which he served from November 1921 to June 1923.[130]

H. C. White, an IWW member, served a prison sentence in San Quentin.[131]

Harry Williams, an IWW member from Scrotia, received a one- to fourteen-year prison sentence, which he served in San Quentin from February 10, 1920, to May 10, 1924.[132]

Ben Wittling, an IWW member from Los Angeles, received a one- to fourteen-year prison sentence, which he served in San Quentin from December 1921 to December 11, 1924.[133]

John Wiza, an IWW member from Sacramento, received a prison sentence.[134]

Robert Woods, an IWW member from Sacramento, received a three-year prison sentence, which he served in San Quentin from September 17, 1923, to January 1925.[135]

Wilt Wright, an IWW member from Portola, received a four-year prison sentence, which he served in San Quentin from October 29, 1923, until his term expired.[136]

Peter Wukusick, an IWW member from Sacramento, received a three-year prison sentence, which he served in San Quentin from December 24, 1923, to 1925.[137]

COLORADO ANTI-SEDITION ACT PRISONERS

Mary Hunt, along with her two sons, was sentenced to the Colorado State Insane Asylum for "pacifist views." The Hunts were Seventh-Day Adventists.[138]

Ralph and Wesley Hunt, sons of Mary Hunt. (See the entry for Mary Hunt.)

GEORGIA ANTI-INSURRECTION PRISONER

Angelo Herndon was an African American member of the Communist Youth League and a paid organizer for the Unemployment Council during the Great Depression. In June 1932, at the age of nineteen, he led a march of over a thousand black and white unemployed workers at the Fulton County Commissioners office in Atlanta, Georgia, demanding the continuation of relief benefits.

Shortly thereafter, Herndon was arrested under a Georgia "anti-insurrection" statute. The law, which subjected Herndon to the death penalty, forbid the "persuasion" or inducement of persons to resist "lawful authority" or to "incite insurrection." The statute was derived from an old Georgia law prohibiting slave uprisings.

At his trial, the prosecution was extremely concerned about Communist Party literature found in Herndon's possession, which called for "equal rights for the Negroes" and "self-determination" for "Negroes in the Black Belt." Herndon was found guilty and sentenced to an eighteen- to twenty-year term on the Georgia chain gang.

Herndon's case became a major civil rights and civil liberties test case.

At the time his case was pending, at least eighteen other persons stood indicted under the Georgia anti-insurrection law. Additionally, scores of other state sedition cases were pending. His case was heard by the U.S. Supreme Court on two separate occasions.

Finally, in a 5–4 decision rendered in 1937, the Court freed Herndon finding the Georgia law an impermissible "dragnet which may enmesh anyone who agitates for a change in government." The Court found that the law, as applied to Herndon, was unconstitutional.

Herndon spent a total of twenty-six months in Fulton Tower Prison before his conviction was reversed.

After 1937 Herndon became a leader in the Communist movement, and during the 1940s edited, along with Ralph Ellison, the *Negro Quarterly: A Review of Negro Life and Culture*. However, by the end of the 1940s he left the Communist Party and reportedly "withdrew from active public participation" in political activities and moved to the midwest where he worked as a salesman.[139]

IDAHO CRIMINAL SYNDICALISM ACT PRISONERS

Charles Anderson, from St. Marie, Idaho, received a one- to ten-year prison sentence.[140]

Bert Banker, from St. Marie, Idaho, received a one- to ten-year prison sentence.[141]

J. L. Brian, from St. Marie, Idaho, received a one- to ten-year prison sentence.[142]

Charles Carlson, from St. Marie, Idaho, received a one- to ten-year prison sentence.[143]

Charles Clifford, from Moscow, Idaho, received a one- to ten-year prison sentence.[144]

Joe Doyle was convicted of violating the state's Criminal Syndicalism Act for taking part in IWW activities. As of 1924, he had served nearly three years in jail.[145]

J. Otis Ellis served a prison sentence, which began in November 1917, for violating the state's Criminal Syndicalism Act by taking part in conversations in which Ellis supported the IWW.[146]

A. S. Embree, an IWW officer and editor, was convicted in Shoshone County, Idaho, on June 1, 1921, of violating the state's Criminal Syndicalism Act. Embree, who received a one- to ten-year sentence, had been editor of the *Nome Industrial Worker* and chairman of the IWW Strike Committee of Bisbee, Arizona. He also served as secretary-treasurer pro tem of the national IWW after the federal raid on the IWW's national office. Embree was paroled on January 9, 1925, and pardoned on January 16, 1926.[147]

Henry Fainer, from St. Marie, Idaho, received a one- to ten-year prison sentence.[148]

Frank Fleury, from St. Marie, Idaho, received a one- to ten-year prison sentence.[149]

T. E. Hawkins, from Moscow, Idaho, received a six-month to ten-year prison sentence.[150]

H. E. Herd, from Moscow, Idaho, received a four- to ten-year sentence on April 15, 1918, for violating the state's Criminal Syndicalism Act. He was arrested in July 1917 during a lumber workers strike in northwest Idaho and began serving the sentence on April 15, 1918. In 1924, after seven years in prison, Herd's health was reported to be "declining on account of ill treatment" and "unsanitary conditions" in the Boise jail.[151]

George Kopp, from St. Marie, Idaho, received a one- to ten-year prison sentence.[152]

Edwin Krier was convicted of violating the state's Criminal Syndicalism Act because he belonged to the IWW.[153]

Joe Martin, from St. Marie, Idaho, received a one- to ten-year prison sentence.[154]

Dennis McCarthy, from St. Marie, Idaho, received a one- to ten-year prison sentence.[155]

J. J. McMurphy received a prison sentence for violating the state's Criminal Syndicalism Act by speaking on behalf of the IWW and having IWW literature in his possession. He began serving time in November 1917.[156]

E. L. Montgomery, from St. Marie, Idaho, received a one- to ten-year prison sentence.[157]

Lyman Moore, from St. Marie, Idaho, received a one- to ten-year prison sentence.[158]

Fred Morgan, from St. Marie, Idaho, received a one- to ten-year prison sentence.[159]

William Nelson, from St. Marie, Idaho, received a two- to ten-year prison sentence for violating the state's Criminal Syndicalism Act by issuing membership cards for the IWW and distributing its literature. Nelson was secretary of the IWW local in St. Marie.[160]

R. Quackenbush received a six-month to ten-year sentence for violating the Criminal Syndicalism Act by belonging to the IWW.[161]

John Shea, from St. Marie, Idaho, received a one- to ten-year prison sentence.[162]

Robert Wilson, from St. Marie, Idaho, received a one- to ten-year prison sentence.[163]

ILLINOIS CRIMINAL SYNDICALISM LAW PRISONERS

Ludwig E. Katterfeld was convicted under the Illinois criminal syndicalism law and received a one- to five-year prison sentence. Katterfeld was a founding member of the American Communist Party and a member of the party's Executive Committee. In 1929, he was expelled from the Communist Party for refusing to submit the magazine he had founded to party control. He was described as a "sincere, honest American radical," who gave "years of his life to the Socialist movement."[164]

KANSAS CRIMINAL SYNDICALISM LAW PRISONERS

C. E. Berquist, an IWW member, served a prison sentence for violating Kansas criminal syndicalism laws.[165]

Harry Breen organized farm workers for the IWW and was arrested during a union drive in Wakensey, Kansas, on July 9, 1920. He received a thirty-year prison sentence for being a member of the IWW. The sentence was thrown out by the Kansas Supreme Court, and Breen was released from prison on September 4, 1922.[166]

Harold Fiske served a prison sentence for violating Kansas criminal syndicalism laws.[167]

Joe Neil, an IWW member, was incarcerated in the insane ward of the Kansas State Penitentiary (from 1922 to 1928) for violating a Kansas criminal syndicalism law prohibiting IWW membership.[168]

MONTANA CRIMINAL SYNDICALISM PRISONERS

Albert Brooks of Dillon, Montana, was sentenced to a seven- to fifteen-year prison term for circulating a book critical of war.[169]

Herbert Mansolf, of Missoula, Montana, was arrested on May 26, 1918 for counselling draft evasion. He was sentenced to prison for a two- to four-year term.[170]

NEW YORK ANTI-ANARCHY LAW PRISONERS

Gus Alonen, an IWW officer from the Bronx, served a sentence in Clinton and Comstock Prisons for violating New York anti-anarchy law. He had been secretary of the Finnish local of the IWW in the Bronx.[171]

Isaac E. Ferguson, an officer of the Communist Party from New York City, received a five- to ten-year prison sentence, which he served in Sing Sing Penitentiary. Ferguson sat on the party's Central Executive Committee.[172]

Benjamin Gitlow, a leader of the American Socialist Party and a founder of the Communist Party from New York City, served approximately thirty-four months of a ten-year sentence in Sing Sing Penitentiary. He was pardoned on December 11, 1925.

Gitlow won a seat in the New York State Assembly after running as the Socialist Party's candidate in 1917. He left the party to found the Communist Party. Gitlow twice ran as the Communist Party's candidate for vice president (in 1924 and 1928) and served in many positions of party leadership, including general secretary. In 1929, the Communist Party expelled Gitlow after he opposed Joseph Stalin's attempt to control the policies of the American Communist Party through the Comintern.[173]

Minnie Kalnin, a Communist Party member, served a sentence in the New York Women's Prison at Auburn and was later pardoned by Governor Alfred E. Smith.[174]

James Larkin, born in Liverpool, England, was an international leader for Irish independence from Great Britain. Larkin was the general secretary and secretary-treasurer of the Irish Transport and General Workers Union, the largest union in Ireland. Together with James Michael Connolly, he helped lead the Easter Rebellion in Ireland and was subsequently deported. Soon after the outbreak of World War I in Europe, Larkin came to the United States. In 1920, he was convicted of violating the New York criminal anarchy law and sentenced to between five and ten years in jail for his activities in helping found the Communist Party in the United States. After serving approximately two years in jail, he was pardoned by Governor Smith and deported to Ireland.[175]

Anna Leisman, a member of the Communist Party, served a sentence in the New York Women's Prison at Auburn. She was later pardoned by Governor Smith. She died of pneumonia almost immediately after her release from prison. According to Elizabeth Flynn, Leisman's pneumonia was the result of her being released from prison "in the freezing cold of January 1923" without any winter clothing. She was "not allowed to wait till her family arrived with heavier clothing. As a result she contracted pneumonia and died."[176]

Paul Manko, a member of the Communist Party from New York City, served a sentence in Sing Sing State Penitentiary, where he went insane. He was pardoned by Governor Smith.[177]

Ignatz Mizher, a member of the Communist Party from New York City, served a sentence in Sing Sing and was later pardoned by Governor Smith.[178]

Carl Paivo, secretary of the Finnish local of the IWW in the Bronx, served a prison sentence.[179]

Charles E. Ruthenberg, a Socialist Party leader from Cleveland, Ohio, served a sentence in Sing Sing for violating New York's criminal anarchy law.

Ruthenberg joined the Socialist Party in 1909 and ran as its candidate for several elective offices between 1910 and 1918 (including state treasurer, mayor of Cleveland and representative to Congress). He was also the editor of the *Cleveland Socialist*. After the outbreak of World War I, Ruthenberg was continually arrested. He served time in the Canton (Ohio) Workhouse for giving a speech at an anti-war meeting.

After the Bolshevik Revolution, Ruthenberg left the Socialist Party to become a leader in the new communist movement, serving as national secretary of the Worker's Party and later of the United Communist Party. He was arrested both in Illinois and in New York for his activities with communist organizations. He died in 1927.[180]

Harry Winitsky, a leader of the Communist Party from New York City, was sentenced to a five- to ten-year prison term for violating the New York anti-anarchy law and served in Clinton Prison and Sing Sing. Winitsky was reportedly betrayed at his trial by Jay Lovestone, another party leader, who accepted the state's offer to drop its prosecution of him on anti-anarchy charges if he testified against Winitsky.[181]

OKLAHOMA CRIMINAL SYNDICALISM LAW PRISONERS

Arthur Berg, a delegate for the Oil Workers Industrial Union of the IWW, received a ten-year sentence for violating Oklahoma's criminal syndicalism laws because he belonged to the IWW.[182]

Homer Ware, a delegate for the Metal Mine Workers Industrial Union of the IWW, received a one- to ten-year prison sentence and served two years in prison before his conviction was overturned.[183]

OREGON CRIMINAL SYNDICALISM LAW PRISONER

Ben Boloff, from Portland, was described as an "illiterate Russian alien and ditch digger." He was sentenced to a term of ten years in prison under the Oregon criminal syndicalism law "merely because he was a member of the Communist Party." In prison he contracted terminal tuberculosis and was denied any medical attention. On January 20, 1932, after fifteen months behind bars, he was released on bond by order of a local circuit judge. An eyewitness at the release hearing described Boloff as "hollow cheeked, haggard, and coughing." He died in the summer of 1932.[184]

PENNSYLVANIA ANTI-SEDITION LAW PRISONERS

Israel Blankenstein, an organizer for the Communist Party, was convicted under Pennsylvania criminal syndicalism laws.[185]

Pete Muselin was a member of the Communist Party from Woodlawn. Muselin, along with codefendants Tom Zima and Milan Resetar, was convicted under Pennsylvania's anti-sedition law and sentenced to five years of hard labor in the Allegheny County Workhouse at Blawnox, Pennsylvania. The conviction stemmed from a 1926 raid of Tom Zima's house and Muselin's barber shop, where a large amount of party literature was confiscated. The three defendants were accused of being "active members" and "leaders" of the local branch of the Communist Party. They were convicted of having "frequently taught by word of mouth" the doctrine of communism. Convicted in 1928, their sentences were unanimously upheld by the Pennsylvania Superior Court and the Pennsylvania Supreme Court. In 1929, the U.S. Supreme Court declined to review their convictions, and they began serving their terms.

The Woodland defendants did not fare very well in Blawnox. Milan Resetar died in jail (see chapter 14). Pete Muselin's family was rendered destitute and impoverished. His wife, Anne Muselin, described their condition in a letter:

I need clothing for both myself and the children. As for myself, I don't care but my children must be clothed. It's better to have them clothed than to pay doctor bills. . . .

You know we must eat. I can't get no work, and even if I did there's no one to care for my children. What must I do?

After almost two years in jail Muselin and Zima became disillusioned. In a letter to the American Civil Liberties Union requesting assistance, they criticized the "miserable failure" and "despicable methods" of the pro-communist International Labor Defense, which apparently would not pay an attorney to obtain their release. They were forced to pay $150 for an attorney to file papers for a pardon.

They asked the ACLU to file for their pardon on the basis of their recanting membership in the Communist Party and pledging to "desist from all further participation and activities in the Communist movement." In December 1931, Muselin and Zima obtained pardons.[186]

Tom Zima was a member of the Communist Party from Woodlawn. (See also the entry for Pete Muselin.)

WASHINGTON CRIMINAL SYNDICALISM LAW PRISONERS

Charlie Brown, a member of the IWW, received a prison sentence for violating the state's criminal syndicalism law because he belonged to the IWW. The court based its conviction of Brown on his teaching, advocating and disseminating of "anarchistic doctrines."[187]

F. A. Brown, a member of the IWW, received a one- to five-year prison sentence for violating the state's criminal syndicalism law because he belonged to the IWW. Brown refused parole in solidarity with fellow IWW inmates and was released at the end of this term on February 14, 1925. (See also the entry for W. F. Moudy.)[188]

Dan Curtin, a member of the IWW, received a prison sentence for violating the state's criminal syndicalism law.[189]

Mike Hennessy received a prison sentence for "unlawfully and feloniously" helping to "organize" the IWW. The indictment stated: "Mike

Hennessy did then and there [November 15, 1919, in Clark County, Washington] print, publish, circulate, distribute, and display books, pamphlets, handbills, documents and other written and printed matter" concerning the IWW.[190]

Frank Hestings received a four- to ten-year prison sentence for violating the state's criminal syndicalism law because he belonged to the IWW.[191]

W. R. Holey, a member of the IWW, received a prison sentence for violating the state's criminal syndicalism law.[192]

Fred Lowery received a prison sentence for violating the state's criminal syndicalism law because he belonged to the IWW. His conviction was based on his teaching, advocating and disseminating of "anarchistic doctrines."[193]

Elias Matson, a member of the IWW, received a prison sentence for violating the state's criminal syndicalism law.[194]

W. F. Moudy received a prison sentence for violating the state's criminal syndicalism law because he belonged to the IWW. Moudy chaired the Criminal Syndicalism Inmate Committee that enacted a resolution against prisoners obtaining parole. They voted to either "be released together" or "remain in prison" for their "maximum terms."[195]

Frank Nash, a member of the IWW, received a five-year prison sentence for violating the state's criminal syndicalism law. He served in Walla Walla Prison and was released at the end of his term on September 28, 1926.[196]

Tom Nash received a ten-year prison sentence in Walla Walla Prison for violating the state's criminal syndicalism law. Nash's constant protest of prison conditions resulted in prison officials placing him in solitary confinement and eventually transferring him to the isolation ward, a unit used to segregate "incorrigible" prisoners from the general prison population.[197]

Kalla Niemi, a member of the IWW, received a prison sentence for violating the state's criminal syndicalism law.[198]

C. F. Payne received a prison sentence for violating the state's criminal syndicalism law because he belonged to the IWW. He served in Walla Walla Prison and was released at the end of his term on September 6, 1922.[199]

Fred Suttle received a five- to ten-year prison sentence for violating the state's criminal syndicalism law because he belonged to the IWW. While in prison Suttle suffered a mental breakdown and was transferred from Walla Walla Prison to the state hospital for the insane. (He was released after nearly seven years in prison on September 24, 1926.)[200]

NOTES

1. "Erwin, Claude, Record of Criminal Syndicalism Convictions in California," Box 135, Folder #1, IWW Collection, Wayne State University [hereafter E]; *People v. Powell*, 236 P. 311 (Calif. App. 1925).

2. IWW General Defense Committee, "To the Beasts in California and in Ancient Rome" [Pamphlet] (IWW, 1924) [hereafter TTB]; E; *Industrial Worker*, October 6, 1923, and October 13, 1923.

3. TTB; E.

4. TTB; E.

5. TTB; E; *People v. Bailey*, 225 P. 752 (Calif. App. 1924).

6. TTB; E.

7. TTB; E; *People v. Wright*, 226 P. 952 (Calif. App. 1924).

8. TTB; E.

9. E; *People v. Powell*, 236 P. 311 (Calif. App. 1925).

10. E.

11. E.

12. TTB.

13. TTB; E.

14. E.

15. E; *People v. Powell*, 236 P. 311 (Calif. App. 1925).

16. *Burns v. United States*, 274 U.S. 328 (1927); *Industrial Worker*, October 18, 1924, November 22, 1924, and May 26, 1928.

17. TTB.

18. E; *People v. Casdorf*, 212 P. 237 (Calif. App. 1922).

19. TTB; E; *People v. Welton*, 211 P. 802 (Calif. 1922).

20. TTB; E.

21. TTB; E; *Industrial Worker*, December 1, 1923.

22. TTB; E.

23. TTB; E; *People v. Connors*, 246 P. 1072 (Calif. App. 1926).

24. TTB; E; *People v. Cox*, 226 P. 14 (Calif. App. 1924).

25. E.

26. TTB; E.

27. TTB; *People v. Thompson*, 229 P. 896 (Calif. App. 1924).

28. TTB; E.

29. E.

30. TTB; E.

31. TTB; E; *People v. Welton*, 211 P. 802 (Calif. 1922).

32. TTB; E; *People v. Eaton*, 213 P. 275 (Calif. App. 1923).

33. TTB; E.

34. E; ACLU, *Annual Report, 1928–1929* (ACLU: N.Y., June 1929).

35. Frank Spector, "Story of the Imperial Valley" [Pamphlet] (New York: International Labor Defense, undated); Joseph Pass, "Forty-Two Years?" *Labor Defender,* June 1931; Vol. 78: 144–147, Archives of the American Civil Liberties Union [hereafter ACLU Archives]; Esther Lowell, "Erickson Speaks from Prison," *Labor Defender,* September 1930; "One More to Free," *Labor Defender,* December 1932; Frank Spector, "California's Parole Racket," *Labor Defender,* September 1932.

36. TTB; E.

37. Spector, "Story of the Imperial Valley"; Pass, "Forty-Two Years?"; Vol. 78: 144–147, ACLU Archives; Lowell, "Erickson Speaks from Prison"; "One More to Free"; Spector, "California's Parole Racket."

38. TTB.

39. TTB; E.

40. TTB; *Industrial Worker,* August 15, 1923.

41. TTB; E; *People v. Bailey,* 225 P. 752 (Calif. App. 1924).

42. E; *People v. Powell,* 236 P. 311 (Calif. App. 1925).

43. TTB; E.

44. TTB.

45. TTB; *Industrial Worker,* June 14, 1924; *People v. Bailey,* 225 P. 752 (Calif. App. 1924).

46. TTB; *Industrial Worker,* August 15, 1923.

47. TTB; E.

48. *Industrial Worker,* July 29, 1922, and August 19, 1922.

49. TTB.

50. TTB; E; *Industrial Worker,* August 15, 1923; *People v. Welton,* 211 P. 802 (Calif. 1922).

51. TTB; E.

52. TTB; E.

53. Spector, "Story of the Imperial Valley"; Pass, "Forty-Two Years?"; Vol. 78: 144–147, ACLU Archives; Lowell, "Erickson Speaks from Prison"; "One More to Free"; Spector, "California's Parole Racket."

54. TTB; E.

55. TTB; E.

56. E.

57. Spector, "Story of the Imperial Valley"; Pass, "Forty-Two Years?"; Vol. 78: 144–147, ACLU Archives; Lowell, "Erickson Speaks from Prison"; "One More to Free"; Spector, "California's Parole Racket."

58. TTB; E.

59. TTB; E.

60. TTB; E; *People v. Johansen,* 226 P. 634 (Calif. App. 1924).

61. TTB; E.

62. TTB; E; *People v. Bailey,* 225 P. 752 (Calif. App. 1924).

63. TTB; E.

64. TTB; E.

65. TTB; E; *Industrial Worker,* June 14, 1924; *People v. Cox,* 226 P. 14 (Calif. App. 1924).

66. TTB; E.

67. TTB; E.

68. TTB.

69. TTB; *People v. Lesse,* 199 P. 46 (Calif. App. 1921).

70. TTB.

71. TTB.

72. E; *People v. Powell,* 236 P. 311 (Calif. App. 1925).

73. TTB; E.

74. E.

75. TTB; E; *People v. Cox,* 226 P. 14 (Calif. App. 1924).

76. TTB; E; *People v. Bailey,* 225 P. 752 (Calif. App. 1924).

77. TTB.

78. TTB; E; *People v. McClennigan,* 234 P. 91 (Calif. 1925).

79. *Ex Parte McDermott,* 183 P. 437 (Calif. 1919).

80. TTB; E; *People v. Cox,* 226 P. 14 (Calif. App. 1924).

81. E.

82. TTB; E; *Industrial Worker*, February 4, 1925; *People v. Welton*, 211 P. 802 (Calif. 1922).

83. E; TTB.

84. E; *People v. Powell*, 236 P. 311 (Calif. App. 1925).

85. TTB; E; *People v. Bailey*, 225 P. 752 (Calif. App. 1924).

86. TTB; E.

87. TTB; E.

88. TTB; E.

89. E; *People v. Powell*, 236 P. 311 (Calif. App. 1925).

90. TTB.

91. TTB; E.

92. TTB; E.

93. TTB; E; *People v. Bailey*, 225 P. 752 (Calif. App. 1924).

94. Spector, "Story of the Imperial Valley"; Pass, "Forty-Two Years?"; Vol. 78: 144–147, ACLU Archives; Lowell, "Erickson Speaks from Prison"; "One More to Free"; Spector, "California's Parole Racket."

95. TTB; E.

96. E.

97. E; *People v. Powell*, 236 P. 311 (Calif. App. 1925).

98. "The Story of James Price," *Industrial Worker*, November 10, 1923; TTB; E; U.S. Attorney General, "In the Matter of the Application of James Price," February 28, 1924, Department of Justice.

99. TTB; E.

100. TTB; E; *People v. McClennigan*, 234 P. 91 (Calif. 1925).

101. TTB; E; *Industrial Worker*, August 15, 1911; *People v. Roe*, 209 P. 381 (Calif. App. 1922).

102. TTB; E.

103. TTB; E.

104. Spector, "Story of the Imperial Valley"; Pass, "Forty-Two Years?"; Vol. 78: 144–147, ACLU Archives; Lowell, "Erickson Speaks from Prison"; "One More to Free"; Spector, "California's Parole Racket."

105. TTB; E; *People v. Wagner*, 225 P. 464 (Calif. App. 1924).

106. TTB; E; *Industrial Solidarity*, March 30, 1927.

107. TTB; E; *People v. Welton*, 211 P. 802 (Calif. 1922).

108. TTB; *Industrial Worker*, August 15, 1923.

109. TTB; E.

110. Spector, "Story of the Imperial Valley"; Pass, "Forty-Two Years?"; Vol. 78: 144–147, ACLU Archives; Lowell, "Erickson Speaks from Prison"; "One More to Free"; Spector, "California's Parole Racket."

111. TTB; E.

112. Spector, "Story of the Imperial Valley"; Pass, "Forty-Two Years?"; Vol. 78: 144–147, ACLU Archives; Lowell, "Erickson Speaks from Prison"; "One More to Free"; Spector, "California's Parole Racket."

113. TTB; E.

114. E; *People v. Steelik*, 203 P. 78 (Calif. 1921).

115. E.

116. TTB; E; *Industrial Solidarity*, March 30, 1927; *People v. Stewart*, 230 P. 221 (Calif. App. 1924).

117. TTB.

118. TTB; E.

119. E; *People v. Powell*, 236 P. 311 (Calif. App. 1925).

120. E; *People v. Taylor*, 203 P. 85 (Calif. 1921).

121. E.

122. TTB.

123. TTB; *People v. Thompson*, 229 P. 896 (Calif. App. 1924).

124. TTB; E.

125. TTB; E.

126. TTB; *People v. Wagner*, 225 P. 464 (Calif. App. 1924).

127. E.

128. TTB.

129. E; *People v. Weiler*, 204 P. 410 (Calif. App. 1921).

130. *People v. Welton*, 211 P. 802 (1922); E.

131. TTB.

132. TTB; E.

133. E.

134. *People v. Bailey*, 225 P. 752 (Calif. App. 1924).

135. TTB; E.

136. TTB; E; *People v. Wright*, 226 P. 952 (Calif. App. 1924).

137. TTB; E; *People v. Stewart*, 230 P. 221 (Calif. App. 1924).

138. ACLU, *Annual Report for 1921–1923*, p. 16 (New York: ACLU, 1923).

139. Herndon Defense Auxiliary Committee, "Facts in the Case of Angelo Herndon" (New York: Herndon Defense Auxiliary Committee, 1936); Charles H. Martin, *The Angelo Herndon Case and Southern Justice* (Baton Rouge: Louisiana State University Press, 1976); Angelo Herndon, *Let Me Live* (New York: Random House, 1937); *Herndon v. Lowery*, 301 U.S. 242 (1937).

140. NCLB.

141. NCLB.

142. NCLB.

143. NCLB.

144. NCLB.

145. *New Solidarity*, January 9, 1924.

146. Sims, "Idaho's Criminal Syndicalism Act: One State's Response to Radical Labor," *Labor History* 15 (Fall 1974).

147. Vol. 233, ACLU Archives; *New Solidarity*, September 20, 1924, and January 21, 1924; Sims, "Idaho's Criminal Syndicalism Act," 511.

148. NCLB.

149. NCLB.

150. NCLB.

151. *New Solidarity*, January 9, 1924; Vol. 233, ACLU Archives; NCLB.

152. NCLB.

153. *New Solidarity*, January 9, 1924.

154. NCLB.

155. NCLB.

156. Sims, "Idaho's Criminal Syndicalism Act."

157. NCLB.

158. NCLB.

159. NCLB.

160. Ibid.; NCLB.

161. *New Solidarity*, December 1, 1923; Vol. 233, ACLU Archives; ACLU, *Annual Report, 1924*, p. 16 (New York: ACLU, 1925).

162. NCLB.

163. NCLB.

164. Theodore Draper, *The Roots of American Communism* (New York: Viking Press, 1957), 204; Theodore Draper, *American Communism and Soviet Russia* (New York: Octagon Press, 1977), 20; Benjamin Gitlow, *"I Confess": The Truth About American Communism* (New York: E. P. Dutton & Co., 1940), 155; *People v. Lloyd*, 136 N.E. 505 (Ill., 1922).

165. *State v. Berquist*, 199 P. 101 (Kans. 1921).

166. *New Solidarity*, October 28, 1922.

167. *State v. Fiske*, 230 P. 88 (Kans. 1924).

168. Mancet Haldeman-Julius, "Joe Neil, Victim of a Great State's Bigotry," June 1928, 344: 6, ACLU Archives; Letter from Lower to Tulin, April 3, 1928 (Joe Neil Parole Matter), 344: 3, ACLU Archives.

169. NCLB.

170. NCLB.

171. Elizabeth G. Flynn, *The Rebel Girl: An Autobiography* (New York: International Publishers, 1955), 200; Gitlow, *"I Confess,"* 105, 117.

172. *People v. Gitlow*, 136 N.E. 317 (N.Y. 1922); *Labor Defender*, October 1925.

173. *People v. Gitlow*, 136 N.E. 317 (N.Y. 1922); *Labor Defender*, October 1925; *Gitlow v. New York*, 268 U.S. 652 (1925); ACLU, *Annual Report for 1925*, p. 14 (New York: ACLU, 1926); Gitlow, *"I Confess"*; Benjamin Gitlow, *The Whole of Their Lives* (New York: Charles Scribner's Sons, 1948).

174. *Labor Defender*, October 1925; Flynn, *Rebel Girl*, 261.

175. FBI File #190-27627; *People v. Gitlow*, 136 N.E. 317 (N.Y. 1922); *Labor Defender*, October 1925.

176. *Labor Defender*, October 1925; Flynn, *Rebel Girl*, 261.

177. *Labor Defender*, October 1925; Gitlow, *"I Confess,"* 119–120.

178. *Labor Defender*, October 1925.

179. Flynn, *Rebel Girl*, 261.

180. *People v. Gitlow*, 136 N.E. 317 (N.Y. 1922); *Labor Defender*, October 1925; *People v. Ruthenberg*, 201 N.W. 358 (Mich. 1925); Flynn, *Rebel Girl*, 257–261.

181. Gitlow, *"I Confess,"* 93–96, 322; Draper, *Roots of American Communism*, 203–204.

182. Robinson, *Anti-Sedition Legislation*; ACLU, *Annual Report, 1925*; *Berg v. State*, 233 P. 497 (1925); *Defense News Service*, August 20, 1924.

183. James A. Robinson, *Anti-Sedition Legislation and Loyalty Investigation in Oklahoma* (Norman, Okla.: Bureau of Government Research, 1956); ACLU, *Annual Report, 1925*, p. 14 (New York: ACLU, 1926); *Wear v. State*, 235 P. 271 (Okla. Crim. App. 1925); *Defense News Service*, August 20, 1924.

184. Eldridge F. Dowell, *A History of Criminal Syndicalism Legislation in the U.S.* (Baltimore: Johns Hopkins Press, 1939), 119–120; *Portland News-Telegram*, January

20, 1932; *Oregonian,* January 21, 1932; *Daily Worker,* February 6, 1932; *News- Telegram, Portland,* February 27, 1932.

185. *Commonwealth v. Blankenstein,* 81 Pa. Super. 340 (1923).

186. *Commonwealth v. Widovich,* 93 Pa. Super. 223 (1928); *Commonwealth v. Widovich,* 145 A. 295 (Pa. 1929); Letter of Anne Muselin, *Labor Defender,* December 1931; Pete Muselin, "The Woodlawn Verdict," *Labor Defender,* December 1929; A. Jakisa, "Woodlawn, 1926–1930," *Labor Defender,* November 1930; Muselin to Harper, letter of September 3, 1931, 42: 38–39, ACLU Archives; ACLU to Harper, letter of September 25, 1931, 42: 145, ACLU Archives.

187. *State v. Lowery,* 177 P. 355 (Wash. 1918).

188. *Industrial Worker,* February 25, 1925.

189. *New Solidarity,* July 22, 1922; *Labor Defender,* August 1926.

190. *State v. Hennessy,* 195 P. 211 (Wash. 1921).

191. *New Solidarity,* September 16, 1922; *State v. Hestings,* 196 P. 13 (Wash. 1921).

192. *New Solidarity,* July 22, 1922; *Labor Defender,* August 1926.

193. *State v. Lowery,* 177 P. 355 (Wash. 1918).

194. *State v. Hestings,* 196 P. 13 (Wash. 1921).

195. *Industrial Worker,* July 22, 1922.

196. *Industrial Worker,* October 9, 1926.

197. *Labor Defender,* August 1926 and September 1926; *New Solidarity,* September 16, 1922.

198. *New Solidarity,* July 22, 1922; *Labor Defender,* August 1926.

199. *Industrial Worker,* September 16, 1922.

200. *Industrial Worker,* September 4, 25, 1926.

Chapter 14

Political Prisoners Who Died While Incarcerated in Federal, Military and State Prisons

Between 1917 and 1931, at least thirty-one young men died as a direct result of imprisonment for their opposition to World War I or for their radical trade union activities. For the most part, these men died in obscurity at a time when the general public ignored the First Amendment abuses that led to their imprisonment and death. Unlike the handful of political activists sentenced to death and legally executed by the state (such as the Haymarket martyrs, Sacco and Vanzetti, Joe Hill and the Rosenbergs), these unfortunate victims of the Red Scare never achieved national notoriety, and their cases have been the subject of little or no historical inquiry.

R. J. Blaine was arrested in California and jailed while awaiting trial in the Sacramento IWW case. He was held in the Sacramento County Jail, where he died in November 1918.[1]

Charles W. Bolly, from Mungo, Indiana, was a Dunkard and objected to military service on religious grounds. He died at Fort Leavenworth.[2]

Frank Burke was a Socialist conscientious objector from Chicago who was court-martialed after the armistice ending World War I was signed. His death sentence was later commuted to fifteen years in prison.

Originally, his prison experiences were typical of other militant Socialists similarly court-martialed: He took part in hunger strikes at Camp Funston, he protested at Fort Leavenworth and was placed in "the hole" on bread and water, and he was subjected to water torture when guards turned powerful fire hoses onto sleeping objectors at Leavenworth. In July 1919, he was transferred from Leavenworth to Fort Douglas.

According to contemporary press accounts, Burke was already very sick when he arrived at Fort Douglas on July 10, 1919. He reported to sick call, sleepless and constipated, but was denied hospitalization until July

25, when his pains reportedly became unbearable. Shortly thereafter a friend visited Burke in the hospital and reported:

I found him in pain and unable to retain any food. He had had his stomach pumped out before being moved. I heard from a corps man that Frank had been calling for dope . . . [An] orderly told me not to bother about Frank's numerous desires, especially his request for a specialist from Salt Lake City. . . .

[Frank] begged me to get a specialist so I went up to see Lieutenant Colonel Graham about getting the services of Major Beer. . . . Major Beer replied that Frank was suffering, but was in no serious condition and that I could see him the next morning about a specialist.

On July 30, 1919, the following day, Frank Burke was dead.[3]

Ed Burns was arrested in California and jailed while awaiting trial in the Sacramento IWW case. He was held in the Sacramento County Jail, where he died in November 1918.[4]

Joe Coya, along with sixteen members of the IWW, was arrested at a union conference in Sacramento in February 1924. While awaiting trial, he, along with other conference participants, was confined in a cell measuring twenty-one by twenty-one feet in the Sacramento County Jail. Because there were no beds in the cell, Coya was forced to sleep on the concrete floor and subsequently contracted pneumonia. He died in prison on May 12, 1924.[5]

Reuben J. Eash, from Thomas, Oklahoma, was a Mennonite and objected to military service on religious grounds. He died at Fort Leavenworth.[6]

Ed Evans was arrested in California and jailed while awaiting trial in the Sacramento IWW case. He was held in the Sacramento County Jail, where he died in November 1918.[7]

Julius Firestone was inducted into the army in 1917. Because of his strong public stance against the war, Firestone was tarred and feathered by soldiers stationed with him at Camp Hancock, Georgia. He became sick and died on November 25, 1918, of pneumonia while incarcerated at Hancock. Firestone was a member of the Central Committee of the Kings County, New York, Socialist Party.[8]

Daniel B. Flory, from Lancaster, Pennsylvania, was an "undenominational" believer and objected to military service on religious grounds. He died at Fort Leavenworth.[9]

Henry E. Franz, from Hooker, Oklahoma, was a Mennonite and objected to military service on religious grounds. He died at Fort Leavenworth.[10]

Ernest Gellert committed suicide at Fort Hancock, New Jersey, on April 8, 1918, to protest the conditions under which conscientious objectors existed in the military camps and prisons.

The twenty-two-year-old Gellert was a sincere idealist and Socialist. He wrote concerning the interrogation soon after his arrest:

He [the military officer examining Gellert] asked me if I thought I was doing any service for humanity by hitting my head against a stone wall. I answered that I realized my own insignificance—that I did not hold the ridiculous idea that I could stop the war as an individual, but that I was willing to give my life if need be as a protest against wars. I was then dismissed.

Transcripts of Gellert's court-martial hearing preserve this exchange between the prosecutor and Gellert:

Question: You state that you are perfectly willing to take any punishment subsequent to violation of orders?
Answer: I am willing to take whatever consequence my attitude may bring.
Question: You have no fear of death itself?
Answer: I am as much afraid of death as anybody else. To me death would mean the end of my existence. Perhaps I should be more afraid of death than ordinary people, but nevertheless, if death should be the alternative, I would submit to death.
Question: You hold life sacred, above everything else?
Answer: When you reduce things to its terms, that is what we come to.
Question: And you place your personal opinions above life?
Answer: My personal opinions and my life are synonymous.

While awaiting court-martial at Upton, Gellert was stripped of his clothing and forced to wear a military uniform or freeze to death. He was housed throughout the winter in an unheated cell and was once forced to stand in place outside during a blizzard.

After his hearing Gellert was transferred to Fort Hancock. There he was denied family visits and subjected to constant ridicule from the enlisted men. According to his attorney, their ridicule was a source of mental torture for the sensitive Gellert.

On April 8, 1918, Ernest Gellert was found dead, a bullet lodged in his breast. A note beside his body read:

I fear I have not succeeded in convincing the authorities of the sincerity of my scruples against participation in the war. I feel that only by my death will I be able to save others from the mental tortures I have gone through. If I succeed, I give my life willingly.

Gellert's death was ruled a suicide by the military authorities.[11]

James Gossard, from Urbana, Illinois, was arrested and scheduled for trial at the mass IWW trial in Wichita. He was held in the Newton County

(Kansas) Jail, where he died while awaiting trial, reportedly because of "improperly treated influenza."[12]

Joseph and Michael Hofer (the Hofer brothers) were members of the Hutterite religious order. Their religion forbade cooperation with the military.

Sent to Alcatraz, the Hofer brothers refused to obey prison officials and were placed in "the hole." The "hole" was a lightless, rat-infested basement cell. The Hofers were stripped of all their clothing, except underwear, and chained to the walls of this dungeon for eight hours a day. Fed only bread and water and denied proper toilet facilities, their health was broken. They were released from "the hole" and transferred to Fort Leavenworth.

Again they refused to work, and although still sick, they were remanded to the Leavenworth solitary cell. Within a few days the brothers' condition further deteriorated into pneumonia. They were sent to the prison hospital, where they died.[13]

Johannes M. Klassen, from Clinton, Oklahoma, was a Mennonite and objected to military service on religious grounds. He died at Fort Leavenworth.[14]

Cornelius Lehane, from Cork County, Ireland. A Socialist and Irish Nationalist, Lehane worked both as a journalist and as a trade union organizer. He was arrested in New York City by federal authorities for anti-war activity and transported to the Hartford County Jail in Connecticut. There he died of influenza after being held in jail for approximately one hundred days.[15]

Ricardo Flores Magón, from Mexico City, Mexico, and Los Angeles, California, was sentenced to twenty-one years and one day in prison for violating the Espionage Act. He began serving his sentence on July 19, 1918. An internationally respected Mexican revolutionary and anarchist, Magón died on November 21, 1922, in Leavenworth Penitentiary. (The circumstances of his death are related in Chapter 6.)[16]

James Nolan was arrested in California and jailed while awaiting trial in the Sacramento IWW case. He was held in the Sacramento County Jail, where he died in November 1918.[17]

Milan Resetar of Woodlawn, Pennsylvania, was one of three Communist Party members convicted under the Pennsylvania sedition law in 1928. (See the entry for codefendant Pete Muselin in Chapter 13 for a description of his case.)

Resetar began serving his sentence in 1929 at the Allegheny County Workhouse in Blawnox, Pennsylvania. In an August 1930 letter from prison he described Blawnox as a place of "appalling" "filth," "swarming with bed bugs, roaches, lice and other vermin."

By September 1931, Resetar had become very ill, but was denied proper medical attention. According to one report:

When he could hardly stand any longer they sent Milan Resetar to the prison infirmary. "Palpitation of the heart," they called his ailment. Five days later they thrust him out again, back to the grim prison workshop and the bleak prison cell. They said he was "improved."

And then the old doctor went off on a vacation and a new doctor took his place. He saw this sick man staggering in anguish. The sweat of death was already on his face. A week after he had been dismissed from the infirmary as healed, they carried him to a bed again.

They found his lungs eaten up by tuberculosis, his heart enveloped in a pus sac.

The state of Pennsylvania declined Resetar's request to be released from prison and transferred to a hospital. He died in jail in October 1931.[18]

Otto Frederick Schmidt, a twenty-six-year-old member of the IWW arrested in Spokane, Washington, was held for ten months in jail as a deportable alien. Originally detained at an immigration station, Schmidt was arrested without a warrant and held without benefit of a trial or hearing. Schmidt was denied letter-writing privileges and was forced to sleep on a "concrete floor" with "no bed." He fell ill at the immigration station and lost his "teeth and hair."

According to his cellmate, A. George Jensen, Schmidt "believed that the working class should organize to better their conditions. He was arrested for trying to make the world a fit place in which to live."

Schmidt was transferred to the Walla Walla County Jail, where conditions remained very poor. When the IWW prisoners collectively protested their condition, the guards responded by hosing them down:

A terrific stream of icy cold water was turned onto the sick, half-starved and helpless men, who were locked in a cage, trapped like so many rats. Men were lifted off their feet and battered against the steel bars by the force of the water. Within a few minutes mattresses and blankets were floating about the floor and five men were stretched out, bleeding and unconscious in the wreckage and water.

Schmidt was one of the inmates found unconscious after the hosing, but he received no medical attention. His body was merely laid on a "bare iron bunk." Later, when prison authorities decided he was sufficiently ill to require medical attention, Schmidt was transferred to the Spokane County Jail. But his condition continued to worsen:

Schmidt was coughing; the froth was over his drawn lips. During his final days he was removed, sent to the Sacred Heart Hospital, where he died on December 2, 1918.[19]

Jacob Schwartz was arrested on August 23, 1918, on Espionage Act charges along with Jacob Abrams, Mollie Steimer and two other anarchists for distributing a leaflet criticizing U.S. intervention in Russia during 1918.

Schwartz reported in a September 5, 1918, letter to a friend that he had been beaten with "black-jacks" while in prison and described himself as "pale-faced and bruised." Schwartz was transferred to Bellevue, where he died on October 14, 1918. The following unfinished note was found in his cell:

Farewell, comrade. When you appear before the court I will be with you no longer. Struggle without fear, fight bravely. I am sorry I have to leave you. But this is life itself. After your long martyr—[20]

Abraham Shocker was an IWW member convicted of violating the California criminal syndicalism law on December 9, 1921. He began serving his sentence in San Quentin on December 11, 1921. On August 9, 1923, Shocker was discovered hanging in his cell. Shocker's death took place within a few days of his release from a forty-three-day stay in solitary confinement.[21]

Van Skedine was sentenced in a federal court to one year in prison for refusing to register for the draft. While incarcerated in the Bridewell Jail in Illinois, Skedine began a hunger strike.

Doctors examined the striking Skedine and declared him sane although "suffering from delusions" because "he believed he was dying for the cause of the conscientious objectors." Skedine died after twenty-two days of hunger striking. The post-mortem report identified the cause of death as "influenza and pneumonia."[22]

Walter Sprunger, from Berne, Indiana, was a Mennonite and objected to military service on religious grounds. He died at Fort Leavenworth.[23]

Carol Swenson, a member of the IWW, committed suicide by hanging on September 19, 1919, while imprisoned in the Spokane County (Washington) Jail, where he was awaiting trial for violating the federal Espionage Act.[24]

Daniel Teuscher, from Fisher, Illinois, was a Mennonite and objected to military service on religious grounds. He died at Fort Leavenworth.[25]

Mark R. Thomas, from Vandergraft, Pennsylvania, was a member of the IBSA and objected to military service on religious grounds. He died at Fort Leavenworth.[26]

Frank Travis was arrested in California and jailed awaiting trial in the Sacramento IWW case. He was held in the Sacramento County Jail, where he died in November 1918.[27]

Daniel H. Wallace was arrested under the Espionage Act for delivering a speech critical of World War I before two thousand people at the Grand Opera House in Davenport, Iowa. Wallace, who had been wounded and gassed while fighting for Britain before the United States' entry into the war, was a staunch opponent of the war.

Upon coming to the United States Wallace told the "terrible truth about the trenches and warfare" in lectures and published materials, and he became organizer-general for the anti-war League of Humanity.

Wallace was convicted and sentenced to twenty years of imprisonment on October 4, 1917. In prison he went "insane" and died.[28]

Ernest D. Wells, from Virginia, was a Christadelphian and objected to military service on religious grounds. He died at Fort Leavenworth.[29]

John M. Wolfe died at Fort Riley on December 6, 1918. In September 1918, Wolfe was among forty-one objectors placed into a "damp, dark basement cell" at Riley. Conditions within this cell, which was designed to hold no more than twenty-two inmates, were deplorable. According to a cellmate of Wolfe, the cell was a "disease breeding place" where "health conditions were impossible."

Wolfe became extremely ill and was transferred to the base hospital. He died from influenza shortly thereafter.[30]

Daniel S. Yoder, from Applecreek, Oklahoma, was a Mennonite and objected to military service on religious grounds. He died at Fort Leavenworth.[31]

NOTES

1. IWW, "With Drops of Blood," Box 1, Record Group 28, National Archives; IWW, "Workers Jailed in Hell Hole" [undated pamphlet].

2. Vol. 71: 67, February 6, 1920, Archives of the American Civil Liberties Union [hereafter ACLU Archives].

3. H. Austin Simons, "Fifth Objector Dies," *New York Call*, October 12, 1919.

4. IWW, "With Drops of Blood"; IWW, "Workers Jailed in Hell Hole."

5. *Industrial Worker*, May 17, 1924, and May 28, 1924.

6. Vol. 71: 67, February 6, 1920, ACLU Archives.

7. IWW, "With Drops of Blood"; IWW, "Workers Jailed in Hell Hole."

8. *New York Call*, November 26, 1918.

9. Vol. 71: 67, February 6, 1920, ACLU Archives.

10. Vol. 71: 67, February 6, 1920, ACLU Archives.

11. Walter Nelles to Woodrow Wilson, letter of May 13, 1918, vol. 76, ACLU Archives; Military Intelligence Division, File #10902-28, National Archives.

12. *New Solidarity*, November 16, 1918; ACLU, "The Truth About the IWW Prisoners" [Pamphlet] (ACLU, 1922); Winthrop Lane, "Uncle Sam: Jailer," *Survey*, September 6, 1919; IWW, "Workers Jailed in Hell Hole."

13. David Hofer, "Desecration of the Dead" [Pamphlet] (Chicago: American Industrial Co., undated), ACLU Archives; Norman Thomas, *Is Conscience a Crime?* (New York: Vanguard, 1927), 197–200.

14. Vol. 71: 67, February 6, 1920, ACLU Archives.

15. Federal Bureau of Investigation [hereafter FBI], "In re: Jim Larkin Memorial Meeting for Cornelius Lehane," February 8, 1919, FBI File #190-27627.

16. Leavenworth Penitentiary Record #14596.

17. IWW, "With Drops of Blood"; IWW, "Workers Jailed in Hell Hole."

18. Paul Peters, "Death in an American Dungeon," *Labor Defender,* January 1932, 7; Resetar death notice, *Labor Defender,* October 1931; Resetar letters printed in *Labor Defender,* August 1930 and September 1931.

19. *New Solidarity,* January 4, 1919.

20. Political Prisoners Defense and Relief Committee, "Sentenced to Twenty Years in Prison" [Pamphlet] (New York: the Committee 1919), National Archives.

21. *Industrial Worker,* August 19, 1923; "Erwin, Claude, Record of Criminal Syndicalism Convictions in California," Box 135, Folder #1, IWW Collection, Wayne State University.

22. *Chicago Tribune,* December 20, 1919.

23. Vol. 71: 67, February 6, 1920, ACLU Archives.

24. IWW, "With Drops of Blood."

25. Vol. 71: 67, February 6, 1920, ACLU Archives.

26. Vol. 71: 67, February 6, 1920, ACLU Archives.

27. IWW, "With Drops of Blood"; IWW, "The Silent Defense" [Pamphlet] (Chicago: IWW, undated), 10.

28. U.S. Attorney General, *Letter of March 9, 1922, re Government Prosecutions Under the Espionage Act,* 67th Cong., 2d Sess., 1922, Senate Doc. No. 159; National Civil Liberties Bureau, *War Time Prosecutions and Mob Violence,* 69: 58, ACLU Archives; League of Humanity, "Twenty-Two Years and $20,000 Fine for Daniel H. Wallace" [Undated pamphlet], 17: 241, ACLU Archives.

29. Vol. 71: 67, February 6, 1920, ACLU Archives.

30. Letter of Maurice Hess, October 20, 1919, ACLU Archives.

31. Vol. 71: 67, February 6, 1920, ACLU Archives.

Chapter 15

Conclusion

In the summer of 1980, shortly before his death, I interviewed the ninety-six-year-old founder of the American Civil Liberties Union, Roger Nash Baldwin.[1] Baldwin had been very active in the defense of the World War I political prisoners and had himself served a prison term for refusing, on moral and political grounds, to register for the draft in 1918.

Although near death, Baldwin's insight into these prisoners was clear and incisive:

What you are writing about has a certain social significance beyond the evidence. Beyond these few men. [These prisoners] are just the surface indication of something greater and stronger than what you write about. It is the affirmation of principle.

The [prisoners] were people [who] expressed, just a chance expression at a particular time, of a force in society that is enduring, that is there all of the time.

If you say, "Here I stand, I can do no other," it is a very important social force. Great human history has been written by people who would not be moved.

Political imprisonment is the most natural form of imprisonment in the history of society. Political imprisonment is always aimed at the opposition. People in power are afraid of the opposition. It leads to treason, revolution and disorder. You stop it before it has a chance to do so. Opinions hostile to the government, subversive as they call them, [have been] penalized more than any other kind in history. . . . The meaning of political imprisonment is the meaning of political opposition.[2]

Baldwin recognized the insidious nature of political imprisonment. He understood how it made people "doubt whether they could possibly be right against the overwhelming [number] of people who thought they were not. It sowed a kind of distrust in themselves. . . . They felt that they were different."

Despite the abuses involved in placing persons such as Eugene V. Debs, Emma Goldman, William Haywood and Kate Richards O'Hare in prison solely on the basis of their nonviolent speech and the terrible loss of human life that resulted from the incarcerations, the U.S. government has never resolved or properly confronted or corrected the past. Congress has never repealed the laws that placed them in jail, the executive's police powers have grown significantly since 1917 and the courts have failed to find these statutes unconstitutional.

In *Brandenburg v. Ohio*, Supreme Court Justices Hugo Black and William O. Douglas agreed with the Court's attempt to strictly limit the application of peacetime anti-sedition laws.[3] But these two justices also recognized how the "clear and present danger" standard articulated throughout the World War I Espionage Act cases had "twisted and perverted" and "eroded substantial parts of the First Amendment."[4] Recognizing these past abuses, Black and Douglas concluded that this standard "should have no place in the interpretation of the First Amendment."[5] Unfortunately, the majority of the Supreme Court has declined to follow this reasoning.

The U.S. government's failure to unequivocally declare sedition laws unconstitutional, through either congressional or judicial action, creates a realistic potential that these laws will again be used to silence dissent. Worse, the blight upon the First Amendment, of which the prisoners discussed in this book are reminders, has never been rectified.

NOTES

1. "Roger Baldwin, 97, Is Dead, Crusader," Obituary, *New York Times*, August 27, 1981.

2. Roger Baldwin, interview with author, New Jersey, summer of 1980.

3. Indeed, in *Brandenburg* the Court set forth a very high standard for obtaining a conviction under state criminal syndicalism statutes:

[T]he constitutional guarantees of free speech and free press do not permit a State to forbid or proscribe advocacy of the use of force or of law violation except where such advocacy is directed to inciting or producing imminent lawless action and is likely to incite or produce such action.

Brandenburg v. Ohio, 395 U.S. 444, 447 (1969).

4. 395 U.S. at 454 (Douglas, J., concurring).

5. 395 U.S. at 459 (Black, J., concurring).

Selected Bibliography

Research into this book began in 1980, with initial Freedom of Information Act (FOIA) requests to the FBI for access to information concerning American activists imprisoned for their beliefs. Since that date I have filed over a thousand separate FOIA requests with a variety of government departments and was forced to undertake two separate lawsuits under FOIA against the FBI. The second suit (D.C. District Court No. 87-3350) was heard by the Honorable Stanley Sporkin, U.S. District Judge. In a hearing on April 12, 1988, Judge Sporkin criticized the FBI's failure to release information and waive copying fees on records related to political prisoners. Shortly thereafter the FBI agreed to settle the suit, which resulted in the release of thousands of documents concerning prosecutions under the Espionage Act and the Smith Act.

Unlike the FBI, the Federal Bureau of Prisons and the U.S. Pardon Attorney readily produced prison records related to hundreds of Espionage and Sedition Act prisoners formerly incarcerated in the federal penitentiaries at Leavenworth and Atlanta. These and other records produced under the FOIA are the principal sources for this book. Additionally, materials from the archival sources listed below were heavily relied upon.

FBI FILES

The following FBI files were processed and declassified at the request of the author. They are available for public review and duplication at the FBI Freedom of Information-Privacy Act Reading Room in Washington, D.C.

Name of File	FBI Freedom of Information-Privacy Act (FOIPA) Request #
Jacob Abrams	271,360
Orville Anderson	263,824
Charles Bennett	271,533
Alexander Berkman	271,548
T. Blodgett	271,359
B. F. Bryant	271,543
Dan Buckley	271,525
Ralph Chaplin	221,610
Stanley J. Clark	232,301
James M. Coldwell	226,180
Roy Crane	271,531
Paul Crouch	226,192
J. M. Danley	271,358
Pete DeBernardi	232,304
William J. Dodge	271,392
Godfrey Ebel	232,311
Orville Enfield	271,410
Mary Equi	221,417
Ben Fletcher	221,612
Sam Forbes	271,434
Harry Gray	232,326
J. K. Hall	271,352
George Harrison	232,321
William D. Haywood	221,505
Edgar Held	271,495
Emil Herman	271,347
Walter Heynachner	271,507
William Hicks	271,504
Clyde Hough	232,330
IWW	99,719
IWW General Defense Committee	221,598
International Labor Defense	95,671
Ida N. Kalkschmidt	271,511
Albert Kaltscmidt	271,512

Harry F. Kane	232,333
Hyman Lachowski	271,367
James Larkin	297,965
Leo Laukki	271,408
Gerard Liebisch	271,319
Samuel Lipman	271,368
Sidney Mader	271,403
Enrique F. Magón	271,317
Walter Matthey	271,312
William V. McCoy	271,306
Herbert McCutcheon	271,377
H. H. Munson	271,288
Walter T. Neff	221,611
Mayer Nehring	271,285
Daniel O'Connell	271,435
Kate Richards O'Hare	221,561
Louise Olivereau	271,443
William O'Rear	271,422
Louis Parenti	232,352
Joseph Pass	271,426
Charles Plahn	232,356
Political Amnesty Committee	221,707
S. J. Powell	271,267
Floyd Ramp	271,364
Walter M. Reeder	271,243
C. H. Rice	271,242
Z. L. Risley	271,339
Joseph F. Rutherford	271,331
Sam Scarlett	232,358
Abram J. Schur	271,314
Archie Sinclair	232,360
Maurice Snitkin	271,303
H. C. Spence	271,492
Rose Pastor Stokes	221,560
Thomas Sullivan	271,257
Pierce C. Wette	232,372
Christian Yearous	271,273
Nicholas Zogg	271,268

ARCHIVES

Archives of the American Civil Liberties Union, Princeton University, Princeton, New
	Jersey.
Industrial Workers of the World Collection, Wayne State University, Detroit, Michigan.
International Labor Defense Collection, New York Public Library, New York, New York.
National Archives and Records Service, Washington, D.C. (Records of the U.S. Pardon
	Attorney, the Military Intelligence Division Records and Department of Jus-
	tice files).
Peace Collection, Swarthmore College, Swarthmore, Pennsylvania.
Socialist Party Collection, Duke University, Durham, North Carolina.
Tamiment Collection, New York University, New York, New York.
The Victor Jerome, Rose Pastor Stokes and Harry Weinberger Collections, Yale University
	Library, New Haven, Connecticut.

NEWSPAPERS/PERIODICALS

Chicago Tribune

Congressional Record

Defense News Service

Federated Press

Harvard Law Review

Industrial Solidarity

Industrial Worker

Labor Defender

Labor History

Labor Unity

The Liberator

Mennonite Historical Bulletin

Mother Earth

New Solidarity

New York Call

New York Leader

New York Times

New York World

Nome Industrial Worker

Providence Sunday Journal

Survey

Wire City Weekly

CASES

Abrams v. United States, 250 U.S. 616 (1919)

Anderson v. United States, 264 F. 75 (8th Cir. 1920)

Anderson v. United States, 269 F. 65 (9th Cir. 1920)

Berg v. State, 233 P. 497 (1925)

Brandenburg v. Ohio, 395 U.S. 444 (1969)

Burns v. United States, 274 U.S. 328 (1927)

Commonwealth v. Blankenstein, 81 Pa. Super. 340 (1923)

Debs v. United States, 249 U.S. 211 (1919)

Dennis v. United States, 341 U.S. 494 (1951)

Dickson v. United States, 278 F. 728 (8th Cir. 1921)

Dunne v. United States, 138 F.2d 137 (8th Cir. 1943)

Enfield v. United States, 271 F. 141 (8th Cir. 1919)

Equi v. United States, 261 F. 53 (9th Cir. 1919)

Ex Parte Bernat, 255 F. 429 (W.D. Wash. 1918)

Ex Parte Jackson, 263 F. 110 (D. Mont. 1920)

Ex Parte McDermott, 183 P. 437 (Calif. 1919)

Ex Parte Moore, 224 P. 662 (Idaho 1924)

Ex Parte Wood, 277 P. 908 (Calif. 1924)

Fiske v. Kansas, 274 U.S. 380 (1927)

Franke v. Murray, 248 F. 865 (8th Cir. 1918)

Frohwerk v. United States, 249 U.S. 204 (1919)

Gerdes v. State, 175 N.W. 606 (Neb. 1919)

Gitlow v. New York, 268 U.S. 652 (1925)

Goldman v. United States, 245 U.S. 474 (1918)

Goldstein v. United States, 258 F. 908 (9th Cir. 1919)

Grubl v. United States, 264 F. 44 (8th Cir. 1920)

Haywood v. United States, 268 F. 795 (1920)

Herndon v. Lowery, 301 U.S. 242 (1937)

Krafft v. United States, 249 F. 919 (3d Cir. 1918)

Magón v. United States, 260 F. 811 (9th Cir. 1919)

Noto v. United States, 367 U.S. 290 (1961)

O'Connell v. United States, 253 U.S. 142 444 (1920)

O'Rear v. United States, 261 F. 257 (5th Cir. 1919)

Pennsylvania v. Nelson, 350 U.S. 497 (1956)

People v. Bailey, 225 P. 752 (Calif. App. 1924)

People v. Casdorf, 212 P. 237 (Calif. App. 1922)

People v. Connors, 246 P. 1072 (Calif. App. 1926)

People v. Cox, 226 P. 14 (Calif. App. 1924)

People v. Eaton, 213 P. 275 (Calif. App. 1923)

People v. Erickson, 226 P. 637 (Calif. App. 1924)

People v. Flanagan, 223 P. 1014 (Calif. App. 1924)

People v. Gitlow, 136 N.E. 317 (N.Y. 1922)

People v. Johansen, 226 P. 634 (Calif. App. 1924)

People v. LaRue, 216 P. 627 (Calif. App. 1923)

People v. Lesse, 199 P. 46 (Calif. App. 1921)

People v. Lloyd, 136 N.E. 505 (Ill. 1922)

People v. Malley, 194 P. 48 (Calif. App. 1920)

People v. McClennigan, 234 P. 91 (Calif. 1925)

People v. Powell, 236 P. 311 (Calif. App. 1925)

People v. Roe, 209 P. 381 (Calif. App. 1922)

People v. Ruthenberg, 201 N.W. 358 (Mich. 1925)

People v. Steelik, 203 P. 78 (Calif. 1921)

People v. Stewart, 230 P. 221 (Calif. App. 1924)

People v. Sullivan, 211 P. 467 (Calif. App. 1922)

People v. Taylor, 203 P. 85 (Calif. 1921)

People v. Thompson, 229 P. 896 (Calif. App. 1924)

People v. Thornton, 219 P. 1020 (Calif. App. 1923)

People v. Thurman, 216 P. 394 (Calif. App. 1923)

People v. Wagner, 225 P. 464 (Calif. App. 1924)

People v. Ware, 226 P. 956 (Calif. App. 1924)

People v. Welton, 211 P. 802 (Calif. 1922)

People v. Weiler, 204 P. 410 (Calif. App. 1921)

People v. Wright, 226 P. 952 (Calif. App. 1924)

Pierce v. United States, 252 U.S. 239 (1920)

Scales v. United States, 367 U.S. 203 (1961)

Schaefer v. United States, 251 U.S. 466 (1920)

Schenck v. United States, 249 U.S. 47 (1919)

Seebach v. United States, 262 F. 885 (8th Cir. 1919)

Snitkin v. United States, 265 F. 489 (7th Cir. 1920)

State v. Aspelin, 203 P. 964 (Wash. 1922)

State v. Berquist, 199 P. 101 (Kans. 1921)

State v. Boloff, 4 P.2d 326 (1931)

State v. Breen, 205 P. 632 (Kans. 1922)

State v. Derke, 172 N.W. 777 (Minn. 1919)

State v. Dingman, 219 P. 760 (Idaho 1923)

State v. Fiske, 230 P. 88 (Kans. 1924)

State v. Hennessy, 195 P. 211 (Wash. 1921)

State v. Hestings, 196 P. 13 (Wash. 1921)

State v. Lowery, 177 P. 355 (Wash. 1918)

State v. Morlen, 167 N.W. 345 (1918)

State v. Pettilla, 200 P. 332 (Wash. 1921)

State v. Tonn, 191 N.W. 530 (Iowa 1923)

Stilson v. United States, 250 U.S. 583 (1919)

Stokes v. United States, 264 F. 18 (8th Cir. 1920)

United States v. Baker, 247 F. 124 (D. Md. 1917)

United States v. Boutin, 251 F. 313 (N.D.N.Y. 1918)

United States v. Krafft, 249 F. 919 (3d Cir. 1918)

United States v. Mayer, 252 F. 868 (W.D. Ky. 1918)

United States v. Nearing, 252 F. 223 (S.D.N.Y. 1918)

United States v. Prieth, 254 F. 946 (D.N.J. 1918)

United States v. Sugarman, 245 F. 604 (D. Minn. 1917)

Von Bank v. United States, 253 F. 641 (8th Cir. 1918)

Wear v. State, 235 P. 271 (Okla. Crim. App. 1925)

White v. United States, 263 F. 17 (6th Cir. 1920)

Whitney v. California, 274 U.S. 357 (1927)

Wolf v. United States, 259 F. 388 (8th Cir. 1919)

Yates v. United States, 354 U.S. 298 (1957)

BOOKS, JOURNALS AND PAMPHLETS

American Civil Liberties Union [ACLU]. *Annual Reports*. Vol. 1, *1920–1930*. New York: Arno Press and the New York Times, 1970.
———. "Conscientious Objectors: The Facts Today." [Pamphlet.] ACLU, 1920. ACLU Archives, Princeton University.
———. "The Truth About the IWW Prisoners." [Pamphlet.] New York: ACLU, 1922.
American Protective League. "Counter Espionage Laws." [Pamphlet.] American Protective League, 1918.
Amnesty International. *Proposal for a Commission of Inquiry into the Effect of Domestic Intelligence Activities on Criminal Trials in the U.S.A.* Nottingham, England: Russell Press Ltd., 1981.
Baldwin, Roger N. "The Individual and the State." [Pamphlet.] ACLU, 1918.

Bell, Daniel. *Marxian Socialism in the United States.* Princeton, N.J.: Princeton University Press, 1967.

Berkman, Alexander. *Prison Memoirs of an Anarchist.* New York: Mother Earth Publishing, 1912.

———. *The Russian Tragedy.* Orkney, England: Cienfuegos Press, 1976 (reprint).

Black, Forest. "The Selective Draft Cases: A Judicial Milepost on the Road to Absolutism." *Boston University Law Review* 11 (1931): 37.

Brock, Peter. *Pacifism in the United States—From the Colonial Era to the First World War.* Princeton, N.J.: Princeton University Press, 1968.

———. *Twentieth Century Pacifism.* New York: Van Nostrand Reinhold, 1970.

Brown, Frederick, S. Kohn and M. Kohn. "Conscientious Objector: A Constitutional Right." *New England Law Review* 21, no. 3 (1985–86): 545.

Cannon, James P. *The First Ten Years of American Communism.* New York: Pathfinder Press, 1973.

Chaffe, Zachariah, Jr. "A Contemporary State Trial—The U.S. Versus Jacob Abrams, et al." *Harvard Law Review* 33 (April 1920): 747.

———. *Freedom of Speech.* New York: Harcourt Brace & Howe, 1920.

———. "Freedom of Speech in Time of War." *Harvard Law Review* 32 (1919): 932.

Chaplin, Ralph. *Bars and Shadows: The Prison Poems of Ralph Chaplin.* Ridgewood, NJ: Nellie Seeds Nearing, 1922.

———. *The Centralia Conspiracy.* Chicago: Charles H. Kerr & Co., 1972 (reprint).

———. *Wobbly: The Rough-and-Tumble Story of an American Radical.* Chicago: University of Chicago Press, 1948.

Committee of One Hundred Friends of Conscientious Objectors. *Who Are the Conscientious Objectors.* Brooklyn, N.Y.: the Committee, 1919.

Constantine, J. Robert, ed. *Letters of Eugene V. Debs.* Chicago: University of Illinois Press, 1990.

Debs, Eugene V. *Walls and Bars.* Chicago: Kerr Publishing, 1927.

Dorsen, Norman, P. Bender and B. Neuborne. *Political and Civil Rights in the United States.* Boston: Little, Brown & Co., 1976.

Dowell, Eldridge F. *A History of Criminal Syndicalism Legislation in the U.S.* Baltimore: Johns Hopkins University Press, 1939.

Draper, Theodore Hart. *The Roots of American Communism.* New York: Viking Press, 1957.

Drinnon, Richard. *Rebel in Paradise: A Biography of Emma Goldman.* Boston: Beacon Press, 1961.

Dubofsky, Melvyn. *We Shall Be All: A History of the IWW.* New York: Quadrangle, 1969.

Eastman, Max. *The Trial of Eugene Debs.* New York: Liberation Publishing, no date.

Eichel, Julius. "The Judge Said 'Twenty Years.' " New York: Julius Eichel, 1981.

Emerson, Thomas I. *The System of Freedom of Expression.* New York: Random House, 1970.

Engdahl, J. Louis. "Debs and O'Hare in Prison." [Pamphlet.] Chicago: Socialist Party, 1919. National Archives.

Evert, J. G. "The Martyrs of Alcatraz." [Undated pamphlet.] Hillsboro, Kans.

Finney, Torin R. "Practical Catholic: The Life and Times of Ben J. Salmon, 1889–1932." Master's thesis, University of Massachusetts at Boston, 1984.

Flynn, Elizabeth G. *The Rebel Girl: An Autobiography.* New York: International Publishers, 1955.

Foner, Philip S. *The Industrial Workers of the World, 1905–1917.* New York: International Publishers, 1965.

Foner, Philip S., and Sally M. Miller, eds. *Kate Richards O'Hare: Selected Writings and Speeches.* Baton Rouge: Louisiana State University Press, 1982.

Ginger, Ray. *The Bending Cross: A Biography of Eugene V. Debs.* New Brunswick, N.J.: Rutgers University Press, 1949.

Gitlow, Benjamin. *"I Confess": The Truth About American Communism.* New York: E. P. Dutton & Co., 1940.

———. *The Whole of Their Lives.* New York: Charles Scribner's Sons, 1948.

Goldman, Emma. *Living My Life.* New York: Dover, 1970 (reprint).

Goldstein, Robert J. *Political Repression in Modern America: 1870 to the Present.* New York: Schenkman Publishing Co., 1978.

Gray, Harold S. *Character Bad: The Story of a Conscientious Objector.* New York: Harper and Brothers, 1934.

Gregg, Richard. *The Power of Nonviolence.* New York: Schocken Books, 1966.

Grosser, Philip. "Uncle Sam's Devil's Island." [Pamphlet.] Boston: 1933.

Hartzler, J. S. *Mennonites in the World War.* Scottsdale, Pa.: Mennonite Publishing House, 1922.

Haywood, William D. *Bill Haywood's Book: The Autobiography of William D. Haywood.* New York: International Publishers, 1929.

Hennesey, Ammon. *The Book of Ammon.* Salt Lake City, Utah: Ammon Hennesey, 1965.

Herndon, Angelo. *Let Me Live.* New York: Random House, 1937.

Herndon Defense Auxiliary Committee. "Facts in the Case of Angelo Herndon." New York: Herndon Defense Auxiliary Committee, 1936.

Hillquit, Morris. *Loose Leaves from a Busy Life.* New York: Macmillan Co., 1934.

Hinds, Lennox S. *Illusions of Justice: Human Rights Violations in the United States.* Iowa City: School of Social Work, University of Iowa, 1978.

Hofer, David. "Desecration of the Dead." [Undated pamphlet.] Chicago: American Industrial Co.

International Workers of the World [IWW]. "An Open Letter to President Harding." [Pamphlet.] Chicago: IWW, 1922.

———. "Opening Statement of George F. Vanderveer." [Undated pamphlet.] Chicago: IWW. National Archives.

———. "The Silent Defense." [Undated pamphlet.] Chicago: IWW.

———. "Smash the IWW." [Undated pamphlet.] Chicago: IWW.

———. "Workers Jailed in Hell Hole." [Undated pamphlet.]

Jaffe, Julian F. *Crusade Against Radicalism: New York During the Red Scare, 1914–1924.* Port Washington, N.Y.: Kennikat Press, 1972.

Jaffe, Philip J. *The Rise and Fall of American Communism.* New York: Horizon Press, 1975.

Kane, H. F. "Why Eleven Members of the IWW Imprisoned at Leavenworth Refused Conditional Pardon." [Pamphlet.] New York: "Printed free of charge by a friend," 1923.

Karsner, David. *Debs Goes to Prison.* New York: Irving K. Davis Co., 1919.

Kellogg, Walter Guest. *The Conscientious Objector.* New York: Boni & Liveright, 1919.

Kohn, Stephen M. *Jailed for Peace.* Westport, Conn.: Greenwood Press, 1986.

Kornbluh, Joyce L., ed. *Rebel Voices: An IWW Anthology.* Ann Arbor: University of Michigan Press, 1964.

Labor Defense Council. "Nine Questions and Eight Answers About the Michigan " 'Red Raid' Cases." [Undated pamphlet.]

League of Humanity. "Twenty-Two Years and $20,000 Fine for Daniel H. Wallace." [Undated pamphlet.]

Marsh, Margaret S. *Anarchist Women, 1870–1920.* Philadelphia: Temple University Press, 1981.

Martin, Charles H. *The Angelo Herndon Case and Southern Justice.* Baton Rouge: Louisiana State University Press, 1976.

Meyer, Ernest L. *"Hey! Yellowbacks!" The War Diary of a Conscientious Objector.* New York: John Day Co., 1930.

Mother Earth Publishing. *Trial and Speeches of A. Berkman and E. Goldman.* New York: Mother Earth Publishing, 1917.

Murry, Robert K. *Red Scare: A Study in National Hysteria, 1919–1920.* Minneapolis: University of Minnesota Press, 1955.

National Civil Liberties Bureau [NCLB]. "The Case of the Christian Pacifists." [Pamphlet.] New York: NCLB, 1918.

————. Memorandum Regarding the Persecution of the Radical Labor Movement in the U.S. New York: NCLB, 1919.

————. "Political Prisoners in Federal Military Prisons." [Pamphlet.] New York: NCLB, 1918.

Nearing, Scott. *The Making of a Radical.* New York: Harper Colophon Books, 1972.

New York State Senate. *Report of the Joint Legislative Committee Investigating Seditious Activities, Revolutionary Radicalism, Its History, Purpose and Tactics.* Albany, N.Y.: J. B. Lyon Co., 1920.

O'Hare, Kate Richards. *In Prison.* New York: Alfred A. Knopf, 1923.

————. *Prison Letters.* Girard, Kans.: New Appeal Publishing Co., 1919.

People's Print. "Before the Court, Nearing-Debs." [Pamphlet.] New York: People's Print. National Archives.

Perry, Grover H. "The Revolutionary I.W.W." [Undated pamphlet.] Chicago: IWW. National Archives.

Political Prisoners Defense and Relief Committee. "Sentenced to Twenty Years in Prison." [Pamphlet.] New York: the Committee, 1919.

Preston, William. *Aliens and Dissenters: Federal Suppression of Radicals, 1903–1933.* Cambridge, Mass.: Harvard University Press, 1963.

Robinson, James A. *Anti-Sedition Legislation and Loyalty Investigation in Oklahoma.* Norman, Okla.: Bureau of Government Research, 1956.

Secretary of War. *Statement Concerning the Treatment of Conscientious Objectors in the Army.* Washington, D.C.: Government Printing Office, 1919.

Seeley, Bob. *To Study War No More, A Bibliography on War, Peace and Conscience.* Philadelphia: Central Committee for Conscientious Objectors, 1979.

Shulman, Alix K., ed. *Red Emma Speaks: Selected Writings and Speeches by Emma Goldman.* New York: Vintage Books, 1972.

Simons, H. Austin. "The Second Strike at Fort Leavenworth." [Pamphlet.] ACLU Amnesty Committee, 1919.

Sims, Robert C. "Idaho's Criminal Syndicalism Act." Vol. 15. *Labor History* 511 (Fall 1974).

Socialist Party. "Being a True Record of the Case of Frederick Krafft." [Undated pamphlet.] Newark, N.J.: Socialist Party.

———. "One Hundred Years for What?" [Undated pamphlet.] Chicago: Socialist Party. National Archives.

Swisher, Carl B. "Civil Liberties in War Time." Vol. 55. *Political Science Quarterly*, p. 329 (September 1940).

Szajkowski, Zosa. "Double Jeopardy—The Abrams Case of 1919." April 1971. American Jewish Archives.

Taft, Philip. "The Federal Trials of the IWW." *Labor History* 57 (Winter 1962).

Thomas, Norman. *Is Conscience a Crime?* New York: Vanguard, 1927.

———. *War's Heretics.* New York: NCLB, 1917.

Thompson, Fred. *The I.W.W., Its First Fifty Years.* Chicago: IWW, 1955.

Townley, Winfield Scott. *Exiles and Fabrication.* Garden City, N.Y.: Doubleday, 1961.

Tranchtenberg, Alexander, ed. *The American Socialists and the War.* New York: Rand School, 1917.

U.S. Congress. House of Representatives. Committee on the Judiciary. *Hearings on Amnesty for Political Prisoners.* 67th Cong., 2nd Sess., 19. Washington, D.C.: Government Printing Office, 1922. Serial 31.

U.S. Congress. Senate. *Letter from Attorney General re Investigation Activities of the Department of Justice, November 17, 1919.* 67th Cong., 2nd Sess., 1917. S. Doc. 153.

———. Senate. Select Committee to Study Government Operations with Respect to Intelligence Activities. *Book II, Intelligence Activities and the Rights of Americans.* 94th Cong., 2nd Sess., 1976. Washington, D.C.: Government Printing Office, 1976. S. Rept. 755.

U.S. Department of Justice. Attorney General H. M. Daugherty to President Warren G. Harding. "In the Matter of the Application for Pardon in Behalf of Eugene V. Debs." Department of Justice Memorandum 35-386-3336, December 23, 1921. Yale University Library.

———. "Interpretation of War Statutes." Washington, D.C.: Government Printing Office, 1917–1920. [Bulletins distributed between 1917 and 1920.]

Weinstein, James. "Anti-War Sentiment and the Socialist Party." Vol. 74. *Political Science Quarterly*, pp. 215–39 (June 1959).

———. *The Decline of Socialism in America, 1912–1925.* New York: Vintage, 1969.

Whipple, Leon. *The Story of Civil Liberty in the United States.* New York: Vanguard Press, 1927. Reprint. New York: Da Capo Press, 1970.

Zahn, Gordon. *War, Conscience and Dissent.* New York: Hawthorn Books, 1967.

Zinn, Howard. *A People's History of the United States.* New York: Harper & Row, 1980.

Index

About the Author

STEPHEN M. KOHN, a partner in the Washington, D.C. law firm of Kohn, Kohn and Colapinto, P.C., and the Chairperson of the Board of Governors of the National Whistleblowers Center, has extensive experience in First Amendment Law. His first book was *Jailed for Peace* (Praeger, 1987). He has since written three books concerning the law of whistleblowing.